Living in a Godly Marriage

Deepen Your Christian Life

From the late 1500s to the early 1700s, Puritan ministers wrote thousands of Christian books that contain massive amounts of biblical, doctrinal, experiential, and practical instruction to energize and deepen your Christian life. During that period, thousands of volumes coming off English presses consisted of Puritan sermon material popularized in book form. Unfortunately, many believers today find it difficult to read the antiquarian Puritan language and, when they attempt to do so, find themselves more frustrated than energized.

This new series, Deepen Your Christian Life, presents in contemporary language the major teachings that several Puritans wrote on subjects that are seldom addressed adequately, if at all, today. Finally, you too will be able to enjoy the Puritans and experience, by the Spirit's grace, that they really do deepen your Christian life.

Living by God's Promises
Joel R. Beeke and James La Belle (2010)

Living Zealously
Joel R. Beeke and James La Belle (2012)

Living with a Good Conscience
Joel R. Beeke (forthcoming)

Living in a Godly Marriage

with Study Questions

Joel R. Beeke and James A. La Belle

Reformation Heritage Books
Grand Rapids, Michigan

Living in a Godly Marriage
©2016 by Joel R. Beeke and James A. La Belle

Reformation Heritage Books
2965 Leonard St. NE
Grand Rapids, MI 49525
616-977-0889 / Fax 616-285-3246
orders@heritagebooks.org
www.heritagebooks.org

Printed in the United States of America
16 17 18 19 20 21/10 9 8 7 6 5 4 3 2 1

Library of Congress Cataloging-in-Publication Data

Names: Beeke, Joel R., 1952- author.
Title: Living in a Godly marriage : with study questions / Joel R. Beeke and
    James A. La Belle.
Description: Grand Rapids, Michigan : Reformation Heritage Books, 2016. |
    Series: Deepen your Christian life | Includes bibliographical references.
Identifiers: LCCN 2015050271 (print) | LCCN 2016004559 (ebook) | ISBN
    9781601784636 (pbk. : alk. paper) | ISBN 9781601784643 (Epub)
Subjects: LCSH: Marriage—Religious aspects—Christianity. |
    Puritans—Doctrines. | Reformed Church—Doctrines.
Classification: LCC BT706 .B44 2016 (print) | LCC BT706 (ebook) | DDC
    248.8/44—dc23
LC record available at http://lccn.loc.gov/2015050271

For additional Reformed literature, both new and used, request a free book list from Reformation Heritage Books at the above regular or e-mail address.

Table of Contents

For

William VanDoodewaard

faithful friend and colleague,
with gratitude for your quiet integrity,
hard and able work,
and your spirit of willingness to help.

— JRB

⸺◆⸺

For

Johnny and Julie Davis,

my dear friends.
May your marriage be filled with the joys
and marked by the blessings
of marrying in the Lord.

— JAL

Foreword

Old stereotypes die hard. Often it is far easier to hang on to misguided caricature than do the tough digging for the truth. The words "Puritan" and "puritanical" offer a good case in point. In the *Canadian Oxford Dictionary*, for example, after a standard historical explanation of these terms has been given, it is noted that the adjective "puritanical" means "one opposed to pleasure." No surprise then that the Puritans are regularly pilloried by our pleasure-loving culture. Sure, some words that have distinct historical associations lose them after they enter into common currency; but not so with these words and their cognates. The journalist and satirist H. L. Mencken (1880–1956) best summed up our culture's perspective on Puritanism when he defined it as "the haunting fear that someone, somewhere, may be happy" and observed that "there is only one honest impulse at the bottom of Puritanism, and that is the impulse to punish the man with a superior capacity for happiness." But the truth, when examined, is quite different. As Marxist historian Christopher Hill (1912–2003), an expert in seventeenth-century British history, once observed, "very few of the so-called 'Puritans' were 'Puritanical.'" Granted, instances of dreary kill-joys can be found in their ranks, but they are not to be taken as representative of the whole.

The Puritans were serious people, but knew when to laugh. Smiles and laughter, Richard Bernard (1568–1641) maintained, were part of a good life. And Bernard's contemporary Richard Sibbes (1577–1635) was confident that "joy is the habitation of the righteous." And as for sex, William Gouge (1575–1653), a prominent Puritan, could encourage married couples to engage in sexual intercourse with "delight, readily and cheerfully," since it was essential to marriage. Another Puritan leader, Richard Baxter (1615–1691), could urge married couples to remember that there is nothing the human "heart is so inordinately set upon as delight." Husband and wife should thus take pleasure in each other. Take joy in your wife, Baxter urged husbands, and then quoted the Bible, "Let her breasts satisfy thee at all times, and be thou ravished always with her love." In fact, as this new study of marriage by Joel R. Beeke and James A. La Belle abundantly demonstrates, the Puritan practice of and perspective on marriage contains desperately needed wisdom for our contemporary culture.

The Puritans were strong in the weakest areas of modern marital thought. They thought long and hard about this divine institution since marriage had been a major battleground in the western European world since the sixteenth-century Reformation. As a result, they are, as noted, thoroughly biblical in their understanding of sexuality within marriage but also solidly scriptural in their condemnation of sexual immorality—both of which our age desperately needs to hear. The Puritans are also strong, and rightly so, on the duties and responsibilities of married life, which cuts against the grain of so much of modern thinking where "duty" is a concept much out of favor. I have long regarded Puritan literature on the matter of marriage as some of the most profound textual material available on this subject in the English language, and, in many respects, a largely overlooked resource for Christian living today—and this book richly confirms this conviction. In a day when marriage is once again a battlefield, this study is must reading.

—Michael A. G. Haykin
The Southern Baptist Theological
Seminary

Biographical Introduction

The Puritans believed that godly marriages were foundational for the future life of families, churches, and nations. Therefore, they wrote prolifically on the subject of marriage, seeking to bring biblical reformation to this subject in a comprehensive way. Martin Luther, John Calvin, and other previous Reformers had begun this task, but the Puritans took it much further, writing a number of detailed treatises on how to live as godly spouses. Out of the wealth of material available to us from the seventeenth century, we have gathered together their insights in this book.

In this introduction, we will briefly summarize the early English authors whom we cite. We list them in alphabetical order. More information about most of them and their writings may be found in *Meet the Puritans*.[1]

Early English Authors

Henry Ainsworth (1569–1622) was a brilliant scholar of the Hebrew Old Testament. As a Congregationalist who separated from the Church of England, he left his homeland to pastor a church in the Netherlands. He is best known for his *Annotations* on the Pentateuch, Psalms, and Song of Songs.

Vincent Alsop (1630–1703), a vigorous and sometimes polemical advocate of Reformed Puritanism, served in the Church of England until ejected from his pulpit in 1662. In addition to his various polemical publications is a short treatise on Titus 2:10 titled *Practical Godliness*.

---

1. Joel R. Beeke and Randall J. Pederson, *Meet the Puritans: With a Guide to Modern Reprints* (Grand Rapids: Reformation Heritage Books, 2012).

Isaac Ambrose (1604–1664), a warm-hearted Presbyterian minister, also served in the Church of England until 1662. His book *Looking unto Jesus* is a classic of Christ-centered Puritan devotions. Other writings, *Prima*, *Ultima*, and *Media*, deal with regeneration, death, heaven, hell, and spiritual growth in this present life.

William Ames (1576–1633) was a systematic theologian of the first rank, as seen in his *Marrow of Divinity*. He also wrote practical divinity, such as his *Conscience with the Power and Cases Thereof*. A Puritan and Congregationalist, he too left England to serve in the Netherlands. His books influenced the Puritans of New England and the Dutch Further Reformation.

Richard Baxter (1615–1691), one of the most prolific of the Puritans, was a Presbyterian whose parish ministry at Kidderminster was instrumental in reviving the whole town. Although his views of justification and the atonement were outside the Reformed mainstream, his practical writings, such as his *Christian Directory* and *The Saints' Everlasting Rest*, are full of insight, comfort, and practical directions.

Robert Bolton (1572–1631) was a gifted scholar and faithful minister whose own heart had been broken over his sins while studying at Oxford. He became a true physician of souls, mingling biblical doctrine with practical counsel to guide sinners to walk before God with a clear conscience.

Thomas Boston (1676–1732) is somewhat unusual among the others listed here, being a Scottish Presbyterian who ministered in the early eighteenth century. Though he pastored small parishes in Simprin and Ettrick and suffered much from the mental illness of his wife, Boston poured his life into a loving discipline of preaching the Word. He stood for the doctrine of salvation by grace alone in the controversy over Edward Fisher's book, *The Marrow of Modern Divinity*. Boston's sermons on the Shorter Catechism form a comprehensive and experiential systematic theology. His *Human Nature in Its Fourfold State* profoundly shaped British and American Christians with its teachings on sin, regeneration, union with Christ, heaven, and hell.

Immanuel Bourne (1590–1672) served as a minister of the Church of England. He sided with the Presbyterians at the beginning of the

Civil War, but conformed at the restoration of the monarchy. His book on marriage, *A Golden Chain of Directions*, was highly recommended by the Presbyterian Puritan Henry Wilkinson.

Nicholas Byfield (1579–1622) faithfully ministered to the parish in Chester, England, despite suffering chronically with kidney stones—which eventually killed him. He wrote several books, including a commentary on 1 Peter, but is best known for his exposition of Colossians, composed of sermons preached intermittently over a period of seven years.

Thomas Gataker (1574–1654), minister and linguist, served in the Westminster Assembly—one of the few divines who favored episcopacy—and wrote the *Annotations* on Isaiah, Jeremiah, and Lamentations. He wrote several theological and polemical works in English and Latin. He also produced a critical edition of the *Meditations* of Marcus Aurelius. A number of Gataker's sermons were collected and published as *Certain Sermons*.

William Gouge (1575–1653), another excellent scholar and member of the Westminster Assembly, preached for forty-five years as the lecturer of St. Anne Blackfriars, London. He published a major commentary on Hebrews, a study of spiritual warfare titled *The Whole Armour of God*, and a classic on family life, *Of Domestical Duties* (modernized recently under the title *Building a Godly Home* in three volumes). This was the major Puritan classic on marriage and child-rearing.

Richard Greenham (c. 1542–1594) was a pioneer in Puritan practical theology, forged in the hardships of his ministry at the village of Dry Dayton. He trained men like Arthur Hildersham and Henry Smith, and influenced many other ministers to apply the gospel to conscience and life. His collected *Works* are full of the wisdom of a model pastor.

William Greenhill (1598–1671) fled to the Netherlands with Jeremiah Burroughs in the late 1630s on account of his Puritanism, where they led a Congregational church. Returning to England, Greenhill participated in the Westminster Assembly and served as a Congregationalist pastor. His large commentary on Ezekiel exhibits much spiritual insight.

Ezekiel Hopkins (1634–1690) served in the Church of England, conforming after the Restoration. In 1681, he was appointed bishop of Derry in Northern Ireland. His *Works* contain many edifying treatises on topics such as the Lord's Prayer, the Ten Commandments, the doctrines of sin, the covenants, regeneration, practical Christianity, and the "almost Christian."

Thomas Manton (1620–1677), a Presbyterian Puritan, favored the return of the monarchy, but was ejected from his ministry because of his refusal to conform to the Act of Uniformity (1662). Much of his *Works* consists of expository sermons through portions of Scripture, including Psalm 119, Isaiah 53, Matthew 25, John 17, Romans 6 and 8, 2 Thessalonians 2, Hebrews 11, James, and Jude.

John Maynard (1600–1665), another Westminster divine, ministered in Mayfield, Sussex, until ejected from his office. In addition to some sermons preached before Parliament, his published works include meditations on the six days of creation and a treatise on the harmony of the law and gospel.

William Perkins (1558–1602) was a patriarch in late Elizabethan Puritanism. His sermons at St. Andrew's Church influenced many students at Cambridge. Today he is best known for his practical treatise on double predestination, *A Golden Chain*. His writings include commentaries on the Sermon on the Mount, Galatians, Hebrews 11, Revelation 1–3; expositions on the Apostles' Creed and the Lord's Prayer; polemical writings against Roman Catholicism; and many treatises on practical Christian living and ministry. They have been translated into multiple European languages and influenced the international Reformed movement. The complete *Works of William Perkins* are now being reprinted by Reformation Heritage Books.

George Petter (c. 1586–1654), after completing his studies at Trinity College, Cambridge, became minister of the village of Bread (Brede) in Sussex, where he served for forty-four years. His brother said that "he conversed much with dead men in his study," and his diligence produced a large commentary on the Gospel of Mark.

Edward Reyner (1600–1660) served as a lecturer (preacher) at Lincoln for more than three decades, except for a brief period in the tumultuous times of the English Civil Wars. He was congregational in ecclesiology. His book *Precepts for Christian Practice* was reprinted several times in the mid-seventeenth century. He also wrote *Considerations Concerning Marriage.*

Daniel Rogers (1573–1652) was a minister of the Church of England until suspended by Archbishop Laud in 1629 for a refusal to conform. He wrote a massive book, *Naaman the Syrian, His Disease and Cure*, and a substantial book on marriage, *Matrimoniall Honour.*

Henry Scudder (c. 1585–1652) was a faithful pastor and Westminster divine. His book *The Christian's Daily Walk* became a classic in English devotional literature (and, in Dutch translation, in the Netherlands), winning praise from Richard Baxter and John Owen.

William Secker (d. 1681?) was the minister of All-Hallows Church in Tottenham, Middlesex (now North London). He published a wedding sermon, *A Wedding Ring Fit for the Finger, or the Salve of Divinity on the Sore of Humanity*, and a volume of sermons, *The Nonsuch Professor in His Meridian Glory, Or the Singular Actions of Sanctified Christians.*

Henry Smith (1560–1591), was a "silver-tongued" Elizabethan preacher mentored by Richard Greenham. Smith did not agree with all the practices of the Church of England, but remained within it, agitating not for structural change so much as spiritual renewal. His published *Works* consist of a collection of fifty-six sermons and went through many editions.

Richard Steele (1629–1692), a Presbyterian minister, suffered ejection for his failure to conform to the Act of Uniformity, harassment by authorities, false accusations against his character, and tuberculosis. Nevertheless, he persevered in faith and the ministry of the word. His published writings include a practical guide for Christians at work, *The Religious Tradesman*, as well as his sermon at the Morning Exercises on the duties of husbands and wives.

Richard Stock (c. 1569–1626), after completing his studies at Cambridge, was the pastor of All-Hallows Church on Bread Street, London. He was a friend of John Davenant and Thomas Gataker, and John Milton grew up in his church. Stock was remembered as "a burning and shining light," both in the truth of his preaching and the holiness of his life. He translated a book by William Whitaker and wrote books on repentance, the doctrine of God, and the prophecy of Malachi.

George Swinnock (c. 1627–1673) ministered in Buckinghamshire until ejected from his position by the Act of Uniformity. He continued to preach privately and to write. Swinnock's writings are not as doctrinally rich as some Puritans, but display a rare talent in illustration. His *magnum opus* is *The Christian Man's Calling*, a practical consideration of how godliness should shape every facet of life.

Jeremy Taylor (1613–1667) was a minister of the Church of England, famous for his devotional spirituality. He was not a Puritan, but being a favorite of Archbishop Laud, he was not well treated during the Puritan Commonwealth. After the Restoration he became a bishop in Northern Ireland and opposed local Presbyterians. His most famous writings were directions for *Holy Living* and *Holy Dying*. Among a series of sermons originally published in 1673 is a message titled, "The Marriage Ring: Or, The Mysteriousness and Duties of Marriage," which we have taken liberty to quote in this book since it is so puritan-minded in substance.

William Whately (1583–1639) was a Puritan preacher known as "The Roaring Boy of Banbury," not for a lack of thought and method, but for the energy with which he delivered his sermons. He authored a number of books, including treatises on marriage, the Ten Commandments, and the new birth.

Andrew Willet (1562–1621) was a Reformed English minister and polemicist against Roman Catholicism. Scholars debate whether to consider him a Puritan, even though his writings certainly reflect a puritan way of thinking. He devoted himself to eight hours of study each day, yet maintained an active family life and productive ministry. He wrote a six-part exposition (*Hexapla*) of each of the following: Genesis, Exodus, Leviticus, Samuel, Daniel, and Romans.

Contemporary Style

We have footnoted direct quotations from these authors, using the abbreviations listed in the table in the next section. Much of the other material in the book summarizes their thoughts in a contemporary form. Due to the target audience of these books—the layperson—we have minimized footnote use. On occasion, we have also used other authors to augment our theme; they are footnoted in full. Modern spelling and punctuation are used throughout. Study questions are offered at the end of each chapter to facilitate group study.

Acknowledgments

We would like to thank our faithful Lord and Savior, the great Bridegroom of His church, for His marital love toward His own. Without Him being the perfect Husband, and Scripture's clear testimony of that fact in Ephesians 5 and many other places, the Puritan understanding of marriage would have been seriously flawed. We look forward to knowing Him better in heaven's eternal, utopian marriage, where Jesus Christ shall truly be all-in-all (Col. 3:11).

We would like to thank our special wives, Mary Beeke and Chantry La Belle, for their loving example of reflecting the church's relationship to Christ as loyal and precious helpmeets. We also thank our dear children for their loving support of our writing ministry. Many thanks to Michael Haykin for his helpful foreword to this book; to Phyllis TenElshof, Greg Bailey, and Misty Bourne for their helpful editing assistance; and to Gary and Linda den Hollander, our excellent proofreading/typesetting couple; as well as Amy Zevenbergen for her cover design.

If this books assists you to understand better the purposes, goals, and duties of marriage, and moves you to live more godly in your marriage in and through Christ Jesus to God's glory, our labor will be well rewarded.

—Joel R. Beeke and James A. La Belle

Abbreviations and Select Bibliography

Ainsworth   Henry Ainsworth, *Annotations on the Pentateuch and the Psalms* (Ligonier, Pa.: Soli Deo Gloria, 1991).

Alsop   Vincent Alsop, "The Sinfulness of Strange Apparel," in *Practical Godliness: The Ornament of All Religion* (Morgan, Pa.: Soli Deo Gloria, 2003), 103–72.

Ambrose   Isaac Ambrose, "Family Duties," in *Media: the Middle Things, in reference to the First and Last Things; or, The Means, Duties, Ordinances, both Secret, Private, and Publick, for continuance and increase of a godly life, (once begun,) till we come to Heaven*, in *The Works of Isaac Ambrose* (London: Rowland Reynolds, 1674), 228–38.

Ames   William Ames, *Conscience With the Power and Cases Thereof* (Puritan Reprints, 2010).

Anonymous   *The New Whole Duty of Man*, The Nineteenth Edition (London: Printed only for John Hinton, at the King's Arms, in Newgate Street, n.d.), 219–32, 394–96. Often attributed to Richard Allestree.

D. B.   *The Honourable State of Matrimony Made Comfortable, or An Antidote Against Discord Betwixt Man and Wife: being Special Directions for the Procuring and Preserving of Family Peace* (London: Francis Pearse, 1685).

Baxter   Richard Baxter, *The Godly Home*, ed. Randall J. Pederson (Wheaton, Ill.: Crossway Books, 2010).

Baxter, *Works*   Richard Baxter, "The Poor Man's Family Book," in *The Practical Works of Richard Baxter* (Morgan, Pa.: Soli Deo Gloria, 1996), 4:234–35.

Bayne   Paul Bayne, *An Entire Commentary Upon the Whole Epistle of St Paul to the Ephesians* (Stoke-on-Trent, England: Tentmaker, 2007), 337–54.

Bolton   Robert Bolton, *General Directions for a Comfortable Walking with God* (Morgan, Pa.: Soli Deo Gloria, 1995), 262–82.

Boston   Thomas Boston, *The Works of Thomas Boston*, ed. Samuel M'Millan (Wheaton, Ill: Richard Owen Roberts, 1980), 2:212–19; 4:209–218.

Bourne   Immanuel Bourne, *A Golden Chain of Directions, with Twenty Gold-links of love, to preserve love firm between Husband and Wife, during their lives. Profitable to all, that are already Married, or that intend to take the Honourable and Holy estate of Marriage upon them hereafter. Advising for a Right Choice in Marriage, and how to keep from those sad consequences [which] have fallen out in too many Families, sometimes upon small dislike between Husband and Wife. That happiness may be the inheritance of parents and posterities, through the grace of God in Jesus Christ* (London: Printed by J. Streater for George Sanbridge, 1669).

Byfield   Nicholas Byfield, *An Exposition Upon the Epistle to the Colossians* (Stoke-on-Trent, England: Tentmaker, 2007), 346–56.

Davenant   John Davenant, *Colossians* (Edinburgh: Banner of Truth, 2005).

Gataker   Thomas Gataker, *Certaine Sermons, First Preached, and After Published at several times, by M. Thomas Gataker B. of D. and Pastor at Rotherhith, and now Gathered together into One Volume* (London: by John Haviland for Phylemon Stephens and Christopher Meredith, 1637).

Gouge   William Gouge, *Of Domestical Duties* (Pensacola: Puritan Reprints, 2006). [Edited and modernized by Scott Brown and Joel R. Beeke as *Building a Godly Home*, 3 vols. (Grand Rapids: Reformation Heritage Books, 2013–14).]

Greenham   Richard Greenham, "A Treatise of a Contract Before Marriage" in *The Works of the Reverend and Faithfvll Servant of Iesus Christ M. Richard Greenham, Second ed.* (London: by Felix Kingston for Ralph Iacson, 1599), 278–88.

Greenhill   William Greenhill, *An Exposition of Ezekiel* (Edinburgh: Banner of Truth, 1994), 441–43.

Hopkins   Ezekiel Hopkins, *The Works of Ezekiel Hopkins*, ed. Charles W. Quick (Morgan, Pa.: Soli Deo Gloria, 1995), 1:413–26.

Manton   Thomas Manton, *The Works of Thomas Manton* (Birmingham: Solid Ground Christian Books, 2008), 2:162–72; 19:436–76.

Maynard   John Maynard, *The Beauty of Order of the Creation. Together with Natural and Allegorical Meditations on the Six Dayes Works of the Creation. With the Addition of two Compendious Discourses* (London: William Gearing, 1668), 175–84.

Perkins   William Perkins, "A Golden Chaine," in *The Workes of that Famovs and Worthie Minister of Christ, in the Vniversitie of Cambridge, M. W. Perkins* (London: John Legate, 1608), 1:60–61.

Petter   George Petter, *A Learned, Pious, and Practical Commentary Upon the Gospel According to St. Mark* (London: F. Streater, 1661), 704–705.

Reyner   Edward Reyner, *Considerations Concerning Marriage: the Honor, Duties, Benefits, Troubles of it. Whereto are added, 1) Directions in two particulars: a. How they that have wives may be as if they had none. b. How to prepare for parting with a dear yoke-fellow by death or otherwise.*

2) Resolution of this Case of Conscience: Whether a man may lawfully marry his wife's sister? (London: by J. T. for Thomas Newbery, 1657).

Rogers   Daniel Rogers, *Matrimonial Honor* (Virginia: Edification Press, 2010).

Scudder   Henry Scudder, *The Godly Man's Choice: or A Direction how single godly persons, who intend marriage, may make choice of a fit and meet yoak-fellow; being the meditations of Caleb Granthamin his single estate, as a rule and guide for himself to walk by; and since his death perused and published with some profitable directions how persons should live as becometh Christians in the married estate* (London: by Mathew Simmons for Henry Overton, 1644).

Secker   William Secker, "The Wedding Ring," in *The Nonsuch Professor—Wedding Ring* (Virginia: Sprinkle Publications, 1997), 245–69.

Smith   Henry Smith, "A Preparative to Marriage," in *The Works of Henry Smith* (Stoke-on-Trent: Tentmaker Publications, 2002), 1:1–40.

Steele   Richard Steele, "What are the duties of husbands and wives towards each other?" in *Puritan Sermons 1659–1689*, 2:272–303.

Ste. B.   Ste. B., *Counsel to the Husband; to the Wife Instruction: a short and pithy treatise of several and joynt duties, belonging unto man and wife, as counsels to the one, and instructions to the other; for their more perfect happiness in this present life, and their eternal glorie in the life to come* (London: by Felix Kyngston, for Richard Boyle, 1605).

Stock   Richard Stock, *A Commentary Upon the Prophecy of Malachi* (Stoke-on-Trent, England: Tentmaker, 2006), 168–91.

Swinnock   George Swinnock, *The Christian Man's Calling*, in *The Works of George Swinnock* (Edinburgh: Banner of Truth, 1992), 1:464–528.

Taylor

Jeremy Taylor, *The Marriage Ring* (1673; repr., New York: John Lane Company, 1907).

Whately,
A Bride-Bush

William Whately, *A Bride-Bush, or, A Direction for Married Persons, plainly describing the duties common to both, and peculiar to each of them. By performing of which, Marriage shall proove a great help to such, as now for want of performing them, doe finde it a little hell* (London: Printed by Bernard Alsop for Beniamin Fisher, and are to be sold at his shop in Paternoster Rowe, at the signe of the Talbot, 1623).

Whately,
A Care-Cloth

William Whately, *A Care-Cloth: or, A Treatise of the Cumbers and Troubles of Marriage; intended to advise them that may, to shun them; [and them] that may not, well and patiently to beare them* (London: Imprinted by Felix Kyngston for Thomas Man, 1624).

Willet

Andrew Willet, *Hexapla in Genesin, that is, a Sixfold Commentary Upon Genesis* (London: Printed by Thomas Creede, for Thomas Man, 1608), 1–44.

Resources on the Puritan View of Marriage

den Ouden

P. den Ouden, *Liefde en trouw bij de puriteinen*, 3rd ed. (Houten, the Netherlands: Den Hertog, 2010).

Packer

J. I. Packer, *A Quest for Godliness: The Puritan Vision of the Christian Life* (Wheaton, Ill.: Crossway, 1994), 259–73.

Parker
and Carlson

Kenneth L. Parker and Eric J. Carlson, *'Practical Divinity': The Works and Life of Revd Richard Greenham*, St. Andrews Studies in Reformation History (Aldershot, England: Ashgate Publishing, 1998).

Ryken

Leland Ryken, Worldly Saints: The Puritans as They Really Were (Grand Rapids: Zondervan, 1986), 39–54, 75–78.

Introduction

Marriage is under attack today, both from without and within. All around us we are witnessing the dissolution and attempted eradication of marriage as created by God and celebrated in His Word. What was once defined as "a communion of life between man and woman joined together according to the ordinance of God"[1] is being redefined today. What our forebears understood to be the fundamental institution of not only every society but of the human race[2] is now being relegated by many to a page in history reserved for the outgrown and useless. What constitutes marriage today, as is evident in the notions and expectations of many people who marry, is often hardly recognizable from the standpoint of God's original ordinance on marriage.

The attack on marriage from *within* is the poisonous fruit of our innate rebellion against God. We are born at enmity with God and rebel against His law by nature (Rom. 8:7–8). There is no fear of God before our eyes (Rom. 3:18) and we do not want Him to reign over us (Luke 19:14). His ways are distasteful to our selfish interests. His law is abhorrent to our pursuit of freedom. His sovereignty is loathsome to our belief in human autonomy. Therefore marriage instituted by God's sovereignty, designed according to God's ways, regulated by God's laws,

---

1. Smith, 1:5.
2. Marriage is "the first relation that was in the world, and from which all others do proceed.... The laws of heaven with respect to [marriage], if observed, would make happy societies, families, &c., and when neglected keep the world in wild disorder" (Boston, 2:212). Cf. also Gataker, 3; Reyner, iii, 45; Steele, *Puritans Sermons*, 2:272.

and aimed at God's glory is often either put on the potter's wheel of man-centeredness and given a new look or entirely rejected simply because it is "of God."

Ironically, most people want the benefits of marriage, such as sexual intimacy, companionship, the comfort of someone with whom to share their joys and sorrows, and children to nurture, carry on the family name, and inherit their estate. But they do not want what they consider to be the yoke, the restrictions, the commitment, and the duties that come with marriage done God's way. They do not want God looking over their shoulders telling them how to "do" marriage. So they oppose marriage as God appointed it and seek to refashion it after their own image, giving free reign to sinful desires, ascribing authority to their own opinions, and doing what is right in their own eyes.

This attack on marriage from within is coupled with an attack from *without* by a culture in which the commitment and boundaries of marriage are considered not only a restraint on personal freedom but also a killjoy. This view regards marriage God's way as a miserable enterprise. Added to this contempt for marriage is the notion that marriage God's way is out of date. We have grown up; we have moved on as a culture and left behind the ball-and-chain marriage of a previous generation. In its place we approve "friendship with benefits," living together, and open relationships in which partners are free to have other sexual partners.

While many are jettisoning marriage and want to get beyond it, others are perverting marriage by redefining it as a union of people in homosexual relationships. These people want both acceptance in the public arena and the right to marry. For them, the "maturing" of our society would mean accepting their sexual orientation as a viable alternative lifestyle and redefining marriage to legally constitute their relationship as a marriage.

Who cannot see that this is an attempt not merely to change God's view of marriage but to eventually eradicate it? What if the attempt is successful? Already the family, the church, our society, and culture at large are suffering because of the attack on marriage. Where will we end up if this rebellion against God continues? Can we kick against the goads without injury or consequences? Marriage was the first human relationship instituted in the world and is therefore the fountain from which all others proceed; its dissolution *cannot* occur without serious consequences for every other relationship in society. The rush to legalize homosexual relationships as marriages suffers from both blindness and numbness—blindness to the dangerous ramifications of the act and numbness to the cries of conscience that such a thing ought not to be done.

Something must be done to recover marriage and restore it to its God-ordained blessedness to family, church, and society, and that something must be done *now*. The rapidly changing landscape of marriage cries out for someone to rescue it and put it back on track before it spins out of control. But what can we do to effect this rescue? How can we restore marriage as an ordinance of God instituted for our good and His glory? How can we restore marriage to its rightful place as a boon to the family, the church, society at large, and the whole world?

Restoration begins with a recovery of what God's Word teaches about marriage. God not only created marriage but created it for His glory. The only hope we have for the restoration of marriage is to go to His Word and let it serve as the final authority for marriage. In His Word God tells us how to think about marriage, how to prepare for marriage, upon what foundation to build a godly marriage, the duties to which marriage obligates us and how properly to perform them, what struggles to expect in marriage and how to address them, and how to persevere in a difficult marriage. God has not left us in the dark on so important and foundational an ordinance as marriage. He has told us what it is, why He created it, how to enjoy it, and how to glorify Him in it.

To discover what God's Word teaches about marriage we will mine the writings and sermons of many Puritans. These Puritans were ministers of the Word from an earlier century who not only manifested a thoroughly biblical understanding of marriage but also called people to enjoy the bountiful blessings of matrimony by aligning their marriages with God's Word and living in them for God's glory.

With their help, we will unfold what Scripture teaches about this fundamental relationship between husband and wife. Whether you are preparing for marriage, are recently married, or are celebrating many years of marriage, it is our prayer that God will enlighten your mind about His purpose for marriage and enable you to enjoy the rich and delightful blessings of marriage by conforming to His will, for He has tied His blessings to your duties.

The Institution and Honor of Marriage

The realigning of our convictions and practices regarding marriage with the teaching of God's Word must begin with an understanding of marriage as God instituted it and an appreciation for the honor He places upon it. While so many people today decry marriage and consider it to be the sepulcher of pleasure, a yoke of bondage, or, at best, a necessary evil, we must remember that God declared marriage to be "very good" (Gen. 1:31) and places an honor upon it which no human cynicism can remove and no broken marriage can disprove (Heb. 13:4). So let's begin by briefly considering the institution of marriage and then look at the many things that make marriage honorable.

The Institution of Marriage

Since we cannot speak of living for God's glory in marriage unless we begin with marriage as God Himself created and defined it, we must turn to Genesis 2:22–25. We can make four observations about the institution of marriage from this passage.

First, note that verse 22 speaks not only of the creation of Eve but also of the marriage of Adam and Eve and therefore of the institution of marriage as an ordinance of God. God did not merely create woman *out of* man but *for* man, a wife for a husband, so that Adam and Eve might serve as our first parents (Acts 17:26) and that marriage might serve as the fountain of all human societies.[1] God brought Eve to Adam

---

1. Reyner, 45.

to be his wife. On this verse Swinnock commented, "[God]…married the first couple that ever were in the world. Their maker was their minister to join them together."[2] Henry Ainsworth said, "God her builder was also her bringer, and so her conjoiner in marriage with the man."[3] George Petter urged his readers to "see the antiquity of the married estate, being instituted by God from the time of man's first creation, at the beginning of the world, even so soon as man was created, yea in the very creation itself.… See [Genesis] 2:22, where so soon as ever the woman was created, God brought her unto Adam to be his wife."[4]

Bringing the woman to the man must be viewed in light of God's previous act of bringing all the animals to Adam. As Genesis 2:19–20 says, "And out of the ground the LORD God formed every beast of the field, and every fowl of the air; and brought them unto Adam to see what he would call them." The purpose of Adam's role in naming the animals was far more than getting to know them and giving them names reflective of their distinctions. The purpose was also that Adam might see for himself that there was no helper suitable for him among those creatures over which he was to exercise dominion (Gen. 1:28). According to Genesis 2:18, the Lord says that it is not good that man should be alone and announces, "I will make him an help meet for him."

In naming the animals, Adam was to realize how unsuitable the creatures were for the kind of helpmate he needed in marriage. Before he entered into marriage, he was to realize that the affinity between husband and wife would be far superior to his relationship with every other thing that God had made. He was to see that God made the woman *for* him to make him more thankful for her and more true to her—two necessary marks of a happy marriage. John Maynard explained it this way: "God is the great Match-maker, and is the Author of marriage. God brought all the creatures before Adam, but among them all he found none that was an help meet for him, and therefore he brought the woman to another end; and in bringing her, did join her to him in marriage; and Adam on the other side, with a glad and thankful heart,

---

2. Swinnock, 1:464.

3. Ainsworth, 1:16.

4. Petter, 704.

accepts her at the hands of God; gives her a name answerable."[5] Regarding the woman's fitness for Adam, Secker said, "The angels were too much above him; the creatures were too much below him; he could not step up to the former, nor could he stoop down to the latter; the one was out of his reach, the other was out of his race: but the woman is a parallel-line drawn equal with him; meet she must be."[6] Thus when God brought the woman to Adam in verse 22 and he named her "woman," it was because he recognized not only her suitability *to* him but also her creation by God *for* him to be his wife and helpmate in his duties before God as his Creator.

In support of this interpretation, consider our Lord's use of Genesis 2:22 in His response to the Pharisees' question about the lawfulness of divorce upon any and all grounds (Matt. 19:3). In Matthew 19:3–6, Jesus declares the unlawfulness of divorce "for every cause" by directing the Pharisees to the institution of marriage by God at creation. Jesus tells them that when a man leaves his father and mother he is to cleave inseparably to his wife in marriage because this marks not only his separation from his parents but also the initiation of his own home and family. When he does so, the man and the woman become one flesh, not only *before* God (v. 5), but *by* God's joining them together in their marriage (v. 6).

Notice that Jesus grounds His argument on God's creation of man and woman from the beginning (v. 4). In other words, to answer a question about the dissolution of marriage Jesus appeals to the divine institution of marriage, which He declares to have happened at the creation of Adam and Eve as male and female (Gen. 1:27), for God *joined* them together in marriage, when He "brought her unto the man" (Gen. 2:22).

A second observation is that, by definition, marriage is God's joining a man and a woman together as one flesh (vv. 22–23). If God joined Adam and Eve together in marriage as soon as He created them, then it follows that God created them male and female *in order that* He might marry them. He created both sexes to institute marriage from

---

5. Maynard, 177–78.
6. Secker, 263–64.

the beginning. He created the two partners of a marriage so that He might both institute the first marriage and declare once and for all that the partners that constitute a marriage are one man and one woman. Swinnock wrote, "In the creation of the world God was pleased to do it by pairs—a heaven and earth, a sun and moon, a sea and land, a night and day, a man and a woman. Marriage must be between one man and one woman, Matthew 19:5."[7]

Any deviation from this arrangement corrupts the ideal and perverts God's holy institution. Therefore same-sex unions simply cannot be marriages because that is contrary to God's institution.[8] On the one hand, they cannot *be* marriages because God did not join man and man or woman and woman together (Gen. 2:22), and on the other hand, they may not be *called* marriages because they are contrary to nature, which testifies that those whom God intended to marry He made fit for marriage by making them two distinct sexes (Gen. 1:27; Rom. 1:26–27). As Petter wrote, "This was the end why they were created male and female: that they might be fit for marriage and capable of it."[9]

In Matthew 19, Jesus concludes by saying, "What therefore God hath joined together, let not man put asunder" (v. 6). To those who plead for same-sex marriage, our Lord's words might also justly be interpreted: "what God has put asunder, let not man join." If marriage was to be established with two of the same sex then God would have made our first parents of the same sex; if it did not matter whether marriage was constituted between two of the opposite or two of the same sex, then God would not have instituted marriage as soon as He created them male and female, for God does nothing without a purpose (Eph. 1:11).

Third, we learn from Genesis 2:22–25 that marriage is to be between *one* man and *one* woman.[10] Ever since Lamech took two wives in Genesis 4:19, there have been polygamous marriages in the world;

---

7. Swinnock, 1:465.

8. This explains why God would pour out His wrath on those who practiced homosexuality (Gen. 18:20; 19:4–5, 24–25) and why God calls homosexuality an abomination (Lev. 18:22)—because it is sinful and contrary to marriage as He instituted it.

9. Petter, 705.

10. Cf. Westminster Confession of Faith 24:1.

men who, as Smith referred to it, "made two ribs of one."[11] But neither antiquity of practice nor the approval of men can make that right, for God's Word shows that polygamy is wrong. If God intended marriage to include more than one wife then He would have made more than one Eve for Adam. On this point Smith said that God "had power to create more, but to show that he would have him to stick to one, therefore he created of one rib but one wife for one husband (Mal. 2:15). And in the ark there were no more women than men, but four wives for four husbands."[12] Likewise Secker pointed out, "In creation God made not one woman for many men, nor many women for one man; every wife should be to her husband, as Eve was to Adam, a whole world of women; and every husband should be to his wife, as Adam was to Eve, a whole world of men. When a river is divided into many channels, the main current starves."[13]

Verse 24 therefore declares that the one man shall leave his father and mother and cleave unto "his wife." The woman is "his wife." She is not another man's wife but his, and he has no other for a wife but her. The one woman whom the one man embraces in marriage is to be his one wife: "they twain shall be one flesh" (Matt. 19:5). The one flesh constituted by marriage is the conjunction of the two whom God joins together. Scripture never directs the man to love his *wives*, only to love his *wife*, being the husband of one wife (1 Tim. 3:2, 12).[14]

That explains why all other women are called strangers in Proverbs to the man who has a wife, because they do not know him as his wife knows him.[15] In marriage the man consents to be intimately and sexually known by his wife, and she consents to be known by him in the same way, giving her husband a singular right to her body just as he gives her a singular right to his—a point Paul makes in 1 Corinthians 7:4: "the wife hath not power of her own body, but the husband: and likewise also the husband hath not power of his own body, but the wife."

---

11. Smith, 1:10.
12. Smith, 1:9.
13. Secker, 269.
14. Smith, 1:10.
15. Ainsworth, 1:17. E.g. Proverbs 2:16; 5:3, 10, 17, 20.

This intimate sexual "knowledge" proper to marriage is so singular and special that it simply cannot admit a third person without perverting the ordinance.[16]

In addition, when the men of God's people took many wives in the days of Malachi, God declared His hatred for such a thing by rejecting the offerings and prayers that Israel made to Him (Mal. 2:13–15). God would not receive worship at their hands (v. 13) because they were perverting His institution of marriage by their polygamy (v. 14). They had taken to themselves other wives, thereby sinning against the wife of their youths (vv. 14–15). And since the wife is a gift from the Lord (Prov. 19:14) and the covenant made between the husband and wife in marriage is made before the Lord as witness to the marriage and maker of the marriage bond, polygamy is a sin against Him (James 2:10–11). "Bigamy and polygamy are both unlawful,"[17] Swinnock wrote. Richard Stock explained: "They had been injurious, not only against their wives, but against God, who was witness of the covenant they made betwixt themselves, which covenant, as it was God's, ordained by Him, that they should be one flesh, so was it made, He being present, and called upon by Him as witness, when he bound himself to take her for his only wife."[18]

Malachi silenced the argument for polygamy as Christ silenced the Pharisees' argument for divorce by appealing to God's original institution of marriage. Verse 15 says, "And did not he make one? Yet had he the residue of the spirit." What Malachi means is this: God marked the oneness of marriage and made it a law of nature that one man is to be joined to one woman. While He could have made more than one woman, He didn't. He gave Adam one woman to marry and Eve one man to marry in order that it might be a perpetual pattern for mankind.[19] Stock said: "After making woman of his rib, he breathed into her breath of life, as it was the remainder of the spirit; and though he had abundance more... [so] that they two should be one, and not more."[20]

---

16. Ames, 198.
17. Swinnock, 1:465.
18. Stock, 173.
19. E. B. Pusey, *The Minor Prophets: A Commentary* (Grand Rapids: Baker, 1950), 2:483.
20. Stock, 177.

Thus both bigamy and polygamy are "simply wicked, impious, and unlawful."[21]

Fourthly, we learn that the only manner in which a man and a woman are to be joined together and become one flesh is by the ordinance of marriage, for this is the means God has instituted for it. Verse 25 is the first mention of nakedness in the Bible and it is placed within the context of "the man and his wife." The sexual union between a man and a woman, with which the Lord is pleased, is associated with the marriage in which He originally placed it (Heb. 13:4). It was this marriage of the man and the woman, who stood naked before God, that received God's approval and blessing: "Be fruitful, and multiply. And God saw every thing that he had made, and, behold, it was very good" (Gen. 1:28, 31).

This divine approval condemns any sexual activity outside of marriage, including that of those living together as boyfriend and girlfriend and having sex as if they were married. However acceptable fornication and living together before marriage may be in our society, both are contrary not only to God's institution of marriage in Genesis 2 but also to God's commandment regarding marriage in Exodus 20:14, "Thou shalt not commit adultery."

The man and his wife were naked and unashamed before God their Creator and Matchmaker, showing that there was no guilt or sin inherently associated with the intimacy and sexuality that God placed within marriage. But it also shows that sexual activity outside of marriage— whether in thought, word, or deed—is shameful and incurs guilt before God because it is sinful. Therefore only the lawful marriage of one man to one woman receives the blessing that God pronounces on marriage in Genesis 1:28, while those who grasp for the blessing of marriage without the ordinance of it invite God's judgment upon themselves (Prov. 5:18–23; Gen. 19:24–25, 27–28, Heb. 13:4).

If we are to live for God's glory in marriage, we must be yoked together as one man to one woman, for that is the kind of marriage that God declared in Genesis 1:31 to be "very good."

---

21. Stock, 181.

The Honor of Marriage

God instituted marriage, and He also honored it. Unlike a picture frame that is extrinsic to the picture it encases, the honor of marriage is not extrinsic to its institution. Rather, it is as essential and natural to marriage as God's institution of it. Regardless of how much we see marriage marred by sin and how hard some strive to defile marriage by perversion, marriage as instituted by God is honorable (Heb. 13:4).

That elevates marriage to a place of excellence and thereby obligates us to seriously consider how we regard it, how we enter into it, and how we live in it, as well as how we honor the marriage vow, the marriage bond, the marriage bed, and the marriage relationship. If marriage is honorable, then we should seek to enjoy and preserve its honor as well as live in our marriage to the glory of Him who made it honorable. Furthermore, if marriage is honorable, there is nothing in it—as God instituted it—but what is good and right, conducive to both our pleasure and eternal advantage.

The Puritans observed that the honor belonging to marriage depends on its relation to God, the circumstances of its institution, its relation to Christ, and its relation to the world. Once these considerations are duly weighed, we will understand why marriage is so excellent an institution.

Marriage Is Honorable in Relation to God
Marriage's honor begins with God as the Author of marriage. He invented it and appointed it.[22] Henry Smith wrote, "Whereas all other ordinances were appointed of God by the hands of men, or the hands of angels (Acts 12:7; Heb. 2:2), marriage was ordained by God himself [who] cannot err. No man nor angel brought the wife to the husband, but God himself, Gen. 2:22; so marriage hath more honor of God... than all other ordinances of God beside, because He solemnized it Himself."[23]

That immediately sets marriage apart from other ordinances, for it is from God's own hand, and therefore marriage should receive the

---

22. Reyner, 2.
23. Smith, 1:5–6.

esteem worthy of its Author. How many laws and human institutions do we hold in high regard for the sake of those who authored them? How many possessions do we prize not for their inherent value but for the sake of the one who gave them to us? And how many works of art or composition are praised because of the reputation of the one who painted it or wrote it? But here is One greater than any author, composer, or benefactor who could be named on earth or in heaven. Here is marriage from the hand of God (Prov. 19:14).

The Author of marriage is the Master of the world, the Lord of heaven and earth, the King of ages, and Father of eternity. Marriage is the work of His hands, depends entirely upon His joining, can only serve its purpose by His blessing, and has the sanction and right of His incontestable authority, for He said, "It is not good that the man should be alone" (Gen. 2:18). Thus, for those who seek God's glory in it, marriage has little meaning outside of He who authors it, little joy outside of He who blesses it, and little peace outside of He who fills it with Himself.

Marriage Is Honorable in the Circumstances of Its Institution
Directly related to the honor God bestows on marriage is the honor marriage receives from several circumstances of its institution. These include the time, the place, the persons, and the manner.

First, marriage is honored by the *time* of its institution. Rather than being instituted as an afterthought, as if to suggest that after God created humans He realized something was missing, God instituted marriage from the very start to show that creation would have been imperfect without marriage. For no sooner did He make man but He took the woman out of the man and brought her to him as his wife. Smith said, "It was the first ordinance that God instituted, even the first thing which he did, after man and woman were created.... Before man had any other calling, he was called to be a husband; therefore it hath the honour of antiquity above all other ordinances, because it was ordained first, and is the ancientest calling of men."[24]

---

24. Smith, 1:6.

Furthermore, God instituted marriage before man's fall into sin. Gouge called it "the most pure and perfect time that ever was in the world, when no sin or pollution of man had stained it."[25] The entrance of sin into the world marred all that God had created by polluting what God had made clean and by corrupting what God had made pure. But marriage was given to man *before* sin entered the world, not as a relief to him in his fallen state but as a perfect addition to him in creation. For when God consented to create man in Genesis 1:28, He did not cease that work until woman was created because she was a necessary part of the marriage which He intended to institute upon man's creation.[26] Therefore there is no sin either in marriage or in the marriage bed, as some have taught, because it was created before sin existed and received the divine approval of Genesis 1:31 that, along with all else the Lord had made, it was "very good."[27]

Second, marriage is honored by the *place* in which it was first celebrated. The first marriage took place in the Garden of Eden, the sanctuary where God manifested His presence to our first parents, making it a heaven on earth.[28] Gouge called it "the most fair, glorious, pleasant, honorable, commodious (i.e., convenient), and every way most excellent place that ever was in this world."[29] Solemn transactions are more highly regarded when they occur in a place of great honor. For example, we go to the courthouse to hold a trial, ministers preach the word of God from a pulpit, and even some couples who have no connection with a church still prefer to hold their wedding ceremony in a church. Thus, by solemnizing the first marriage in His own garden of delights, God placed a high honor upon it.

Third, marriage is honored by the *persons* who were the first to marry, Adam and Eve, our first parents and the common parents of all mankind, including kings, queens, princes, and nobles. Even Jesus Christ, according to His humanity, was the son of Adam (Luke 3:38).

---

25. Gouge, 151.
26. Rogers, 5.
27. Reyner, 3.
28. Reyner, 3.
29. Gouge, 151.

Gouge described Adam and Eve as "the most honorable that ever were, even the first father and mother of all mankind, they who had an absolute power and dominion over all creatures, and to whom all were subject. None but they ever had a true monarchy over the whole world."[30] Furthermore, their marriage had a peculiar honor in that He who married them was the Lord God who dwelt with them in paradise. The Lord brought the woman to the man to be his wife (Gen. 2:22) and blessed their union (Gen. 1:28) as that which fulfilled His purpose for man and served man's need (Gen. 2:18).

Finally, marriage is honored by the *manner* in which it was instituted. Consider first of all the manner in which the triune God instituted marriage. It was, as Gouge pointed out, "with as great deliberation as ever was used in instituting any ordinance."[31] For what do we read at this point in the creation narrative (Gen. 2:18)? "The LORD God said." He spoke to the other divine Persons of the Trinity. And what had they determined that He now saw fit to proclaim? "It is not good that the man should be alone." Man was in need of a companion. And what did He do about man's need? "I will make him an help meet for him." He immediately proceeded to make a woman for the man that she might be his wife.

Consider secondly the manner in which God brought the woman forth both as a suitable companion and as a helpmate for the man. Genesis 2:22 says, "And the rib, which the LORD God had taken from man, made he a woman." The Hebrew word used for "made" literally means "to build." God built a wife suitable for the man, fashioning her according to the man's needs, even as He had already fashioned the man to meet the needs of the woman whom He would bring forth from him. Smith wrote, "He is not said to *make* man a wife, but to *build* him a wife, signifying that man and wife make as it were one house together, and that the building was not perfect until the woman was made as well as the man."[32] Willet put it this way: "By this is meant, both that man was

---

30. Gouge, 151.
31. Gouge, 151.
32. Smith, 1:7.

yet as an imperfect building before woman was made, and that by the woman the house and family is built by procreation of children."[33]

Moreover, the verse says that God made the woman from Adam's rib. This showed the man what honor he was to place upon his marriage if he was to honor God, for the woman was not made from man's head as if she were to rule over him, because the man is to be the head of the woman (Eph. 5:23). Neither was she made from man's foot as if she were to be set at man's feet as his servant. Rather, she was made from man's rib to show that she is his helpmate, that she is to lie in his bosom, and that she is to be close to his heart.[34] Willet offered several reasons why God made woman out of man's rib and not out of the earth as He did man:

> That hereby might appear the preeminence that man has over woman, as the apostle notes (1 Cor. 11:7–8)…therefore also the woman has her name and denomination of man…. Another cause of this work was that it might be a surer bond of love, that the man knowing the woman to be taken out of him, might more firmly set his affection upon her…. Other reasons are…not out of his head, that she should not be proud, nor out of his feet, as though she were man's vassal, but from his side, to show the love and conjunction between them.[35]

The woman's creation out of man's side testified that the woman was unlike the rest of creation and therefore was to have man's special regard, care, love, and nearness.

Is it any wonder, then, that a prudent wife is said to be a gift from the Lord in Proverbs 19:14? Honors and riches may be inherited from our parents, but a good wife is a present from heaven, as if she had written on her: *the gift of God*. So precious is this gift of God that Smith wrote, "Beasts are ordained for food, and clothes for warmth, and flowers for pleasure, but the wife is ordained for man; like a little Zoar, a city of refuge to fly to in all his troubles (Gen. 19:20); and there is no peace comparable unto her but the peace of conscience."[36] Rogers also

---

33. Willet, 38.
34. Smith, 1:8.
35. Willet, 37.
36. Smith, 1:8.

spoke of the woman as the gift of God when he said that "it is the use of the Holy Ghost to style excellent things [to be] God's things…because excellency cannot own anything that is base. God's greatness gives no common gifts, so that a wife is no common blessing: she is God's woman…a true gift of God, an excellent piece, [for] which a man may bless God while he lives…. Happy is he upon whose head such a crown is set, to whom heaven has given such a gift."[37]

Thus marriage is honorable in relation to several circumstances that attended its creation. It is honorable because it was instituted right away as part of man's very creation and in the state of man's innocence before his fall into sin. It is honorable because it was instituted in Paradise where everything was agreeable to man's satisfaction and delight. It is honorable because the first man and woman who married were the first parents of all mankind and He who married them was the Lord God Himself. It is honorable because it was the result of the Trinitarian counsel to provide for man's need. It is honorable because the woman was made perfectly suitable to the man's need and the man perfectly suitable to the woman's. It is honorable because the woman was made from man's rib to signify the honor which he was to place both upon his wife and his marriage to be a good steward before God.

Gouge therefore concluded, "Let all the forenamed branches concerning the first institution of marriage expressly recorded by the Holy Ghost be well weighed, and we shall easily see that there is no ordinance now in force among the sons of men so honorable in the institution thereof, as this."[38] Likewise, Rogers asked, "Now that which a God of pureness ordains by a perpetual decree of pureness, in an estate of pureness, how can it choose but to have an engraved character and formal nature of preciousness and honor in it?"[39]

---

37. Rogers, 4.

38. Gouge, 152. Gouge goes on to address the *ends*, *privileges*, and *mystery* of marriage, all which he persuasively argues contribute to the great honor God has placed upon marriage. We have chosen not to speak of these points here because we will take them up in subsequent chapters.

39. Rogers, 5–6.

Marriage Is Honorable in Relation to Christ

God the Father honored marriage and so did God the Son. Christ honored marriage in five ways: by His birth, His presence, His commendation, His relationship with His church, and His disciples.

First, Christ honored marriage by being born as the seed of the woman (Gen. 3:15; Matt. 1:18–25). If Christ became incarnate to accomplish our redemption and chose to be conceived and born of a woman who was espoused to a man, then surely this honors marriage by acknowledging it as the only proper context for the bearing of children. It was to the married couple that God gave the mandate to "be fruitful, and multiply" (Gen. 1:28).

Second, Christ honored marriage by His presence at the marriage in Cana of Galilee where He worked His first miracle by turning the water into wine (John 2:1–11). Christ was pleased to be present at this wedding feast and to do His first miracle on this occasion to show how He honored the marriage bond and the joyous celebration of it. Just as the first blessing of God recorded in Scripture was the benediction He placed upon the first marriage (Gen. 1:28), so the first blessing of Christ recorded in the Gospels was His presence at the marriage in Cana (John 2:11).

Third, Christ honored marriage by using it as a symbol of the kingdom of heaven. In Matthew 22:2, Christ compares the kingdom of heaven to a wedding feast which a king gave for his son and to which all were invited. And then, in verses 11–14, Christ compares one's rightful presence in the kingdom of heaven to being clothed in a wedding garment. Marriage is therefore commended as being a suitable comparison to the joys, communion, and fellowship that we enjoy with Christ in the kingdom of heaven.

Fourth, Christ honored marriage by choosing it to illustrate His relationship with His church. In Ephesians 5:32, after speaking of the duties of the wife to her husband and the duties of the husband to his wife and comparing their relationship to the relationship between Christ and His church, Paul declares, "This is a great mystery: but I speak concerning Christ and the church." Marriage illustrates better than any other human relationship the manner in which Christ intimately relates to His church, comforts His church, delights in her, and will glorify Himself in her and with her forever.[40] We are the bride of Christ, joined to Him by the Father just as God brought the woman to Adam. The Father gives us to the Son to be His bride (John 6:37) and, with sovereignty, draws us to the Son by an irresistible attraction and love (John 6:44) and grants us the grace to come to the Son that we might know His love (John 6:65).

Thus, when Scripture celebrates our union with Christ as our Savior, it often uses the metaphor of our being married to Him. We read of our marriage to God in Hosea 2:19: "And I will betroth thee unto me for ever; yea, I will betroth thee unto me in righteousness, and in judgment, and in lovingkindness, and in mercies." God accomplishes this marriage by joining us to Christ as our Bridegroom, to which Paul refers in 2 Corinthians 11:2: "for I have espoused you to one husband, that I may present you as a chaste virgin to Christ." Furthermore, the entire Song of Solomon celebrates the mystical union between Christ and His bride in the language of the love, passion, and intimacy enjoyed between a man and a woman in marriage. Also, Psalm 45 is a psalm of love which sets forth the glory of Christ as a bridegroom in verses 1–9 and the glory of the church as His bride in verses 10–17. Therefore marriage is honored by Christ by His choosing it of all ordinances to illustrate "the sacred, spiritual, real, and inviolable union betwixt Christ and his church."[41]

Finally, Christ honored marriage by the manner in which His servants spoke of it in His name. In Revelation 19:7–9, the heavenly host speaks of the consummation of our faith in Christ as "the marriage of the Lamb" and of the joys of that communion and fellowship as "the marriage supper of the Lamb." All believers will be gathered together as one on that day and presented as a bride to the Son arrayed in His righteousness. It will be our wedding day! Thus, in Revelation 21:9–10 when the angel shows John the church that God has prepared for His Son, he calls it "the bride, the Lamb's wife…descending out of heaven from God." By contrast, those who have rejected the invitation to be joined

---

40. Reyner, 4. We will speak of this in greater detail in a subsequent chapter.
41. Gouge, 153.

to the Lamb of God in holy matrimony are said to commit fornication with "the great whore" of the world (Rev. 17:1–2).

Paul also honors marriage in his writings. Not only does he speak of it with great honor in Ephesians 5, but he also shows in 1 Timothy 2:14–15 how the curse placed upon the fallen woman (that she should travail in childbirth, Gen. 3:16) is turned into blessing as, even in her fallen estate, she is able to bring forth children within the context of marriage and eventually the very Son of God who would be her Savior (Gen. 3:15; Isa. 9:6).

Marriage is therefore made honorable by virtue of its relation to Christ. He chose to be born of a woman espoused to a man. He honored the marriage union with His presence at a wedding feast in Cana and by manifesting His glory in the performance of His first public miracle at that feast. He honored marriage by using it as an illustration to represent the communion we will have with Him in the kingdom of heaven. He honored it more significantly by using it to set forth His relationship with His church, His expressions of love to her, and her duties to Him.[42] And He honored it by the teachings which He gave to the church through His disciples which echoed and built upon His own. How, then, can we consider marriage as anything less than honorable when our Savior has placed such a great honor upon it?

Marriage Is Honorable in Relation to the World
Marriage also has a special honor in providing the means by which the world is to be populated (Gen. 1:28; Mal. 2:15). Without marriage, men and women have no righteous way of fulfilling the mandate given by God to our first parents. If they sought to fulfill it outside of marriage it would be sexual immorality, which is contrary to the Lord's appointment and therefore abominable in His sight (Mal. 2:13–14). On this point, Whately argued,

> Take it away and the world must needs…come to an end within
> one age…. Debar marriage and you bring the being of the world
> to a full point, yea, to a final conclusion. Debar marriage and you

---

42. Reyner, 4–5.

shall have no families kept, no names maintained amongst men; but either this great habitation, the world, must fall, for want of lawful heirs, to beasts and birds alone to possess it, or else, which is worse, be intruded upon by base and mis-begotten men. We must have no world or but a beastly and confused world, if marriage were not.[43]

"What should the world be," Rogers wrote, "save a dungeon without it? And what is [the world] but an emptiness and vanity without the usefulness of marriage?"[44] Referring specifically to the benefit that marriage bears to the wellbeing of the world, he wrote, "Marriage is the preservative of chastity, the seminary of the commonwealth, seed-plot of the church, pillar (under God) of the world, right-hand of providence, supporter of laws, states, orders, offices, gifts, and services; the glory of peace, the sinews of war, the maintenance of policy, the life of the dead, the solace of the living, the ambition of virginity, the foundation of countries, cities, universities, succession of families, crowns, and kingdoms."[45]

To recap, marriage is honorable in relation to God who instituted it, in relation to the many circumstances that attended its original institution, in relation to Christ who crowned it in several ways, and in relation to the world which it provides with perpetual substance. How should this affect how we think of marriage, how we enter upon marriage, how we continue in marriage, and what we chiefly aim for in marriage?

Consider the following counsel. First, if God has made marriage honorable, we must not think lightly of it or consider it an estate lower than God has declared it to be;[46] nor must we judge marriage by what men's sins or opinions have made it to be. A crown is still a crown though it be cast in the dirt.[47] Therefore we must judge marriage as what God made it to be and declare that it is still honorable (Heb. 13:4).

Second, if marriage is honorable, then we must not enter into it carelessly as many do in our day. Those who enter into marriage should

---

43. Whately, *A Care-Cloth*, 22–23.

44. Rogers, 6.

45. Rogers, 6.

46. Reyner, 5.

47. Rogers, 5.

not do so with little thought of the duties incumbent upon them, little regard for the fruit that God expects of those who marry, and the difficulties that face those who marry. If we are to honor marriage as God expects, we must seek to *procure* the honor of marriage by entering it with due preparation and with a wisely chosen spouse. Only then can we expect the Lord's blessing.

Third, if marriage is honorable and we have procured the honor of marriage by a good entrance into it, then we who marry must seek to *preserve* that honor by the faithful observance of those duties which must be performed to each other within that marriage. Marriage must be guarded jealously, tended to with all diligence, and attended by the graces of God necessary for dealing with the infirmities of one's spouse. Only then will our marriages flourish to the glory of God and their honor maintained without fading "until death do us part."[48] How sad it is to see so many couples, either by pollution from without or corruption from within, lose the honor of their marriages which they had at the beginning. For, as Rogers observed, there is nothing so miserable than to *have been* happy.[49] They cast their crown in the dirt only to wonder why they no longer enjoy the blessings and benefits of marriage.

Fourth, if marriage bears the honor that God places upon it, we who marry must make God and His glory the beginning, aim, and end of our marriages. We must begin by calling upon God's name, continue by relying upon God's grace and looking to His law, and persevere to the end, looking always to Him. As Baxter said, "Those who sincerely follow God's counsel and aim at His glory and do it to please Him, will find God owning and blessing their [marriage]."[50] In other words, it is only when we begin our marriages with honor that we can proceed in them with piety and end them with glory to God.[51]

To help you *procure* and *preserve* the honor of marriage, the remaining chapters are put before you. We pray that God may use them to guide you with good counsel so that you might enter marriage with an

48. Rogers, 115–16.
49. Rogers, 115. Emphasis added.
50. Baxter, 47.
51. Taylor, 5.

eye to God's glory, order your marriage according to His Word, depend upon His presence and blessing in your marriage, and nurture your marriage to promote your salvation and Christian walk all your days.[52]

Study Questions

1. What is the foundational text in the Bible for understanding marriage as God's creation? What four basic principles does this text teach about marriage?

2. Why are same-sex unions not true marriages?

3. How is marriage dishonored or despised in our culture today?

4. How do the circumstances of God's institution of marriage honor the marriage relationship?

5. How should Proverbs 19:14 increase our gratitude if we have good spouses?

6. How did Jesus Christ honor marriage? List specific passages of Scripture.

7. What honorable functions in society does marriage have?

8. What does the honor of marriage imply about how we should go about seeking a spouse and getting married?

---

52. Reyner, 8–9.

9. How should a married couple preserve and enhance the honor of their marriage?

10. What are some ways that an honorable marriage gives honor to its Creator, the Lord?

The Purposes and Benefits of Marriage

The Puritans believed that the purposes and benefits of marriage flow naturally out of God's institution of marriage at the time of creation. This gives marriage an honorable place in the world and in the plans God has for mankind since He does nothing arbitrarily (Eph. 1:11). Therefore marriage must have a *purpose* as great as the primacy given to it in God's creation (Gen. 1:26–27; 2:21–22). It must also be *beneficial* to mankind, for God created marriage after declaring that it was not good for Adam to be alone (Gen. 2:18, 20, 23). In the previous chapter we addressed God's institution of marriage and the honor that He places upon it. We will now speak about the purposes for which God ordained marriage as well as the benefits that flow from it when a husband and wife seek God's glory.

The Purposes of Marriage

The Puritans believed the three main purposes for which God instituted marriage were the benefit of a good companion, the procreation of children, and, since the Fall, the avoidance of fornication.[1] Henry Smith said, "Now it must needs be, that marriage, which was ordained of such an excellent author, and in such a happy place, and of such an ancient time, and after such a notable order, must likewise have special causes for the ordinance of it."[2]

---

1. Swinnock, 1:464.
2. Smith, 1:8.

However, as the account of man's creation in Genesis 2:7, 15–23 is an expansion of what we read in Genesis 1:26–27, it is clear that God's statement in Genesis 2:18 that it is not good for man to be alone *preceded* the creation of woman and the mandate given to our first parents in Genesis 1:28 that they be fruitful and multiply. That shows us God was first of all concerned for man's mutual help, society, and comfort, and only *after* Eve's creation did He bless our first parents with the mandate to bring forth children.

God's initial concern was that man was alone and that was not good for him, so the Lord created Eve as a helper for Adam. Therefore the benefit of companionship takes precedence over the procreation of children as a purpose for marriage. Hence, as the teaching on marriage developed among the Puritans, it is not surprising that the benefit of a good companion became the first reason offered for the institution of marriage.[3]

For example, in Andrew Willet's commentary on Genesis, companionship took the primary place in his explanation of why God said it was not good for man to be alone: "This is so said, 1) in respect of mutual society and comfort; 2) in respect of the propagation of the world; 3) especially for the generation and increase of the church of God; 4) but most of all it was meet that woman should be joined to man, because of the promised seed of the woman, of whom came our Saviour Christ after the flesh."[4] In his sermon titled "The Marriage Ring," Jeremy Taylor also said companionship was the first priority. He said, "The first blessing God gave to man was society: and that society was a marriage, and that marriage was [joined] by God himself, and hallowed by a blessing."[5] We will therefore consider three purposes of marriage in this order.

1. Companionship

Just as man was created in response to the deliberate counsel of Genesis 1:26, "Let us make man in our image, after our likeness," so woman was made after the deliberate counsel of Genesis 2:18, "It is not good that

---

3. Ryken, 47–48.
4. Willet, 35.
5. Taylor, 1.

the man should be alone; I will make him an help meet for him." Thus the first cause of the woman's creation was that man was alone among all the creatures God had made. God decided it was better for man to lose a rib than lack a wife, better to lack part of himself than be without a second self who would complement his whole self.[6]

Marriage was therefore ordained in response to a natural necessity.[7] As Smith explained, Eve was given as a wife "to avoid the inconvenience of solitariness signified in these words, 'It is not good for man to be alone.' [It is] as though He had said, This life would be miserable and irksome, and unpleasant to man, if the Lord had not given him a wife to company his troubles."[8] Smith continued, "If it be not good for man to be alone, then it is good for man to have a fellow; therefore as God created a pair of all other kinds, so he created a pair of this kind."[9] Ainsworth said that God made man's companion "one that should be as his second self, like him in nature, knit unto him in love, needful for procreation of seed, helpful in all duties, present always with him, and so very meet and [convenient] for him."[10]

This does not mean there is no place for a single life, that singleness lacks real advantages, or that a life of celibacy is not pleasing to the Lord. At a time when the early church anticipated being scattered and broken into pieces by persecution, many of God's people found it more prudent to live a single life, lest being married cause undue suffering and hardship on a family when one parent was taken away by necessity or force (cf. 1 Cor. 7:25–31). In a time of persecution marriage might even become "an accidental impediment to the dissemination of the gospel,[11] which called men from a confinement in their domestic charges to travel, flight, poverty, hardship, and martyrdom."[12] As Taylor said, during such a time the apostle Paul recommended "the advantages of single life, not by any commandment of the Lord, but by the spirit

---

6. Reyner, 39.
7. Taylor, 6.
8. Smith, 1:12.
9. Smith, 1:12.
10. Ainsworth, 1:15.
11. I.e., by reason of the circumstances and not by reason of itself.
12. Taylor, 3.

of prudence…for the present and then incumbent necessities, and in order to the advantages which did accrue to the public ministries and private piety."[13] Singleness was not in itself a better service to God, but it might be more useful during the times of affliction in which the early church was living. "Saint Paul indeed commends single life," said Richard Bernard, "not simply, but with respect unto the then present times, full of troubles and persecutions."[14]

When God calls a person to be single, that condition has many advantages which are described by the apostle Paul in 1 Corinthians 7:35 as attending upon the Lord "without distraction," that is, with undivided devotion. By necessity, though not at all in a way unpleasing to the Lord, a married person is *divided* between attending to his spouse and serving his Lord (vv. 32–34). The advantage of singleness is therefore the "undivided" or undistracted devotion of which the apostle speaks in verse 35. Taylor said of this advantage, "Single life has in it [such] privacy and simplicity of affairs…that there are more spaces for religion *if* men would use them to these purposes. And because it *may* have in it much religion and prayers and *must* have in it a perfect mortification of our strongest appetites, it is therefore a state of great excellency."[15]

Yet marriage is still recommended as "honourable in all" (Heb. 13:4), whereas that is not said of singleness. What is more, singleness is never commanded in Scripture, whereas, in some cases, marriage is (1 Cor. 7:9, 36). While marriage has its *troubles*, the single life has its *desires*, which can be more troublesome, dangerous, and liable to result in sin, while the troubles of marriage call for the exercise of marital duty and piety. Though it may be argued that a single life has the advantage of chastity and devotion, it must be remembered that neither of these graces is absent from the married condition. Both chastity and devotion must be exercised in marriage to preserve the honor of marriage, and both must be exercised in trials that do not trouble the single life.

---

13. Taylor, 3.

14. Richard Bernard, *Ruth's Recompence: Or, A Commentary Upon the Book of Ruth* (Stoke-on-Trent, England: Tentmaker Publications, 2006), 66.

15. Taylor, 5. Emphasis added.

Some say that the single life is full of perpetual sweetness because it lacks the bitter trials of the married life. This may be true to some extent; but it is still a life of singularity and—what is sometimes more dominant—a life of hardship because by definition it is a life without the companionship that only a spouse can provide. Ecclesiastes 4:10 tersely summarizes the hardship of being alone when it says, "Woe to him that is alone when he falleth; for he hath not another to help him up." Applying this verse to marriage, Charles Bridges summarized the Puritan view of the advantages of marriage, saying:

> To begin at the beginning—with that ordinance, where God declared his own mind—"It is not good for man to be alone".... If it was "not good" in paradise, much less is it in a wilderness world. What claim, then, has a monastic or a celibate life to higher perfection? When *two* are brought together by the Lord's providence (Gen. 2:22)—and specially when each is fitted to each other by His grace—"dwelling together as heirs of the grace of life" (1 Pet. 3:7), in abiding union of hearts—having one faith—one hope—one aim—who can doubt the fact—*Two are better than one*? Love sweetens toil, soothes the sting of trouble, and gives a Christian zest of enjoyment to every course of daily life. The mutual exercises of sympathy give energy to prayer, and furnish large materials for confidence and praise.[16]

Therefore, if a single life has more time for singular devotion, married life is more complicated and thus has more need to exercise more graces (those peculiar to the marital estate) in more ways towards one's spouse and family. For example, what can a single woman know of submission to her husband "as unto the Lord," and what can a single man know of loving his wife as Christ loves His church? What can a celibate know of the duties of parents and the exercise of love towards in-laws, or of the union of hands and hearts and the pleasures of the undefiled marriage bed? What can a single person know of the privilege of being the nursery of heaven and the earthly picture of the marriage of Christ and His bride? In so many ways, marriage is recognized as an excellent blessing from the Lord.

---

16. Charles Bridges, *Ecclesiastes* (Edinburgh: Banner of Truth, 1992), 90.

While marriage has its thorns, so does every relationship this side of heaven. This world is a wilderness in which every condition is beset by the troubles and afflictions of sin. According to Job, man's days are few and full of trouble (14:1). Therefore no condition on earth is entirely happy, if happy means "free of trouble." But marriage has the particular advantage of support in times of sorrow because of the companionship it offers. God brought two together "that the infinite troubles which lie upon us in the world might be eased with the comfort and help one of another."[17] "Though man's corruption has filled [marriage] and every state of life with snares and troubles, yet from the beginning it was not so," said Baxter. But "God appointed it for mutual help, and as such it may be used.... A married life has its benefits, which you are thankfully to accept and acknowledge to God."[18]

A single person lacks a companion as close as a spouse with whom to share his crosses. All his troubles must be carried in his own heart and borne on his own shoulders. If a man is afflicted, who will console him? If a woman is sick in bed, who will take care of her? Upon such considerations Solomon pronounced a "woe" upon a man who is alone (Eccl. 4:9–12). Smith wrote of such a person, "Thoughts, and cares, and fears will come to him because he has none to comfort him, [just] as thieves steal in when the house is empty."[19] A single person may have friends to help him in such times of need, but he lacks a companion as intimate as a spouse, a companion so close as to be *one* with him, who can provide comfort and solace.

A married man has a companion who enters his heart, partakes of all that happens to him, is touched by all his disasters, and does everything in her power to sweeten his condition, ease his mind, cheer his heart, and share his troubles. Husbands and wives can help one another in keeping troubles at bay; and when that proves impossible, they can help by bearing one another's burdens, supplying each other's wants, and being helpers to each other's joy.[20] Gouge said a spouse helps

17. Smith, 1:12.
18. Baxter, 46.
19. Smith, 1:12.
20. Scudder, 63–64.

bring forth and raise children, helps in ordering prosperity and bearing adversity, helps in health and sickness, helps in all of life, and even helps in death, seeing it as the occasion of giving thanks to the Lord for the days and years they have spent together in helpful companionship.[21]

Therefore, in the married estate we can expect "the greatest earthly comforts attainable in this life, even much spiritual comfort, if the yokefellows do truly fear God…so that they apply themselves to be helpful, and to do good, and give all lawful [satisfaction] unto each other, in all the good offices which they owe as husband and wife, and as heirs together of the same grace of life."[22] That conviction moved Scudder to inquire if there was a greater blessing than "to enjoy a meet help, one who may rejoice thy heart in this thy pilgrimage, one who may accompany thee, and cheer thee up in the way, when thou art treading many a weary step to the land of rest?"[23]

2. Procreation

The second purpose of marriage flows out of Genesis 1:28, "And God blessed them, and God said unto them, Be fruitful, and multiply, and replenish the earth, and subdue it: and have dominion over the fish of the sea, and over the fowl of the air, and over every living thing that moveth upon the earth." Within matrimony, our first parents were blessed by God with dominion over all creation and the mandate to bring forth children.

Just as God created all of life to reproduce according to its kind—whether plants or animals—so His image bearers, man and woman, were also created capable of reproduction. In their headship over every living creature in the world, God's image bearers were the apex of all that He had made, but this goal could not be realized unless man increased and multiplied over the face of the vast earth that God created for him. For man was not only to multiply but was also to "have dominion" over all creation as God's vice-regent, exercising his lordship under God and in the name of God. Creation would instinctively recognize the Cre-

---

21. Gouge, 152–53.
22. Scudder, 64.
23. Scudder, 6.

ator's image in man and bow in service to him, whether it was an ox yielding its neck to the yoke or the ground yielding itself to the plow that it might bring forth abundant crops in season. Such global dominion and vice-regency necessitated that man be fruitful and multiply.

Consequently, once God brought the woman to the man in marriage (Gen. 2:22), He immediately charged them to bring forth children. What does this charge on the sixth day of creation prove, if not that procreation was one of the very purposes for which God made and married Adam and Eve? Hence one of the purposes of marriage was procreation. God made them, explained Smith, "not both male nor both female, but one male and the other female; as if he created them fit to propagate.... And therefore when He had created them so, to show that propagation of children is one end of marriage, He said unto them, 'Increase and multiply,' (Gen. 1:28); that is, bring forth other children, as other creatures bring forth their kind."[24] Smith wrote, "For this cause marriage is called *matrimony*, which signifies *motherage*, because it makes mothers of those who were virgins before, and is the seminary of the world, without which all things [in creation] should be in vain, for want of men to use them; for God reserves the great city [heaven] to Himself; and this suburb He has set out unto us, which are regents."[25]

This mandate was given to our first parents before they yielded to sin. This shows that God sought more than just the natural, animal-like multiplication of men upon the earth, for fallen men can accomplish this well enough. Rather, God desired "a religious and holy posterity, such as might worship [Him]."[26] Hence in Malachi 2:15, when the prophet rebuked the people for perverting the ordinance of marriage by taking more than one wife, he said the reason God joined one man to one woman in marriage was that He sought "a godly seed."

By calling our parents to be fruitful and multiply *prior to* the entrance of sin, God was calling them to propagate so that His church, of which they were the only members at the time, might cover His earth. They were to glorify God by raising a seed set apart to worship Him.

---

24. Smith, 1:9.
25. Smith, 1:9.
26. Stock, 177.

Stock put it this way: "Though sin had never come, yet this end was ordained of God (Gen. 1:28): propagation of mankind, but specially the church; nay, by [the family in Gen. 1:28] is only meant the church, seeing [Adam and Eve] were in their perfection; and if then they had given themselves to propagation or had continued in their first estate, they had brought forth still holy men in their perfect image, who should have been the seed of God."[27]

Now both Scripture and experience teach us that no marriage can bring forth children who are holy and godly by nature, for we are all conceived and born in sin and are children of wrath (Pss. 51:5; 58:3; Eph. 2:3). Though our first parents were created after the image of God and would have brought forth children after that image had they obeyed God in the probation (Gen. 2:16–17), Genesis 5:1–3 tells us that because of the fall into sin, Adam's posterity (all born *after* the Fall) are born after his *fallen* likeness and image. Also, Paul declares in Romans 3:10 that "there is none righteous, no, not one," and Ecclesiastes 7:29 states unequivocally that man fell from his original estate of righteousness: "Lo, this only have I found, that God hath made man upright; but they have sought out many inventions." Thus holiness and sanctification do not come by nature, but rather only by grace for Christ's sake.

Did the fall of mankind into sin make procreation null and void, since it is impossible for two married sinners to bring forth anything other than sinners like themselves? Not at all. This purpose of marriage has not changed because God does not change (Mal. 3:6). One of the purposes of marriage today is still that we raise a godly seed for the Lord. Baxter wrote, "It is no small mercy to be the parents of a godly seed; and this is the purpose of the institution of marriage (Mal. 2:15)."[28] Ephesians 6:4 tells fathers to bring up their children "in the nurture and admonition of the Lord"; Proverbs 22:6 directs parents to train their children up in the way they should go, which can be no other way than the way of the Lord; and Ephesians 6:1–2 commands, "Children, obey your parents in the Lord: for this is right. Honour thy father and mother."

---

27. Stock, 183.
28. Baxter, 46.

God commands believing fathers and mothers to raise their children for Him and He also urges those children to honor their parents for His sake. Gouge encouraged believers to have children so that "the world might be increased; and not simply increased, but with a legitimate brood, and distinct families, which are the seminaries of cities and the Commonwealths. Yea also that in the world the Church by a holy seed might be preserved and propagated (Mal. 2:15)."[29]

Of course this purpose is not expected of parents who are not believers since unbelieving parents cannot raise children for God. But if the parents are believers and by the grace of God are enjoying the honor of a marriage lived for His glory, this purpose is revealed in the covenant that God makes with them and with their children (Gen. 17:7; Isa. 44:3; Acts 2:39). For it is by virtue of the covenant that our children are borne to the Lord (Ezek. 16:20) and are said to be holy (1 Cor. 7:14).

Thus our children are *God's* children, whom He has entrusted to us to raise for Him. He has a special claim on them as the One who blessed and opened the womb (Ruth 4:13; 1 Sam. 1:19–20). He holds us accountable to teach our children about Him, direct them to Him, urge them to believe in Him, and take Him as their own God. Having expressed His willingness to be their God in their baptism as infants, God holds us parents accountable to encourage them to consent to the marriage between Christ and their souls. He holds us accountable to raise children who, so far as it depends on us, are not strangers to Him but are embracers of the true religion and worshipers of the true God. His grace alone can save, sanctify, and make our children holy by uniting them to Christ. As He calls on us to see that our children are raised within the covenant family, we look to Him that by His grace they might become professors in the one true God and religion.[30]

That explains why God forbids (1 Cor. 6:15–16; 2 Cor. 6:14) and reproves (Gen. 6:1–2, 5; Ezra 10:10–11) unequal marriages between a believer and an unbeliever, and why He commands us to marry "only in the Lord" (1 Cor. 7:39). As Stock pointed out, though the number of mankind might be increased by such marriages, the more central

---

29. Gouge, 152.
30. Stock, 183.

purpose of a godly seed will be frustrated by these unequal matches because the yoke is being pulled in two different directions.[31]

Such marriages may raise children apart from God, ignorant of God, and in rebellion against God. Such child-rearing outside the covenant, rather than fostering neutrality in children's minds and hearts, motivates them against God and the authority of His Word, against Christ and the salvation He offers to them as sinners, and hardens them in the ways of ungodliness and destruction. If we leave God out of the center of our children's training, then it will take a miracle for God to find a saving place in them as adults, for God usually saves by bringing up children in the Word (Prov. 22:6; Rom. 10:17).[32]

God still seeks a seed to worship him, a seed raised within the covenant, a seed raised to profess Him as God and trust Him for salvation; and He still holds parents responsible to train their children to love, obey, and serve Him with all their heart and soul, as much as to feed, clothe, and care for their bodies.

Thankfully, though God remains a sovereign dispenser of His saving grace and is under no obligation to bestow it upon any of our children, He promises to bless our seed (Isa. 44:3; Prov. 22:6) and declares that He is pleased to impart His saving grace to our children when we acknowledge our responsibility and strive to raise them for Him (Ex. 34:6–7; Ps. 103:17). We must train our children in the ways of the Lord, trusting that He will bless our efforts and that when we appear before Him we'll be able to say, "Behold I and the children which God hath given me" (Heb. 2:13).

3. Avoidance of Sin

The third purpose of marriage surfaced after the Fall when man's lust strove against the purity and chastity to which God called him and broke out into fornication, adultery, and uncleanness. God graciously brought His institution of marriage forward in opposition to the deceitful plea-

---

31. Stock, 183.

32. Cf. "Parental Responsibilities" in *Discussions by Robert L. Dabney, D.D.* (Harrisonburg: Sprinkle Publications, 1982), 1:676–93.

sures of sin to serve as a remedy.[33] With this third purpose in mind, Swinnock defined marriage as "the lawful conjunction of one man and one woman for the term of their natural lives, for…the avoiding of sin."[34]

The apostle Paul declares this purpose of marriage in 1 Corinthians 7:2 when he says, "To avoid fornication, let every man have his own wife, and let every woman have her own husband." Hence Reyner wrote, "Though marriage was instituted before there was sin, and Adam needed it not as a remedy against [lust], yet upon another account… since the fall, it is of necessary and sovereign use to prevent sin and to procure or promote our sanctification, that we may possess our vessels in holiness and honor, not in the lust of concupiscence: this is the will of God [1 Thess. 4:3–5]."[35]

God calls us to avoid fornication and adultery so He appointed marriage to be the most sanctified alternative to those sins (1 Cor. 7:9). Marriage is designed by God, Paul says, to satisfy the sexual appetite as husband and wife render "due benevolence" to each other (1 Cor. 7:3). When this benevolence is lovingly rendered (1 Cor. 7:5), "marriage is a haven to such as are in jeopardy of their salvation through the gusts of temptations to lust."[36]

In Proverbs 5, Solomon tells men to keep far away from a wanton woman (v. 8) and not be ravished by a stranger (v. 20). Rather than assuaging our thirst away from home, he says we are to drink water out of our own cistern and our own well (v. 15), to rejoice in the wife of our youth (v. 18), delighting in her beauty and ravishing her with love (v. 19). Of these verses, Charles Bridges wrote, "Tender, well-regulated, domestic affection is the best defense against the vagrant desires of unlawful passion."[37]

Some, like the apostle Paul (1 Cor. 7:7), have the gift of celibacy and can remain chaste and content in an unmarried estate; but since celibacy is a gift of God, it cannot be commanded of all (v. 6). Each

---

33. William Arnot, *Studies in Proverbs* (Grand Rapids: Kregel, 1998), 133.
34. Swinnock, 1:464.
35. Reyner, 40.
36. Gouge, 152.
37. Charles Bridges, *Proverbs* (Edinburgh: Banner of Truth, 1968), 58.

person must know his calling from the Lord and honor Him in it (v. 17). Therefore any man or woman is free to marry in the Lord as a remedy for lust since marriage is the means God has appointed to quench that fire (v. 9). "For those that have not the gift of [celibacy] this is the only warranted, and sanctified remedy," said Gouge.[38] Taylor called this third purpose of marriage "the enemy to hell and an antidote of the chiefest inlet to damnation."[39]

In light of the Lord's goodness to man in providing him with marriage as a remedy for his lustful desires, it is grievous to see so many people either reject marriage for the deceitful pleasures of fornication, destroy their marriages with adulterous relationships, or, worse still, pervert this blessed institution with homosexual relationships. Have we forgotten how heinous all forms of sexual immorality are and how the Lord will punish those who indulge in them (Heb. 13:4)?

The clearest view of a virtue's beauty is seen by setting it beside its opposite vice. The infamy of sexual immorality is committed *prior to* as many marriages as it happens *during* and therefore prevents as many marriages as it destroys. The wide acceptance of all forms of sexual immorality today makes marriage seem like a mere formality. It may even seem foolish to address a practice so fixed in our society that one would have a better chance of turning the tide back with his own hands. But the truth of God must be declared whether men hear us or not, and we rest content that His sheep will hear His voice (Ezek. 2:3–5; John 10:27).

No greater harm can be done to a marriage, to those who are preparing for marriage, or to those who are unmarried than to indulge in sexual sin. Some argue that stolen waters are sweet, but as sin is always against God and God alone is good, sin can never be sweet in itself. When we taste of sin and find it to be sweet, this response says more about the nature of our palate rather than the nature of sin. Sin is, can only be, and always will be poisonous and destructive. Whatever sweetness our sinful flesh finds in this sin, it will always prove to be bitter in the end.

---

38. Gouge, 152.
39. Taylor, 13.

To determine how heinous adultery, fornication, and all forms of sexual immorality are, consider what William Greenhill wrote in his exposition of Ezekiel 18:5–6.[40] First, sexual sin violates the institution of an infinitely wise God in which He appointed two to be one flesh, and not three or more (Gen. 2:24; 1 Cor. 6:16). And while people try to commit such deeds in secret and remain undiscovered by others, God sees and knows what is happening (Prov. 5:20–21).

Second, adultery stains the ordinance of God that Scripture declares to be honorable in itself (Heb. 13:4) and which serves as an earthly picture of the marriage between Christ and His church (Eph. 5:31–32). Adultery defiles the marriage bed and, when committed by those who belong to the Lord, shamefully joins Christ's holy bride to another (1 Cor. 6:15–16).

Third, adultery reduces rational men, who are the height of God's creation, to irrational beasts by making them forget reason and chase after their lusts (Hos. 4:11; Jer. 5:7–8; 13:27).

Fourth, in adultery and fornication man sins: against his own body (1 Cor. 6:18), making himself one with an adulteress and defiling his body with uncleanness (Matt. 15:19–20); against his name and credit, for he brings dishonor and reproach upon himself (Prov. 6:33); against the peace and comfort of his own conscience, for he will be sorely wounded with guilt, shame, and the accusations of God's law (Prov. 7:26); and against his own soul, which is to be prized more than the whole world (Prov. 6:32; 7:27; 23:27; Mark 8:36–37).

Fifth, adultery is a great offense to the innocent party, whether husband or wife (Prov. 23:27–28). When a husband goes to another woman, he breaks the covenant he made with his wife before the Lord to be hers and hers alone. When a wife goes to another man, she forsakes the husband to whom she promised her faithfulness and love before God. Is this not the greatest wrong a man can do to his wife or a woman to her husband, in tearing themselves away from the spouse of their youth and giving their hearts, affections, and bodies to another (1 Cor. 7:3–4)?

Sixth, adultery is a sin that brings ruin upon a family (Job 31:12).

---

40. Greenhill, 441–43.

Seventh, adultery involves, if not causes, many other sins as those who work to commit it also work to either deny it or keep it hidden (2 Sam. 11). "No sin goes alone," Rogers wrote, "but to be sure, [adultery] cannot avoid many [other sins] to accompany it. Once over the shoes in this puddle, rarely will Satan leave off, till he has by degrees got you over head and ears."[41]

Finally, adultery is sin against the seventh commandment of a most holy and pure God. Therefore it shuts a person out of heaven by His just judgment and invokes God's eternal wrath, from which no escape and against which no appeal shall be admitted if there is no repentance (Mal. 3:5; Heb. 13:4; 2 Pet. 2:9–10; 1 Cor. 6:9–10; Rev. 21:8; 22:15; 2 Thess. 1:9).

Though adultery is so great an evil and brings upon a person so many hurtful and deadly consequences (unless grace intervenes), most adulterers are unwilling to turn away from this evil conduct.

But God has provided a remedy for adultery in the blessed estate of marriage. And God has provided a Savior through whom all who see their need for deliverance from this sin can be saved! Lust is a many-headed monster and a spring which may divide itself into many rivers in a person's life; but Christ is the King of kings and Lord of lords whose throne is above heaven and earth and whose power is over all. He alone can break the power of lust and will do so for all who come to Him (Matt. 11:28–30). He alone can give you a love for purity and chastity, a desire to live for God's glory, and the grace to mortify the sin of uncleanness and yield all the members of your body unto righteousness and cleanness.

> If you are guilty of the terrible sin of adultery, humble yourself under God's just judgment and seek refuge in the Savior who is willing to forgive, has power to save, and has a love for sinners which constrains both. "Beg of the Lord to turn a terrified heart into a melting one…to mold an unclean soul into a clean and chaste one," said Rogers. "No hammer can do this; mercy must dissolve it in the furnace of grace."[42] And look to God's promises:

---

41. Rogers, 318.
42. Rogers, 343.

first, that all your sins shall be forgiven and never imputed to your account (Jer. 3:1–2; 1 John 1:9), for the Lord has opened such a fountain in Jesus Christ that the chief of sinners can be pardoned and all of his sins can be washed away. Second, that once the Lord forgives you of your sins, though they were very grievous and you lived a long time in them, yet He will never look at you that way again; rather, He will see you in His Son as one of the members of His body, holy and acceptable (1 Cor. 6:9–11; Eph. 1:6).

The Benefits of Marriage

As God instituted marriage and made it honorable so God also blessed marriage and made it beneficial. Hence the *benefits* of marriage coincide with the *purposes* of marriage. God instituted marriage with particular goals in mind, but also with a particular good in mind, and our enjoyment of the latter depends upon our pursuit of the former. If we abuse marriage contrary to His purposes, then it can render little benefit to us since God has not promised to bless our abuse. Only when we acknowledge the purposes for which He appointed marriage—and seek His help that our marriages may serve those ends—can we look to Him for the experience of them.

What is the good which God had in mind for marriage and the benefits that He crowns upon the married estate? Two Puritans are of great help here: Edward Reyner and Thomas Gataker. Reyner addressed this question in a treatise on marriage, and Gataker addressed it in several sermons. Those sermons spoke of the good that comes via a good wife, but much of what Gataker said can easily be applied to husbands as well. Before presenting Reyner's approach, let us explain more fully the relationship between the purposes and benefits of marriage, because some of what Reyner describes as benefits have already been presented as purposes, and it is important that we understand the difference.

A *purpose* of marriage is a reason why God instituted it. For example, one purpose is that man might have the benefit of a good companion (Gen. 2:18). Another is that godly seed might be raised up for the Lord (Mal. 2:15). A *benefit* of marriage, however, is a fruit of marriage which we enjoy by God's mercy and blessing when we honor Him by living for His glory in our marriages. Consequently, listing a purpose as a benefit makes the point that when we honor God in our marriages we will enjoy the blessing of fulfilling the ends for which He appointed marriage.

That is not to say that an unbelieving couple who lives without regard to God's glory in their marriage cannot enjoy some of the benefits of marriage. Under the umbrella of God's common grace, many unbelieving couples are recipients of some of the blessings of marriage. However, there is a vast difference between being blind recipients of the blessings of marriage and knowingly receiving the blessings of marriage from the hands of a loving and wise Father in heaven.

Unbelieving couples may know such blessings as companionship and bearing children, but they may not see these things as blessings from God and so do render thanks to God for them, acknowledging the wisdom and love of God in the distribution of His blessings. They also cannot fully benefit from these blessings because they do not see them as instruments in the hands of God for their sanctification. Instead, these very blessings often turn out to be thorns and snares to them instead of blessings, hindrances instead of helps, unsatisfactory instead of fulfilling, and taxing instead of occasions of praise. On the other hand, a Christian couple can pray to God for the benefits of marriage, praise and thank God for the benefits bestowed, exercise faithful stewardship before God for those benefits, and trust that whether benefits are given, restricted, or entirely withheld, God is working all things for their good for Christ's sake (Rom. 8:28). An unbelieving couple does not truly taste and see that the Lord is good. They are inclined to bite the hand that feeds them and deny the Giver a return upon His gifts.

Reyner suggested that the benefits of marriage may be divided into five categories: personal, familial, political, ecclesiastical, and universal.[43] We will consider these briefly, starting with the *personal* benefits to those who marry. One is that a couple has the benefit of companionship. The constitution of the body as well as the disposition of the mind show that human beings are made for relationship. A husband and wife complement and complete each other as suitable companions

---

43. Reyner, 38–48.

and help mates (Eccl. 4:9–10). Second, they enjoy the benefit of preserving chastity. Marriage provides them with God-given satisfaction of their sexual desires and therefore bridles lust (1 Cor. 7:2, 9). Third, those who marry enjoy the benefit of mutual help. They can be a solace to each other in adversity, sickness, and poverty as well as in joy and prosperity (Esth. 4:14). Baxter said of this, "If God calls you to marriage, take notice of the helps and comforts of that condition, as well as the hindrances and troubles, that you may cheerfully serve God in it, in the expectation of His blessing…. God appointed it for mutual help, and as such it may be used."[44]

Fourth, in marriage a couple may enjoy the privilege of promoting their relationships with Christ, who is the heavenly Husband of them both (Jer. 3:14; Eph. 5:31–32). The greatest benefit of marriage is to provide mutual help in religion. As Swinnock said, "God did not institute marriage to be a hindrance, but to be a help in religion. Good company should make us walk the more cheerfully in the way of God's commandments."[45] Marriage directs wives to Christ for the spiritual love, kindness, tenderness, comfort, nourishing, and cherishing that they owe their husbands. Marriage teaches us as Christians to reserve our hearts wholly for Christ, so that we embrace only Him, subject our desires and will to His, surrender ourselves wholly to His disposal, open our hearts to Him, be "sick with love" for Him and grieve for His absence, forsake all that is dear to us to follow Him, and leave all and cleave to Him. This is to "spiritualize marriage and to improve it to a high, holy, and heavenly use, the benefit whereof will extend to the days of eternity."[46]

The second category of the benefits of marriage is *familial.* Believing husbands and wives enjoy the benefit of building a family which may extend to several generations. Just as Rachel and Leah were used to build up the house of Israel (Ruth 4:11), so marriage provides the only lawful means to make men and women fathers and mothers, to raise sons and daughters to carry on after them as living monuments

---

44. Baxter, 46.
45. Swinnock, 1:465.
46. Reyner, 44.

and representations of themselves.[47] Without marriage, a family's great name may perish quickly (Judg. 11:34, 38); but a family name may be long remembered by the help of the children who mirror the things for which their forbears stood and serve the God for whom they lived (2 Tim. 1:5; 3:14–15; Ruth 4:12).

The third category of benefits is *political*. Marriage lays the foundation "of cities, countries, nations; of laws and civil government; of common-wealths and kingdoms," Reyner said.[48] Marriage is thus the basic building block upon which every political structure is built. With its offspring, marriage furnishes these structures with the people needed to fill them.

The fourth category is *ecclesiastical*. Marriage replenishes Christ's church on earth with members and provides living stones and pillars for Christ's church in heaven.

The fifth category according to Reyner is *universal*. Marriage preserves and increases the human race. This was one purpose of the marriage of our first parents before the Fall (Gen. 1:28) and was included in God's benediction upon their marriage after the Fall (Gen. 3:15; 4:1). Assuming that human beings did not transgress God's commandment and have children out of wedlock, Reyner said that, "were it not for marriage, the world would come to an end."[49]

Reflecting on these several benefits of a God-honoring marriage, Reyner urged three responses. First, this should make us *thankful* to God that He has provided so beneficial a relationship as marriage. "It is a bundle of benefits," Reyner said. "How many both private and public are bound up together in it as in one volume?"[50] It should also make us thankful for all the help and comfort that the Lord affords us from our spouses. Well may husbands bless God for their wives and well may wives bless God for their husbands, because there is no help in all of life's troubles equal to that of a godly spouse. As Gouge said, "No such

---

47. Gouge, 153.
48. Reyner, 45.
49. Reyner, 45–46.
50. Reyner, 46.

help can man have from any other creature as from a wife, or a woman as from a husband."[51]

Second, Reyner said this should teach us to *improve* our marriages so that we might enjoy all the benefits for which God appointed them. We should strive to glorify God in our marriages so that we might enjoy the comfort He promised in them. We should strive to make our marriages serve the good of our souls as well as our bodies so that they serve our needs here on earth and promote our readiness for heaven. We should strive in marriage to build godly families whose members know, fear, and serve God. We should strive in marriage to send forth offspring that will serve the church and society to God's glory.

Third, Reyner said the benefits of a God-honoring marriage *reprove* those who marry without intending to glorify God. Such couples enjoy few of the benefits of marriage. Instead, when they marry for their own ends, their homes are often places of discord that may end in divorce. When they marry for lust's sake, they are never satisfied by their spouses; their eyes remain full of adultery (2 Pet. 2:14) and they are quickly drawn to another. When they marry without an eye on God's glory, they expect no help from heaven but view it as a hindrance. They neglect to raise a seed for the Lord, so they often get children as ungodly as themselves, if not worse. They do not care whether their children honor the Lord and their families are often built upon the children's whims; thus, their children are often no help in society, but become prodigals and squanderers of what their parents gave them. When they marry without a desire to love and serve one another for the Lord's sake, they often prove to be thorns in each other's sides and provoke each other to anger. They marry without reference to the Lord of marriage, so they know nothing about how marriage is supposed to reflect God before a lost world.[52] Can there be anything more important than to honor God in marriage and to live for God's glory throughout our days?

Thomas Gataker also spoke of the *benefits* of marriage. His sermon "A Wife in Deed" is based on Proverbs 18:22: "Whoso findeth a wife findeth a good thing, and obtaineth favour of the LORD." In that sermon,

---

51. Gouge, 153.
52. Reyner, 47–48.

Gataker explained six benefits of having a godly wife. In his summary of those benefits, Gataker wrote that a good wife is "the best companion in wealth; the fittest and readiest assistant in work; the greatest comfort in crosses and griefs; the only warrantable and comfortable means of issue and posterity; a singular and sovereign remedy ordained by God against [lust]; and the greatest grace and honor that can be, to him that has her."[53] Secker put it more simply when he wrote, "Good servants are a great blessing; good children are a greater blessing; but a good wife is the greatest blessing."[54]

Gataker began as Reyner did, with the benefit of *companionship*. This benefit tops the list of both the purposes and the benefits of marriages written by the Puritans. While they did not condemn celibacy for those who were called to it, the Puritans were convicted that man was made for society and that solitude was uncomfortable and "inconvenient" or troublesome (Gen. 2:18; Eccl. 4:9–11). They believed a man desires company with whom he may share his thoughts and life; and the more likeminded the company is, the better will be the benefit and joy gained from it, and the more he will desire and seek it out again.

A wife is therefore a man's best companion and friend. Gataker suggested that Adam was *truly* happy in Eden, but he was not *fully* happy until God had provided him with a wife and he was joined to the woman as his closest friend and companion in all of life. Gataker said, "There is no society more near, more entire, more needful, more kindly, more delightful, more comfortable, more constant, more continual, than the society of man and wife."[55] He was convinced that a house was "half [furnished] and unfinished, and not fully happy but half happy, though otherwise never so happy," until it was completed with a wife.[56]

Second, a godly wife brings the benefit of *assistance*. Eve was provided for Adam not merely as a mate, but as a helper. As man was created to work and to glorify God in activity, he needed help (Gen. 2:18). Therefore, God provided an assistant for him. If man needed this

---

53. Gataker, 166.
54. Secker, 269.
55. Gataker, 161.
56. Gataker, 161.

help before his fall into sin when work was neither a burden nor painful to him, how much more do we need the help of another when our work is wearisome, our sin burdensome, and our troubles cumbersome? Hence Solomon argued that two are better than one (Eccl. 4:9). If one falls the other can lift him up; if one is cold the other can warm him; if one is weak, the other can strengthen him; if a task is too much for one, it may be carried more easily by two.

Who is better suited to help man in his tasks and trials than the wife whom God created to be his helper? A wife is so suited to a man and his needs that she is almost his second self (Gen. 2:24). A marriage has four eyes seeing, four hands working, and four feet walking.[57] What ways of prudence cannot be discovered when so many eyes are looking for them? What work cannot be accomplished when so many hands are given to it? What paths of righteousness cannot be traversed and paths of wickedness avoided when so many feet are walking together in step? Additionally, if one pair needs a rest, the other may watch; if one pair fails, the other may recover the loss and save them both.

Such a benefit simply cannot be found in a friend or brother, but is peculiar to a spouse since marriage makes the two to be one flesh (Gen. 2:24). A friend cannot be available in every hour of need. A friend may live far away and not be able to come quickly. A friend may himself be in need and therefore be unable to give assistance to another. A friend may have his affections drawn away by another so that his love for you withers. But a spouse is a help always near, a help always ready, and a help always able, because a spouse is close, dear, and careful. Furthermore, how many needs does a spouse have that require the tenderness, intimacy, and unconditional love that only a spouse can supply? As close as a friend or a brother may be, he can never be *as* close to a man as a wife and to a woman as a husband.

Third, a godly wife brings the benefit of *comfort*. To be sure, a friend is a blessing at all times, but what need is greater than facing trial and grief? In danger and distress the presence of a stranger will only discourage and disappoint, but the sight of a friend will lift the spirits,

---

57. Gataker, 162.

inspire courage, and rekindle hope. That friend might ease the burden or even remove it entirely. If all he can do is sit on the ash-heap and join his tears with ours, it would be no small comfort.

But who is better suited to comfort and solace a husband in times of affliction and adversity than his godly wife? She can comfort her husband in his sickness and accompany him in his weakness. She will gladly yield her own neck to the yoke which he pulls and her shoulders to the burden which he bears. Without a thought for herself, she will stoop to do what she can to comfort and console her husband. As Gataker said, "There is no need of mercy where there is no misery; nor use of comfort where no cross is. And if in Paradise...a place all of delight, a garden of pleasure, there was yet need of help and society, and of the help and society of [a wife]...how much more then in this world, in this vale of tears, where crosses are so [common]...and where the more crosses man is encumbered with...the more need of comfort and assistance he has?"[58]

Fourth, Gataker said a godly wife brings the benefit of *children*. Genesis 1:28 says, "God blessed them, and God said unto them, Be fruitful, and multiply," showing that the ability to bring forth children is His blessing upon marriage. And what a great blessing that is! Man had the preeminence in creation, for he was made first (Gen. 2:7). But it was also a great honor when God made the man and his wife to bring forth children to propagate the earth. He who created out of nothing could have easily continued to do so, but instead He chose to appoint man and woman as His instruments to do so.

After the Fall when human beings became mortal and corrupted by sin, God might have removed this honor, yet He did not. Rather, He continued to use men and women to bring forth every successive generation (Gen. 5:1–3). In the face of our mortality (Gen. 5:4–31), this blessing is a great comfort because it gives us a kind of immortality, as our names and possessions can be carried on by our posterity. A man in his old age is comforted by knowing that, though he must go the way of

---

58. Gataker, 163, quoting Bernard.

all the earth (1 Kings 2:2), he has an heir to carry on in his stead (Gen. 15:2). It is no small blessing for a dying man to have begotten children.

If children are so great a blessing, how much greater is the blessing of marriage which brings them forth? Marriage is the root from which the fruit of children spring. How great then is the blessing of a wife? For, as Gataker wrote, without a woman there can be no children at all; without a wife, there can be no children lawfully; and without a good wife, there can be no children cheerfully.[59]

Fifth, a godly wife brings the benefit of a *remedy* against lust. Before the Fall, when man was well and in good health, he had no need of such a remedy. But now that man has fallen into sin, marriage provides a remedy against the sin of fornication (1 Cor. 7:2). Marriage provides a legitimate place where a man may, in a manner designed by God (Heb. 13:4), enjoy the wife of his youth, being "ravished always with her love" (Prov. 5:19). By God's grace, marital sex goes a long way towards keeping a man's desires at home and away from the house of a stranger, either in thought or in deed (Prov. 5:8, 15, 20).

Finally, a godly wife brings the benefit of grace and *honor* to her husband. Of all the things that might be reckoned to a man's honor, whether riches or rewards or reputation, a godly wife exceeds them all, for she is like a crown upon her husband's head (Prov. 31:10–12, 28) as he is upon hers. They are the jewels of each other, a testimony of how rich the other is, and the delight of each other's eyes. How great, then, must the benefits of marriage be if so many blessings come wrapped up in a wife! She is such a help that Secker urged the following counsel: "Let him seek for her that wants one; let him sigh for her that has lost one; let him take pleasure in her that enjoys one."[60]

Like Reyner, Gataker proposed several responses to the Lord's beneficence. First, these blessings should warn us of the great power of sin that can turn an ordinance so full of blessings into a state so full of woes. How many have never known what misery was until they were married? How many have found a wife or a husband to be their greatest burden in life? How many have entered marriage only to regret it

---

59. Gataker, 164.
60. Secker, 269.

all their days? If we hope to reap the fruits and find the benefits which come from marriage, then we must be sure that we begin by marrying as God directs and continue therein, not letting sin ruin our marriages. Any misery, trouble, or cross we might bear in our marriages cannot be ascribed to marriage itself but only to our own sinfulness, since marriage is honorable (Heb. 13:4).

Second, if we have honored the Lord in our choice of a mate and in getting married, we should look for the benefits in our marriage. Sadly, many couples enter marriage expecting a world of cares, an ocean of troubles, and an inexplicable labyrinth of annoyances, as if it could bring forth nothing but thorns and thistles![61] Though marriage certainly has its cares and its troubles, it also has its comforts, blessings, and pleasures. It is an ordinance of God and can therefore be expected to be crowned with the blessings He has promised us if we seek them from His hand.

Third, if a wife can be so beneficial to her husband, then let wives strive to be so. The more good they can do their husbands, the more delight they will find in their marriages, and the more comfort they will receive from them.

Finally, let husbands strive to walk worthy of a godly wife and encourage her to be a storehouse of blessings by providing her with the comfort, love, protection, and provision that she needs. Husbands must give to their wives the very blessings that their wives offer to them. For whatever the Lord requires on a wife's part is likewise required of her husband.

Marriage is a blessed institution filled with blessings and comforts for this life. But these blessings are not so tied to the married estate that all who marry will automatically reap them. Rather, marriage is *God's* institution; and the purpose of marriage is to glorify *God*, so the blessings of marriage can only flow into a marriage which humbly seeks to honor God. Marriage can only find its true purpose when it is consummated between two people who love and fear God.[62]

---

61. Gataker, 172.
62. den Ouden, 22.

Study Questions

1. What are the main purposes of marriage? Prove each from Scripture.

2. What considerations might make it prudent to remain single? What hardships attend singleness?

3. Read Malachi 2:15. What does this reveal about God's purpose for procreation? How should that shape our parenting?

4. What does Proverbs 5 teach about sexual relationships?

5. What factors did William Greenhill present to show the horror of adultery?

6. According to the Puritans, what are the personal benefits of a good marriage?

7. Why is it true that marriage is "the basic building block upon which every political structure is built"?

8. In what practical ways can a godly wife be:
   - a blessed companion to her husband?

   - an assistance to her husband?

   - a comfort to her husband?

9. How should a husband respond to God's gift of his wife with gratitude and appreciation?

Securing a Good Entrance into Marriage

We have seen that marriage is a divine ordinance which God has honored in several ways. We have also seen that God ordained marriage with several purposes in mind and is therefore pleased to bless it with several benefits. Why, then, do so many marriages neither manifest this honor nor enjoy these benefits? The cause can most often be traced to those who marry without regard to the Lord of marriage. If we rush into marriage rashly, foolishly, and without seeking the Lord's blessing, then we cannot expect to find it the delightful experience it was intended to be.

Our entrance into marriage is the root and foundation of it. If the foundation is faulty, then the house cannot be stable; if the root is rotten, then the branches and fruit will be also. To procure the honor that the Lord has placed upon marriage and enjoy its benefits we must approach the married state with due preparation and choose our spouses wisely.

Due Preparation

Most everyone understands the value of preparation. When we have an important task before us such as a test at school, a job interview, or a visit to the job site from a supervisor, we do whatever is necessary to prepare for it and not be caught off guard. But if we choose to "wing it," one failure or embarrassment is usually enough to cure such indifference and teach us a valuable lesson.

Other factors can make preparation an absolute necessity. For example, the need for preparation increases in proportion to the effect the outcome will have on us and others. Some things that we do are relatively insignificant in comparison to others that have a rippling effect on us and those around us. Also, a limited opportunity may also determine how important preparation is. The incentive to prepare increases exponentially if we know we only have one shot at something.

Scudder argued for the value of preparation, saying, "Mariners learn their skill before they launch into the deeps; all artists study the theory before the practice; wise men are long in contemplation before they adventure upon action. It's a known rule, deliberation must be long where determination can be but once; and where there is no admission of second thoughts to reverse a former error, the first thoughts must be careful, that error be prevented."[1]

Marriage *warrants* preparation. It is "the tying of such a knot, that nothing but death can unloose."[2] It has a determinative effect on the joy or woe of our lives; and it is an institution upon which God has been pleased to bestow many precious blessings. Furthermore, marriage warrants *proportional* preparation. Without preparation for marriage, said Whately, we might as well try to fly without wings, walk without legs, and see without an eye.[3] The right way of entering into the honorable state of marriage is "a matter of greatest consequence concerning man's weal or woe in this life, according as it is well or ill done."[4]

What kind of preparation, then, is necessary to secure a happy and godly marriage? Two things are absolutely necessary to lay the foundation for a comfortable enjoyment of marriage all your days. First, by God's grace, you must choose God for yourself; and second, you must seek your spouse from God.

1. Choose God for Yourself

The blessings and honor of marriage depend upon honoring and glorifying God in it. The primary concern of a person entering marriage is to see that he, by grace, chooses God before choosing his spouse. "The

---

1. Scudder, iii–iv.
2. Secker, 265.
3. Whately, *A Care-Cloth*, i.
4. Scudder, xiv.

personal covenant with Christ should precede the marriage covenant," said den Ouden.[5] "We must be married to Christ," said Manton, "before married to one another; the marriage covenant should be begun and concluded between Christ and you."[6]

What marriage requires of us is far beyond our natural abilities and strength. Husbands and wives need divine help and grace to fulfill their duties to each other. Furthermore, every blessing and comfort that marriage yields demands a response of praise and thankfulness to God. Therefore the first stone to be laid in the foundation for a good marriage is trusting in Christ as our Savior. In the dedicatory epistle to Henry Scudder's treatise *A Godly Man's Choice*, Jeremiah Whittaker wrote, "before the Lord incline your heart to think of any choice [of a spouse] on earth, be entreated to make your choice in heaven; that the Lord Jesus may be the guide of your youth and so the God of your [old] age."[7]

How can a man be a faithful husband to his wife if he lacks the example of Christ's headship towards him (1 Cor. 12:12–13, 27; Eph. 5:25–27)? How can a man be a good father to his children if he fails to understand the example of God's Fatherhood? To lay the foundation for his faithfulness as a husband and father in marriage, a man must surrender himself to the love, care, and headship of Christ before he seeks a spouse. In the same way, how can a woman be a submissive and supportive wife to her husband if she is a stranger to submitting to and honoring Christ (Eph. 5:22–23)? How can a woman be a faithful mother to her children if she is a stranger to the care, love, and nurturing that God gives to His children? To lay the foundation for her own faithfulness as a wife and mother in marriage, she must surrender herself to the love, care, and nurturing of God before she seeks to be married.

Furthermore, though marriage offers incomparable benefits and comforts, it can also bring troubles and cares on a couple that are absent in the single life. How can a person be ready for the self-denial, service, sacrifice, and love required in marriage unless he is already accustomed to such conduct as a disciple of Christ (Mark 8:34)? How can a person

---

5. den Ouden, 22.
6. Manton, 2:165.
7. Scudder, iv.

exercise the forgiveness required in marriage unless he first experiences the forgiveness of God (Eph. 5:32)? How can a person have the patience, kindness, and faithfulness required of a spouse and a parent unless he first possesses the Spirit of God (Gal. 5:22–23)? How can a person exercise chastity and purity in the marriage bed unless the lusts of his heart are subdued by the beauty and kingship of the Lord Jesus Christ (Job 31:1–4)? How can a man or a woman venture into marriage without salvation, which both equips them for their duties and arms them against its troubles (Phil. 4:13)?

It is therefore indispensable that we be married to Christ in salvation prior to marrying an earthly spouse. Our love for Him and our marriage to Him will not only guide our choices in pursuing a spouse but will serve as the root and ground of our marriages, causing them to bear fruit that honors God, to please our spouses, and to be witnesses to the world, all the while giving our marriages stability amidst all the storms and trials of life. "As touching your faith in Jesus Christ," wrote Greenham, "understand that marriage is holy unto them only, whose hearts are sanctified by faith in His name. And although God will always approve His own ordinance [of marriage], yet it must need prove hurtful in the end unto them who call not for His blessing."[8]

2. Seek Your Spouse from God

The second thing necessary for a godly marriage is to seek your spouse from God. For if, as James 1:17 declares, "Every good gift and every perfect gift is from above, and cometh down from the Father of lights," and as Proverbs 19:14 testifies, "a prudent wife is from the LORD," then good and fit spouses are held in God's hand and must be sought from Him. God is, Scudder said, "the great Patron, in whose family are all the prudent, wise, virtuous, religious persons that are to be desired; and if thou wouldst have one of these, apply thyself to obtain His favor [and] so shalt thou find a good wife (Prov. 18:22)."[9]

Every goal has a way that leads to it. But, as Proverbs 14:12 says, "There is a way which seemeth right unto a man, but the end thereof are

---

8. Greenham, 281.
9. Scudder, 3.

the ways of death." There are many crooked and indirect ways that may fulfill a man's goal, but they include much trouble, regret, and unnecessary labor. Alternatively, there is also a way that will bring a man comfort and pleasure to his desired end (Prov. 11:8; 21:23).[10]

What is the sure way that leads to a godly spouse and a happy marriage? Scudder advised: "Now if to marry, and to marry in the Lord, a wife and a good wife, one with whom thou mayst begin thy days with joy, continue them in quiet, and end them with comfort, if this be the end of thy thoughts, then surely the most direct and straight way to obtain it, will be to seek her of God."[11] Reyner said this "making God the beginning of our marriages" involves several considerations: "Seeking earnestly to God for counsel and direction therein; for guidance of our affection to a right object; for the choice of a fit yoke-fellow; for making the woman a comfortable help and the man a suitable head; expecting to receive one another as a special gift and token of favor from the hand of God."[12] A good and fit spouse is therefore the Lord's gift to you and the Lord's choice for you, not the fruit of your diligent search.

To encourage you to seek your spouse from God's hand, consider the following truths. First, consider that God, the Searcher of all hearts (1 Chron. 28:9), is best able to guide and direct you to a good and fit spouse. Because our choices can only be made on the basis of appearance, which so often is not a true representation of the heart (e.g., 1 Sam. 16:6–7), it is necessary to seek the help of the One who sees and knows the heart. As Scudder said, a good and fit spouse is "a flower that grows not in every garden, an herb that is not in every field; [one that] is not to be found in every house. You may seek long enough ere you find, and finding be deceived, unless God direct you."[13]

Second, the Lord best knows you and your needs. A good marriage joins together two complementary people. And who knows what kind of a person will best complement you better than the Lord? Humbly

---

10. Scudder, 1–2.
11. Scudder, 2.
12. Reyner, 7.
13. Scudder, 2–3.

submit yourself to the wisdom of the all-wise and all-knowing God (Job 36:5; Ps. 147:5).

Third, seeking a spouse from the Lord is the easiest way to find one. How easily Adam found Eve! Not only did he sleep while she was in the making, but God Himself brought her to him (Gen. 2:21–23). When we seek a spouse from the Lord we can leave the matter in His hands and, with confidence, peace, and patience, wait upon His leading. He will not disappoint those who wait upon Him (Prov. 3:5–6; Ps. 27:14). He will not lead astray those who seek Him but will order their steps and establish their ways (Ps. 37:23–24). Indeed, He will first make our match in heaven and then, without fail, lead us to our spouses and our spouses to us. "No marriages are consummated on earth, that were not first concluded and made up in heaven; and none are blessed here, that were not in mercy made there," noted Gataker.[14]

Fourth, consider that no one has found a good and fit spouse in a better way than from the Lord's hands. Many have found a rich spouse, a spouse of high social standing, a beautiful or handsome spouse, and a civil or kind spouse; but without the goodness and fitness which the Lord provides in a spouse, the other qualities soon prove vain and fade. Consider the anxiety, discontent, disappointment, and even shock that fill those who seek a spouse apart from God. Only those who seek a spouse from the Lord "enjoy much pleasure and quiet in seeking, contentment in finding, and comfort in the possessing."[15]

Fifth, acknowledge God's supreme governance over all things and submit to His guidance and direction in a matter that affects not only our happiness and obedience to Him (Eph. 5:22, 25) but also the children we are to raise in His name (Mal. 2:15). Scudder said, "If we rush into such weighty business and venture ourselves upon things of so great concernment without acquainting [God] with it, or seeking to Him for it, or imploring His aid and assistance for the accomplishing of it, what is it but to pluck our necks from His yoke, casting off all obedi-

---

14. Gataker, 137–38.
15. Scudder, 8.

ence and subjection to Him, as if we had no dependence upon Him; and therefore would [fly in] all directions from Him?"[16]

Sixth, however a marriage turns out, the only way we can take comfort in our choices is if we can say with all peace of conscience that our husbands or our wives were sought and received *from the Lord* (Prov. 16:9; Prov. 3:5–6). If your wife turns out to be the virtuous and godly woman that you sought, then "comfort will flow in on every side; great comfort will redound to you, that God was graciously pleased to bend His ear unto you and give you so favorable a pledge of His lovingkindness. Every time you cast your eye upon her, you may with rejoicing cast up your eyes to God, and say, 'Lo, this is the wife that Thou hast given me,' and bless Him in that you have so goodly an heritage."[17]

But if your wife turns out to be a troublesome and difficult woman, you still may find comfort, Scudder said, *if* you have "the inward testimony of your conscience, bearing you witness, that you did sincerely commit your way unto the Lord, and roll yourself upon Him for direction in it. Lo, here you may assuredly take comfort that all shall be for your good. He who brought you to this condition, shall support you in it; He will either lighten the weight of your burden or strengthen the weakness of your shoulders."[18] On the contrary, continued Scudder, if this marriage was "a web of your own weaving," then you brought this cross upon yourself and must "lay your hand upon your mouth [and] patiently submit; repentance is fitter for your comfort."[19]

Seventh, if you sought your spouse from the Lord and can acknowledge His hand in your marriage, you will be enabled to be thankful to Him for your spouse and armed against the temptation to regret your choice. As Scudder wrote, "It will keep you from repenting of your match, from wishing that you had not married this person, and from wishing that you had married such and such. You cannot now say unto, or taunt one another with this, that I might have had such an one so beautiful, so personable, so rich, so well qualified. No, now you see you

---

16. Scudder 8–9.
17. Scudder, 9–10.
18. Scudder, 10.
19. Scudder, 11.

could have had none other; this is the man, this is the woman, that God has given me. You must say, I will therefore thankfully and contentedly satisfy myself in this my lot and portion."[20]

Finally, consider the benefits of receiving a spouse from God's hands.[21] First, it will encourage you to give God all the glory for the comfort and delight you find in your spouse. We often forget that the hand behind all our blessings is the Lord's (Ps. 103:2–5) and we do not sufficiently praise Him for His mercies. But when you receive your spouse from God's hands, your heart will be stirred to praise Him throughout marriage. Second, you have a greater obligation to glorify God in your marriage when you realize that your spouse is from Him, for it makes your marriage a stewardship from Him. Marriage is a "talent" that we must invest for His glory. Third, the crosses and trials of marriage will be lightened by knowing that you did not rush into this relationship blindly and passionately, but rather received your spouse from the Lord. He who gave you a spouse will also support you in your marriage that it may work the good He intended for it. Fourth, it enables you to pray for the needs of your spouse, temporal or spiritual, as the one whom God gave to you. Fifth, it will help you part from each other at death more willingly when you acknowledge the Lord's hand in your marriage. What He freely gives He is free to take away, and we may be comforted knowing that both the giving and taking are acts of His wisdom and His love.

In summary, the happiness of our marriages has much to do with whom we marry. If we are careless or sinful in our choices, we no doubt will regret them, for the Lord's blessings will fly from us. Therefore we must seek our spouses from God if we wish to be thankful and content in marriage.

How to Seek a Spouse

How does one go about seeking a spouse from God? By the same means by which all other mercies are sought from God: prayer. "If Abraham's servant prayed unto the Lord to prosper his business (Gen. 24:12),

---

20. Scudder, 70–71.
21. Manton, 2:166–68.

when he went about to choose a wife for another," wrote Smith, then "how should you pray when you go about [choosing] a wife for yourself, that you may say after, 'My lot is fallen in a pleasant ground'?"[22]

A spouse must be obtained from the hands of the Lord in response to fervent and directed supplication. As Chrysostom said, "When you are in search of a wife, flee to God; for He is not ashamed to act as your bridesman.... When you are anxiously employed in seeking a husband, pray to God, and say, 'Lord, bestow me as Thou wilt, and [me] on whom Thou wilt.'"[23] Ambrose put it this way: "Let [a man] ply the throne of grace with fervency of prayer; a good wife is a more immediate gift of God.... Such a rare and precious jewel [as a godly wife] is to be sued and sought for at God's mercy-seat with extraordinary importunity and zeal; and if she be procured at God's hand by prayer, he shall find a thousand times more sweetness and comfort [in her], than if she be cast on him by an ordinary providence."[24]

What exactly should one ask of the Lord? Scudder suggested the following.[25] First, ask that God would give you wisdom and understanding so that when you meet a prospective spouse, your heart might not be distracted either by beauty, riches, or natural endowments, and thereby neglect what should be your main concern, namely, grace in the heart. "Do not first love, and then consider; but first consider, and then love. Chiefly fix your observation on the soul of the party," Steele wrote.[26]

Second, ask the Lord not to knit your affections to someone whose affections are not already knit to Him and that your love may not be given to one whose love is not given to Him. Since we may be deceived by a fair appearance, we must ask the Lord that He search and try our hearts and not allow our affections to be led astray by a "painted fire."

Third, if after your affections go out toward another you discover that the truth of grace is not in his or her heart, then you must earnestly beg of God for grace to withdraw your affections from that person, lest

---

22. Smith, 1:13.
23. *Puritan Sermons*, 2:300n, quoted from Chrysostom.
24. Ambrose, 228.
25. Scudder 12–26.
26. Steele, *Puritan Sermons*, 2:300.

you sinfully keep your affections upon one who will draw you away from the Lord. "Beg of God," Scudder said, "that He who subdues all things to himself, would subdue your affections and bring them into subjection to His will, that they might be like the Captain's servant, to go and come at His pleasure."[27]

How can anyone hope to find a spouse from whom to expect pleasure and comfort and with whom to glorify God unless he or she first consults the Lord in much prayer? God is still the great and wise Matchmaker (Gen. 2:22). Why would we even attempt to seek a spouse without His help and guidance (Prov. 18:22)? Steele urged, "When you find that you are called to [marriage], be sure to recommend it earnestly to God by prayer, as Abraham's servant did (Gen. 24:12). In this way, you 'acknowledge him, and he shall direct thy paths.' No business [is] so critical, none so weighty; and therefore no business so calls for solemn and earnest prayer."[28]

Let us therefore go to God, who gives to all men liberally and upbraids not (James 1:5), and ask Him not only to grant us a spouse but to match us to one who is fit for us. Let us go to God and ask Him that He would knit us to a spouse not merely by the ordinance of marriage but by the hand of His good, wise, and loving providence.[29] For, as Manton wrote, "God will order things for the best, when we do not lead, but follow Him...and dare not undertake anything but what is agreeable to His will."[30] "It is a blessed thing," he continued, "to be under God's conduct, to be led on or led off by so wise, and powerful, and all-sufficient a guide; for such He delights to do them good, and takes pleasure in His resolutions to prosper them."[31]

How to Find a Spouse Fit for Us

We must seek our spouses from the Lord by prayer, but we must also examine those whom He brings across our path to see if they are fit

---

27. Scudder, 16. Cf. Matt. 8:8–9.
28. Steele, *Puritan Sermons*, 2:300.
29. Gataker, 143.
30. Manton, 2:168.
31. Manton, 2:168.

for us. That is to say, it is not enough to seek a spouse by prayer; we must also prayerfully seek a spouse. Our primary concern must be that God leads and guides us in our choices; but under the protection of His providence, we must look for the qualities in a person which make someone a fit companion.

Two things must now occupy our concern. First, what distinguishes a *good* spouse? Second, what are the marks of an *agreeable* spouse? The Puritans were concerned that neither of those considerations be overlooked and that the former take precedence over the latter, since a person must first be qualified as a good spouse before considering agreeableness. Smith wrote, "When these [two considerations] are warily observed, they may join together, and say, as Laban and Bethuel said (Gen. 24:50), 'This cometh of the Lord, and therefore we will not speak against it.' How happy are those in whom faith, love, and godliness are married together, before they marry themselves!"[32]

Many people bring trouble upon themselves because they reverse this order. They set their affections upon one who is unqualified to be a good spouse in hopes that love will right every wrong, but no amount of love can qualify someone who is unqualified. That is to say, no amount of love from us can turn their hearts towards God so that we might lawfully consider them.

The Mark of a Good Spouse

The mark of a good spouse is the presence of true saving grace or godliness, that is, a personal relationship with the Lord Jesus Christ as Savior. Those who lack this mark, no matter how amiable, beautiful, or lovely, are wrong for us, for we who belong to the Lord Jesus simply have no business courting, dating, or marrying them. Can He in whom there is no darkness at all give us a spouse in whom is nothing but darkness and no light at all? Why, then, would we entertain a romantic relationship with such a person? According to the apostle Paul, oneness with Christ is *the* criterion of a good spouse. We are, Paul says to the church in Corinth, "at liberty to be married to whom [we] will; only in the Lord" (1 Cor. 7:39).

---

32. Smith, 1:18.

It is a sin for a believer to marry an unbeliever, for Scripture urges us to marry "only in the Lord." The importance of this mark is reinforced by the following advice from several Puritans. To marry in the Lord, wrote Daniel Rogers, "is to use our uttermost discreet diligence to seek out such companions as (in charity and likelihood) are either already espoused to the Lord Jesus their husband by faith, and in token thereof, sit close to Him in obedience; or [are] an endeavorer thereto." "But beware," he continued, "lest you attempt any marriage in which neither of these can be perceived."[33]

When Robert Bolton advised how to secure a good entrance into marriage, he began with this mark as the first and foremost point of consideration. He wrote,

> For the first point: let your choice be in the Lord, according to blessed St. Paul's rule, "only in the Lord," (1 Cor. 7:39). Let piety be the first mover of your affection, the prime and principal consideration in this greatest affair; and then conceive of personage, parentage, and portion, and such outward things and worldly additions, as a comfortable accessory, considerable only in a second place. Let the world say what it will; to a mind truly generous and ennobled with grace, the most absolute concurrence and greatest exquisiteness of beauty, gold, birth, wit, or what else besides may be found most remarkable and matchless in that sex, should be nothing, nor hold scale with the lightest feather upon any lady's head, compared with a gracious disposition and godly heart. Religion, or the fear of God, as it is generally the foundation of all human felicity, so must it specially be accounted the ground of all comfort and bliss which man and wife desire to find in the enjoying of each other. There was never any gold, or great friends, any beauty, or outward bravery, which tied truly fast and comfortably any marriage knot. It is only the golden link and noble tie of Christianity and grace, which has the power and privilege to make so dear a bond lovely and everlasting, which can season and strengthen that nearest inseparable society with true sweetness and immortality.[34]

---

33. Rogers, 19.
34. Bolton, 262–63.

Immanuel Bourne proposed "twenty golden links of love" to preserve strong love between a husband and wife. At the head of these links, making the rest dependent on it, was that *special care* be taken to be certain that one marries a fellow believer, that is, not one who merely professes to be a Christian but one who lives religiously and in the fear of God. "For thus," Bourne wrote, "marriages are contracted more prosperously and a blessing may be expected when the married parties both fear God. Such being pronounced blessed by the Holy Ghost (Ps. 112:1–3).... But on the contrary...without the fear of God...a curse may rather be expected than a blessing."[35]

Jeremy Taylor gave similar directives: "Begin therefore with God. Christ is the President of marriage and the Holy Ghost is the Fountain of purities and chaste loves, and He joins the hearts. And therefore let our first suit be in the court of heaven and with designs of piety, or safety, or charity. Let no impure spirit defile...let all such contracts begin with religious affections." Taylor continued, "We sometimes beg of God, for a wife...and He alone knows what the wife shall prove, and by what dispositions and manners...but we shall not need to fear concerning the event of it if religion, fair intentions, and prudence manage and conduct it all the way."[36]

The anonymous author of *The New Whole Duty of Man* taught that the salvation of the prospective spouse must be the chief consideration in marriage because it will not only make the marriage happy but will also best suit one's own relationship with Christ. "Whoever intends to marry, should not so much regard the outward shape or beauty, wealth, etc. as [much as] the spiritual qualifications of the person to whom they desire to be joined; which will make that state of life truly holy, and serve to the great end of the soul's salvation. Although a competency for the ease of life is to be regarded, yet a virtuous man or woman is of more value than all the wealth and honors the world can afford."[37]

William Whately wrote rather candidly of the troubles and challenges in a marriage; but he counseled his readers that since many of

---

35. Bourne, 3–5.
36. Taylor, 12.
37. *The New Whole Duty of Man*, 231.

marriage's troubles stem from sin, many can be cut off at the beginning if we take care to marry in the Lord. Consequently, he directed the unmarried man to "enter discreetly and religiously upon marriage, observing such due care therein, that he may in his very entrance cut off the root and stop the fountain of very many troubles.... The most important matter in building is to lay a good foundation. Doubtless it is so in this matter of marriage, whereinto he that makes a godly and wise entrance shall find his proceeding to be much more easeful and comfortable than any aftercare could make it, without this first care."[38]

Whately later wrote, "To have a fit yoke-fellow will prevent many matrimonial troubles and will make all easier. Now in a yoke-fellow, the main matter to be desired is virtue and godliness; and he that in choosing, vouchsafes that the first place, shall surely be blessed in his choice; but whosoever sets other and baser things before that, does deal preposterously and foolishly, and setting the cart before the horse... can never drive comfortably in the way that he would go."[39] He warned, "Young men and women, destroy not yourselves by seeking a good outside, but let both parents and children judge as God judges and follow His counsel that says, 'Not the rich, not the fair, but the righteous is more excellent than his neighbor.' He takes the best course to gain [happiness] in marriage that chooses not the finest body, the sweetest face, the greatest state, [or] the largest portion, but the holiest heart, the richest soul, the beautifulest spirit, and the most virtuous man or woman. This is the foundation of [happiness] in marriage; lay this at first, [for] you can never else rear up a comfortable building."[40]

Richard Steele offered several ways to help a person be faithful to his or her marital duties. When charging his listeners to be most considerate in the choice of a spouse, Steele urged, "Chiefly fix your observation on the soul of the party. Many marry to lay hands to lands, or money to money; but see that his or her soul lie well for yours. For no beauty, friends, or portion, will settle upon you a comfortable life, if pride, passion, or any other lust predominate in the soul. And why

---

38. Whately, *A Care-Cloth*, 68–69.
39. Whately, *A Care-Cloth*, 71–72.
40. Whately, *A Care-Cloth*, 73.

will you espouse a perpetual cross for some present profit or delight? It concerns therefore the man, and especially the woman, to endeavor to marry a member of Christ, a religious person; [from whom] they may most rationally expect the conscionable discharge of their respective duties. If such be not the best husbands and wives, it is not by reason of their piety, but their defect of it."[41] Charging his hearers to resign themselves wholly unto God so they might themselves *be* good spouses, Steele said, "Until you be savingly regenerated and sanctified, you cannot please God, nor be entire blessings to one another. You may indeed live together like civil pagans; but what is this to the life of Christians? Religion will most firmly bind you to God, religion will most firmly bind you to one another. A good temper may do much; but a new nature superadded to it will do more."[42]

Henry Smith offered this advice in choosing a wife (which of course applies equally to choosing a husband). The first advice was that she be godly, "because our spouse must be like Christ's spouse, that is, graced with gifts and embroidered with virtues, *as if we married holiness herself.* The marriage of a man and woman is resembled [by] the apostle to the marriage of Christ and the church (Eph. 5:29). Now the church is called holy…undefiled…fair within…. So our spouse should be holy, undefiled, and fair within. As God respects the heart (1 Sam. 16:7) so we must respect the heart, because that [we] must love, and not the face."[43] Later Smith observed, "Though heresy and irreligion be not a cause of divorce, as Paul teaches, yet it is a cause of restraint…. Christ says [in] Matthew 19:6 and Mark 10:9, 'Let no man separate whom God hath joined;' so I may say, Let no man join whom God separates. For if our father must be pleased with our marriage, much more should we please that Father which ordained marriage."[44]

William Secker said a wife (again, equally applicable to a husband) must be holy, belonging to the Lord as a Christian. "If adultery may separate a marriage contracted, idolatry may hinder a marriage not

41. Steele, *Puritan Sermons*, 2:300.
42. Steele, *Puritan Sermons*, 2:301.
43. Smith, 1:13. Emphasis added.
44. Smith, 1:20.

perfected. Cattle of diverse kinds were not to engender, 2 Corinthians 6:14, *Be not unequally yoked, &c.* It is dangerous taking her for a wife, who will not take God for a husband. It is not meet that one flesh should be of two spirits. Is there [not] a tree you like in the garden, but that which bears forbidden fruit?"[45]

Finally, Richard Baxter wrote, "Do not let carnal motives persuade you to join yourself to an ungodly person. Rather, let the holy fear of God be preferred in your choice before all worldly excellence whatsoever. Do not marry a swine for a golden trough, or an ugly soul for a beautiful body."[46]

If there is such great benefit to marrying only in the Lord, then there must also be great *danger* in marrying apart from the Lord. To avoid this danger, Secker warned against three things which commonly lead suitors astray: "Choose not for beauty; choose not for riches; and choose not for dignity. Because he that looks for beauty buys a picture; he that loves for riches makes a purchase; and he that leaps for dignity matches with a multitude at once."[47] Concerning beauty he warned: "If a woman's flesh has more of beauty than her spirit has of *Christianity*, it is like poison in sweetmeats, most dangerous: Genesis 6:2…. Take heed of sinning at the fairest signs."[48] Concerning riches he warned: "Some are so degenerate as to think any good enough who have but goods enough. Take heed, for sometimes the bag and baggage go together…. When Themistocles was to marry his daughter, two suitors courted her together; the one rich, and a fool, the other wise, but poor. And being demanded which of the two he had rather his daughter should have, he answered…I had rather she should have a man without money, than money without a man."[49] Concerning the dignity of birth or social standing he warned: "A good old stock may nourish a fruitless branch. There are many children who are not the blessings, but the blemishes of their parents. They are nobly descended, but ignobly minded…. Piety is a greater honor than parent-

---

45. Secker, 265.
46. Baxter, 41–42.
47. Secker, 266.
48. Secker, 266.
49. Secker, 267.

age. *She is the best gentlewoman that is heir of her own deserts, and not the degenerated offspring of another's virtue.*"[50]

Baxter cited several problems that befall those who marry outside the Lord.[51] First, he said, you will cause great suspicion that you are ungodly since Christians who know both the misery of an unbelieving soul and the excellence of a soul in which the image of God can be clearly seen can never be indifferent whether they are joined to the godly or the ungodly. Therefore, "He who deliberately prefers riches and beauty in another before the image and fear of God gives a very dangerous sign of a graceless heart and will. If you value beauty and riches more than godliness, you have the surest mark that you are ungodly.... Does this not show that you either do not believe the Word of God, or else that you do not love and regard His interest? Otherwise, you would take His friends as your friends and His enemies as your enemies.... Can you so easily marry an enemy of God?"[52]

Second, those who fear God desire a spouse who will be a helper to the soul and further them in the way to heaven as well as pray with them and stir them up to love God and be heavenly minded. If you marry an ungodly person, either you have no such desire or else you must know that you have not chosen anything wiser for yourself than if you chose water to kindle a fire or a bed of snow to keep yourself warm.[53] The fruits of an unequal match will be nothing but hardship, for the two will try to pull the same yoke in different directions. As one Puritan wrote, "where the match is unmeet, the conjunction unequal, the united in body disunited in spirit; of contrary affections, hearts, and religions; duties unperformed, each crossing [the] other, or any of the twain [so] unwise that [they] will not be admonished, what are the fruits there? but wrath, bitterness, contention, controlling, contradiction; taking all things in the evil part; jealousy, upbraiding, discontentment, false dealing, secret juggling, conspiring; wants without pitying each other, toil without helping each other; seeking each one his [own] credit with dis-

---

50. Secker, 267.
51. Baxter, 42–43.
52. Baxter, 42.
53. Baxter, 42.

credit unto both, with many other [fruits] as grievous to be spoken of as any [aforementioned]."[54]

Third, if you marry an unbeliever, you will have no helper on the way to heaven, but you may have a hinderer. An unbelieving spouse will call you back from your prayers with worldly diversions, cast worldly thoughts into your meditations, and stifle your heavenly conversation with worldly talk. "One such hindrance so near you in your bosom," Baxter warned, "will be worse than a thousand further off. As an ungodly heart that is next to us is our greatest hindrance [Rom. 7:21–24], so an ungodly husband or wife is worse to us than many ungodly neighbors."[55]

Fourth, an ungodly companion will be a continual temptation to sin.

Fifth, such a spouse will be a continual grief to you when you think of how you must be separated at death and in what torment he or she will be while you rest in heaven.

Sixth, an ungodly spouse will be incapable of the principal part of your love. You may love such a husband or wife, but you will be prevented from ever loving him or her as a brother or sister in Christ.

The Marks of an Agreeable Spouse

A spouse must not only be good, but also be *agreeable,* that is, well suited to you as a companion. "For as you may not make choice of any who is not godly," Scudder cautioned, "so neither may you choose of every one that is. She may be good, yet not good for you; she may be a fit wife, yet not fit for you. Further therefore enlarge your requests, that God would provide for you not only a good wife, but a meet wife, meet in every respect."[56]

If godliness is the first rule of choosing a wife, then fitness is the second. "It is not enough to be virtuous," wrote Smith, "but to be suitable; for divers women have many virtues, and yet do not fit to some men; and divers men have many virtues, and yet do not fit to some women; and therefore we see many times even the godly couples jar when they are married, because there is some unfitness between them.... They

---

54. Ste. B., 3–4.
55. Baxter, 42–43.
56. Scudder, 19.

which are alike strive not; but they which are unlike, are fire and water. Therefore one observes, that concord is nothing but likeness; and that all strife is for unfitness, as in things when they do not fit together."[57]

To be married is to be yoked together; but how will a couple pull the yoke of marriage harmoniously if they are incompatibly yoked? "Take therefore," Whately said, "a yoke-fellow meet for thee; for the agreement of the married folk is the best help against all troubles, and this is the surest way to procure agreement."[58] Marriage itself cannot make two people compatible. It is naive, if not foolish, to imagine that two people who find themselves incompatible before marriage will be compatible after marriage, as if marriage was a sort of cure-all that washed away all blemishes in one's character and behavior and reconciled two persons that beforehand were as ill-suited to one another as night and day. On the contrary, marriage exposes one's true character and behavior. Whatever causes friction before the marriage will only cause more friction during marriage.

It is critical therefore that we consider the fitness of a person *before* marrying him or her. We must observe a person in different contexts, judging fitness by taking several different measurements. Those who jump into marriage without judging a partner's fitness soon regret their choices and find the daily grind of their relationships to be painful, cumbersome, and grievous. Such marriages are seldom happy and often lead to divorce as the only way to correct an unwise choice.

So, what are the marks of fitness? What should a person look for in discerning compatibility? Isaac Ambrose offered the following: "Let him observe and mark these six points in his choice: the report, the looks, the speech, the apparel, the companions, the education. These are like the pulses that show the fitness and godliness of any party with whom he ought to marry."[59] Let us consider how these marks might help determine the fitness of another, whether man or woman.

---

57. Smith, 1:14.
58. Whately, *A Care-Cloth*, 74.
59. Ambrose, 228.

1. *The Report.* What kind of reputation does he have? How do people speak of him in his absence? What kind of credit does he have in the community, workplace, or school? Proverbs 22:1 tells us that "a good name is rather to be chosen than great riches, and loving favour rather than silver and gold." Look for those who are highly spoken of, have a good report among men, and cannot be accused of living in sin. If he is well spoken of by the world, is it because he is of the world or because the world is attracted to his goodness? If he is godly, the church's report of him should bear that out. It was said of Zacharias and Elizabeth, "They were both righteous before God, walking in all the commandments and ordinances of the Lord blameless" (Luke 1:6). A good report is far from infallible, but it is a wise place to start and we must beware of those who do not have a good report among God's people.

2. *The Looks.* Reflecting upon Ecclesiastes 8:1 Smith said, "godliness is in the face of a man, and folly is in the face of a man, and wickedness is in the face of a man."[60] Thus a person's countenance reveals much of his character. Does he have the proud look we read of in Proverbs 6:17? Does she have the haughty look that the Lord rebukes in Isaiah 3:16? Does his countenance reveal an angry and discontent heart? Do his eyes reveal a wanton and lustful heart? We must beware of faces that reveal a proud, angry, lustful, or discontented heart and look for godliness that springs from a godly heart.

3. *The Speech.* Christ declared in Matthew 12:34 that the mouth speaks out of the abundance of the heart. Speech is a trustworthy measure of a person. The "fruit of the lips" will either condemn or commend him (Matt. 12:37; Prov. 16:23; 18:7). Is there uncleanness in the speech? Then there is uncleanness in the heart. Is there self-love in the speech? Then there is self-love in the heart. Is there flirtation in the speech? Then there is lust in the heart. On the contrary, is there tenderness and

---

60. Smith, 1:16.

compassion in the speech? Then there is mercy and love in the heart. Is there gentleness and contentment in the speech? Then there is a quiet and contented spirit within. Those who cannot bridle their tongues have a vain or worthless religion (James 1:26), and therefore we must beware of those whose speech is not the language of Canaan which we love.

4. *The Apparel.* How a person dresses reveals how he sees himself and how he wants others to see him. Is he dressing so others will think better of him than he is? "Look not for better within than you see without," Smith wrote, "for every one seems better than [he] is; if the face be vanity, the heart is pride."[61] Is he dressing for men or for the Lord? Is a woman dressing to attract the eyes of men? If she enjoys enticing men's eyes, what does this reveal of her heart's desires? Or is she dressing modestly to reflect her humility before the Lord, so that her beauty, which is a gift from the Lord for her husband, does not prove a stumbling block to others? Apparel is often a sure window into the heart's desires and inclinations. Therefore beware of those who dress to be seen as servants of men and not as the servants of God (Isa. 3:16).

5. *The Companions.* Smith said, "Birds of a feather will fly together, and fellows in sin will be fellows in league, as young Rehoboam chose young companions, 1 Kings 7:8. The tame beasts will not keep with the wild, nor the clean dwell with the leprous. If a man can be known by nothing else, then he may be known by his companions; for like will [stick] to like.... So when David left iniquity, he said (Ps. 6:8), 'Away from me, all ye that work iniquity;' showing, that a man never abandons evil until he abandon evil company.... Therefore choose such a companion of your life as has chosen company like you before."[62] What kind of friends does a potential spouse keep? With whom does he spend his spare time? Take notice not only of his friends, but

---

61. Smith, 1:17.
62. Smith, 1:17.

how he behaves in their presence. Do you recognize him as the same man that you saw at church last Lord's Day? Or does he behave differently with his friends during the week? Is she the same in all company or do her friends bring out another side of her that is unpleasant to you? Beware of a person who delights in wicked friends and who changes like a chameleon to suit present company.

6. *The Education*. The importance of this mark is the effect a person's education has on his thinking and behavior. "Nurture and education put a stamp on someone's personality. Great disparities in habits, culture, and development can eventually form a source of irritations and misunderstandings, which have a negative effect on the marriage."[63] Knowing the manner in which a person was educated can alert us to the factors that shaped his character and can help us know whether someone may be fit for us or not.

These are the common marks by which fitness can be measured. It takes time and much observation to make these various measurements, but it will prove worthwhile when we can marry (or refrain from marrying) a person with confidence and peace in our choice. "All these properties are not spied at three or four comings," noted Smith, "for hypocrisy is spun with a fine thread, and none are deceived so often as lovers. He which will know all his wife's qualities before he be married to her, must see her eating, and walking, and working, and playing, and talking, and laughing, and chiding, or else he shall have less with her than he looked for, or more than he wished for."[64]

When we are sure of a person's sincere *godliness* and have measured a person's *fitness*, we will be able to enter marriage with our hearts completely taken up with each other. The husband will be able to love his wife and settle his affections upon her as the fittest woman that the world can offer; the wife will be able to love her husband as the best fit

---

63. den Ouden, 24.
64. Smith, 1:18.

for her over any other in all the earth. And with such contentment in the choice, the husband will be to his wife as a shield over her eyes and a seal upon her heart, that she might not lay her eyes on any other man or let another steal his way into her heart; and the wife will be so pleasing to her husband's eyes and so near to his heart, that he might look upon her to her dying day as the delight of his eyes and the love of his heart and therefore not be enticed by another woman.

One more mark of fitness the Puritans offered was the consent of parents. This requirement is nearly lost in our culture where every man does what is right in his own eyes (cf. Judg. 21:25) and the commandments of God are largely disregarded; but it was a necessary precondition in the minds of the Puritans and should be recovered because of the godliness, wisdom, and motive that undergirds it.

Based on the fifth commandment, the Puritans said a child is obligated to ask the permission of his parents to marry so a couple might have their blessing and support in marriage. Also, the parents are obligated to help their son or daughter make a good and a fit choice, that their child might not be deceived in his or her choice, miss his or her way, and thereby bring hardship into the next generation. Thus Abraham provided a wife for his son Isaac (Gen. 24:2–3); Isaac provided a wife for his son Jacob (Gen. 28:2); and Hagar provided a wife for her son Ishmael (Gen. 21:21). Moreover, Caleb consented to his daughter's marriage (Josh. 15:17); Saul consented to his daughter's marriage (1 Sam. 18:27); and Naomi provided a husband for Ruth (Ruth 3:1). Based on such examples in Scripture, the Puritans said part of a child's godliness is to submit to his parents' guidance in the matter of marriage, since that honors the Lord and His commandment (Ex. 20:12). In so doing, the blessing promised in the fifth commandment will come upon the marriage as well as the couple's relationship with their parents. While the Puritans agreed that there *may* be some exceptions in which a spouse may lawfully be taken in marriage without the parents' consent, it should be the exception which proves the rule.

We should make every effort to secure the consent of our parents and refrain from marrying anyone whom they cannot commend, because our parents do not represent God in vain. Additionally, our submission to them may overcome and soften their hearts so that they may eventually consent to the one we love, while our willful opposition to them will risk ruining both our relationship with them and our peace of conscience before the Lord.[65] Moreover, we should make every effort to secure their consent because where else will we go when trials come but to our parents? If we married without their consent how can we go to them later for help? Also, we should make every effort to ensure that when our marriage falls into trouble we will not find ourselves plagued with thoughts, as Joseph's brothers were (Gen. 42:21), that such a trial has come upon us because of our sin against our parents.

What if our parents are unreasonable or selfish in resisting our marriage? What if, as far as we can see, there are no grounds for their denial? We must remember that we are called to honor and obey our parents in the Lord (Eph. 6:1–3) which is something that the Lord will surely take notice of and honor. When we feel that our choices are of the Lord and yet our parents disagree, we must normally submit to them in godly submission and prevail with God by prayer that He may soften their hearts by the same Spirit who has knit our hearts to our choices. For if God is in the choice, then God must likewise be in our parents; so, after praying, seek your parents' consent since God declares that you must have it (Ex. 20:12) and they must give it (Deut. 7:3; Jer. 29:6).

In addition, fly to the throne of grace and beg of God that He will grant us children with submissive and content hearts, and parents who are wise and godly; that He will grant children with loving and trusting spirits, and parents with tender and thoughtful counsel; and that He will grant children and parents alike with obedience to His Law (Ex. 20:12). For while children should submit to their parents, parents should not compel their children to marry an unbeliever or someone in whom they see no compatibility and whom they cannot love entirely. Furthermore, while parents should not advise their children to marry someone for their beauty, riches, or high station, neither should children ask their parents to approve their marriages to someone with whom they are merely infatuated. For a marriage quickly made is often grounded

---

65. Rogers, 79–80.

on a faulty foundation and soon regretted. Parents must therefore help their children choose with discernment and wisdom someone they can love entirely and constantly from the day of their wedding until the day of their parting.

Therefore let parents begin in their children's youth to win their hearts and prove to them that they work for their good, discipline for their good, and pray for their good, so that when their children look for guidance in choosing a spouse and for consent to marry their parents may not meet with rebellion and obstinacy if they must disagree. Yet, let parents beware of neglecting their duty to their children by failing to provide guidance for them or abusing their authority and position by withholding their consent without biblical grounds. Let them rather walk, as they expect of their children, in the way of duty, remembering that the Lord has charged them to be faithful in this.

A Final Exhortation

We cannot end this chapter without a final exhortation to marry only in the Lord. One who marries outside the Lord will have no peace. Marriage has the potential to secure the greatest blessings as well as to bring on the greatest hardships and crosses, depending on one's entrance into it. Why, then, would anyone venture upon a marriage without the Lord and His blessing? Consider the following counsel from Daniel Rogers.[66]

First, deny yourself by renouncing the wisdom of your own will as if you needed no advice and were able to make an unerring choice in marriage. Instead, submit yourself to the Lord by prayer and patience, and do not rush into marriage at the first inclination or opportunity. It may be that the Lord has called you to a single life or that He has called you to marriage but just not at the present time. Seek the Lord's will in the matter and use all means to devote yourself wholeheartedly to the Lord in undistracted devotion until He makes it clear that He is calling you to marry.

Second, if you find that the Lord has called you to marriage, prepare yourself for it. Pray for the Lord to teach you self-denial, humility, wis-

---

66. Rogers, 43–54.

dom, and chastity. Marriage puts a person outside of himself and calls him to love, serve, stand by, wait upon, prefer, and submit to another. If you are accustomed to serving yourself, preferring yourself, and loving yourself, then marriage will prove a very hard yoke to draw.

Third, be warned against the common disease which has so blurred the eyes of men that they can see nothing but the outward appearance of things. Do not allow beauty, riches, station, or education to deceive you by bribing your judgment and leading your affections to thrust godliness from the criteria. Beware also of covetousness, pride, and ambitious thoughts that lead so many to think themselves the catch of a thousand and therefore too good for any but those in whom beauty, riches, and intelligence rate higher than in most. As Rogers said to men seeking a wife, "Think not too highly of yourselves when there is little worth in you to equal the lowliest women…but moderate your spirits and marry in the Lord. [If] nothing hinders, but the Lord and outward means may concur…then the question is ended. But if it is so, that a match of five hundred pounds is offered with the Lord, and another of seven or eight hundred without him…what then shall be done? I answer. Other conditions being concurrent in any tolerable proportion, despise the greater offer, and take the lesser, counting the loss of your gain happy, and the gain of her grace with that loss, happier."[67] Think therefore not only of what you would give, but what you would forego for a good and fit companion, because marriage is honorable and you must procure its honor by a good entrance into it at all costs, lest you forfeit its honor and therefore its blessing.

Fourth, ask the Lord fervently for the blessing of a good marriage. Let the Lord see by your fervency and frequency at His throne that you are deeply concerned for a good marriage and seek to honor Him in it, and He will not deny you. Either God will hear you and answer you, or He will give you a reason for His denial, which will otherwise satisfy you. Only remember that a good spouse is a precious gift from the Lord and that He is not accustomed to let His prized gifts go easily, but likes to be importunately entreated for them (Matt. 15:22–28). In addition,

---

67. Rogers, 47.

add a vow to your prayers that if the Lord would be so gracious as to provide a wife for you of His choosing and giving, then you would choose her over a thousand who stood beside her from the world.

Fifth, seek the advice of the most judicious, impartial, and godly friends, lest you be deceived by either your own wisdom or by the advice of a flatterer. God has promised that He will lead you in your choice but He has also provided the brethren for your encouragement and support.

Sixth, be observant and careful in your mutual conversations with one whom you think may be a good and fit spouse that you may learn not only the speech of a person but the soul. Talk not only about religion but about the power of religion upon the soul. Talk about the work of God upon the heart, the subduing power of Christ over your sin, the enabling power of the Spirit over your flesh, and the working grace of God in your soul. Look not only for gifts but for graces. Look for the fruits of the Spirit and especially for humility and modesty. Slight defects in each other will soon be made up by religion where love is genuine, but the lack of religion cannot be made up with any amount of outward gifts and talents.

Finally, if any object that waiting for a spouse of the Lord's choosing may cause some to miss out on marriage altogether, we repeat our counsel: wait upon the Lord, commit your way unto Him, for He knows best what you need (Pss. 27:14; 37:5–6). Those who wait will fare far better than those who do not, for the former wait upon Him who cannot fail them, while the latter presume to be wiser than their Creator and Lord. And if any object that a good and fit spouse cannot be found in our day, we remind you that the Lord who calls you to wait for such a spouse knows very well who and where that person is and will not fail to bring such a spouse to you.

Do not be tempted to follow the stream and fashion of the world; for He makes none a son of Abraham, if He calls him to marry, for whom He will not also make a daughter of Abraham so that he might marry in the Lord. "Use means to find [a good and fit spouse], and having so done, prefer pearls before pebbles, and the Lord shall bring the good to the good, for He is a God of order, not of confusion."[68]

Study Questions

1. Why is it important, by God's grace, to "choose God for yourself" before seeking a spouse?

2. What are some Scriptures showing us why we should seek a spouse *from God*?

3. How should we pray for the affections of our hearts when we seek a spouse? Why?

4. List several reasons why a believer must choose another godly person for a spouse.

5. Henry Scudder said, "She may be good, yet not good for you; she may be a fit wife, yet not fit for you." What does this mean? Give some examples.

6. What six points did Isaac Ambrose offer for evaluating a potential spouse? Can you enlarge upon these points?

7. How might a potential spouse's reputation among godly Christians confirm or correct our opinion of him or her?

---

68. Rogers, 53.

8. What role should parents play in evaluating a potential spouse?

9. How crucial is parental approval to getting married? Why?

10. Why is self-denial an important quality to cultivate when seeking a spouse?

Preserving the Honor
of Marriage

When we marry in the Lord we honor the Lord of marriage and can therefore look to Him for the many blessings which He delights to bestow upon marriage. Yet, as a man who has worked so hard to procure a fortune gives much thought to how to preserve it, so the task now is to address the means by which we might preserve and maintain the honor of marriage. Rogers said, "Those who have found an honorable marriage must wait upon it and keep it so."[1]

If marriage's honor is *from* the Lord and is to be procured by marrying *in* the Lord, then it necessarily follows that the only means of preserving its honor is to walk faithfully *before* the Lord in marriage. Otherwise, unfaithfulness will mar the honor of marriage before men, pierce the hearts of our spouses, and cause the Lord to withdraw His blessings from us. Accordingly, Scripture teaches us not only to marry in the Lord (1 Cor. 7:39), but also how to live together in faithfulness before the Lord (Eph. 5:22–33; Col. 3:18–19; 1 Pet. 3:1–7).

To walk faithfully before the Lord in marriage is to heed the mutual and respective *duties* of marriage. Marriage is a stewardship from the Lord and is entered into with vows to one another before the Lord. Marriage should therefore be considered primarily from the standpoint of duty and obligation. Marriage entails uniting not so much with someone you passionately love at the moment as with someone you are committing to always love faithfully and dutifully.[2]

---

1. Rogers, 115.
2. den Ouden, 40–41.

When God unites a man and a woman in marriage, He calls them to honor Him by faithfully performing the duties incumbent upon them in the relationship into which He has brought them (e.g., Eph. 5:22–33; 1 Pet. 3:1–7). As these duties are assigned by God in His Word, faithfully performing them not only honors Him directly but also helps preserve and maintain the honor which He places upon the marriage. Gouge therefore spoke of both the need and benefit of being faithful in fulfilling marital duties when he said, "These [duties] are either *absolutely necessary* for the *being* and *abiding* of marriage; or needful and requisite for the *well being* and *well abiding* of it, that is, for the good estate of marriage, and for a commendable, and comfortable living together."[3]

However, God does more than assign us duties and call us to faithfully obey them. He wants those duties so impressed upon our minds and instilled in our hearts that we walk in them willingly and cheerfully out of the conviction that both His glory and our happiness are bound up with our faithfulness. He therefore *impresses* these duties upon us by grounding the ordinance of marriage on two scriptural principles: the Christ-church principle and the covenantal principle. So, before addressing the respective duties of marriage in the following chapters, we will first discuss these two principles which provide the ground and motivation for *duty* itself in a marriage. Once we do that, we can faithfully yield to all that duty to which the Lord calls us which, by His grace, will in turn *preserve* the honor of our marriages.

The Duty of Mutual Submission

Gouge's *Of Domestical Duties* is based on Ephesians 5:21–6:9, which describes the duties of husbands and wives, parents and children, masters and servants. Prior to explaining those duties, Gouge wrote an introduction explaining this passage phrase by phrase so that in each particular station one may know and understand his or her duty before the Lord, which is to *submit one to another* (Eph. 5:21).

In Ephesians 5:21, Paul charges his readers to submit themselves "one to another in the fear of God." Gouge explained that no matter

---

3. Gouge, 155.

what particular role or station the believer fills, he or she is called by God to *submission*. An inferior submits to those over him by honoring them and serving them in the fear of the Lord (1 Pet. 2:13–17), while a superior submits to those under him by ruling over them with love and humility in the fear of the Lord (1 Pet. 5:1–4), and equals submit to one another by putting the interests of others above their own in the fear of the Lord (Phil. 2:3–4).

The logic behind such mutual submission is twofold. First, each of us has been assigned a place by God, not so much for our own good as for the good of others. Rather than being called to self-gratification or self-exaltation, we are called to service and duty. The apostle therefore describes the church or body of Christ as being so composed by God that each one may care for one another (1 Cor. 12:24–25) and thereby serve not his own interest, but the common good (1 Cor. 12:7). God gives the members of Christ's body different roles according to what is good for the whole body rather than for individual members. In our particular callings we are to regard the good of others more than our own (Phil. 2:3–4). For those in authority, Gouge said, the callings of superiors "are in truth offices of service, indeed, burdens under which they must willingly put their shoulders, being called of God, and of which they are to give an account concerning the good which they have done to others, for the effecting whereof, it is needful that they submit themselves."[4]

Second, in being assigned our places by God, each of us is responsible to be faithful to Him. No matter what our station is, we must fulfill our duties in the fear of the Lord because, said Gouge, that is the "*efficient cause* that moves a true Christian willingly to perform all duty to man."[5] Mindful of how good God is to us, and how happiness consists of enjoying His favor, a proper and holy fear of the Lord makes us willing to do all that He requires of us and unwilling to do what displeases Him.

In the fear of the Lord we submit to one another in performing the duties of our stations. Wives submit to husbands and husbands love their wives (Eph. 5:22, 25); children obey parents and parents nurture their children (Eph. 6:1–4); and servants obey masters and masters

---

4. Gouge, 4.
5. Gouge, 5.

govern their servants with Christ-like care and kindness (1 Pet. 2:17; 2 Chron. 19:5–9). As Gouge wrote, "He that obeys not those who are over him *in the fear of God* shows no respect for God's image; and he who governs not those who are under him *in the fear of God,* shows no respect for God's charge."[6]

Some may argue that mutual submission denies the difference between those who are in authority and those who are under authority. But the reverse is seen to be true if we remember that the form submission takes will differ with the roles we occupy. He who is in authority submits by governing those under him with humility and love. Likewise, he who is under authority submits by lovingly and faithfully performing his duties, giving honor to whom honor is due. And the Lord receives the greatest honor of all for we are all servants of one another according to our respective stations, equally accountable to Him, and equally motivated by fear of Him as members of His body.

Gouge therefore charged believers, saying: "Wherefore let all of all sorts set the *fear of God* as a mark before them to aim at in all their actions…. Let superiors (Num. 11:29) neither do anything to [satisfy] their inferiors, nor suffer any thing (1 Sam. 24:8) to be done for their sakes by their inferiors, which cannot stand with the *fear of God.* And let inferiors (Gen. 39:10; 1 Sam. 22:17) [neither] do, nor forbear (Acts 4:19) to do at the will of their superiors any thing swerving from the fear of God; but *every one submit themselves one to another in the fear of God.*"[7]

Christ and His Church

In the context of mutual submission, Gouge followed the apostle Paul who, in Ephesians 5, addresses the duties incumbent upon wives and husbands in the Lord. As a basis for their duties, Paul introduces the first major principle of marriage: the *Christ-church principle.* According to this principle, the husband is to love his wife as Christ loves the church, and the wife is to show reverence and submission to her husband as the church submits to Christ. Paul invokes this principle, said

---

6. Gouge, 9.
7. Gouge, 10.

Gouge, so that both husband and wife might be "the better directed" and "the better provoked."[8]

The husband's headship over his wife parallels Christ's headship over His church (Eph. 5:23). As Christ loves His church, so the husband must love his wife. He is to love her absolutely (v. 25), purposefully (v. 26), realistically (v. 27), and sacrificially (vv. 28–29). He must exercise a "true, free, pure, exceeding, constant love" to his wife, nourishing and cherishing her as Christ does His gathered people (v. 29).[9] Christ's love for His church is the pattern for a husband to follow.

To be sure, Christ's love for His church is as excellent, perfect, and infinite as His divine person. Thus a husband is unable to love his wife equal to the measure of Christ's love. As a sinner, he will always fall short of the infinite reach of Christ's love (v. 25). Yet, Christ's love for His bride is to be every husband's goal and pattern.[10] He is to walk as closely as he can to it. Such Christ-like love, said Gouge, will serve "as sugar to sweeten the duties of authority which appertain to a husband," and thereby enable his loving wife to more easily submit to him.[11] His faithfulness will encourage her faithfulness and his love will draw out her submission.

Likewise, the wife's submission to her husband parallels the church's submission to Christ (Eph. 5:22–24). "A wife must submit herself to a husband," Gouge wrote, "because he is her *head*; and she must do it *as unto the Lord*, because her husband is to her, as Christ is to the Church."[12] Thus the Christ-church principle provides both the *reason* for a wife's submission as well as the *manner* in which she is to render it. She is not to submit to her husband in *anything* that contradicts her submission to Christ (v. 22), but in *everything* that is in keeping with her submission to Christ, because she submits to her husband as she submits to Christ (v. 24).

---

8. Gouge, 18 and 30.
9. Gouge, 31.
10. Gouge, 31.
11. Gouge, 94.
12. Gouge, 19.

If a wife submits to her husband in things contrary to Christ, then she is not submitting *as unto the Lord*. Conscientious wives must therefore remember, wrote Isaac Ambrose, "that they have a husband in heaven, as well as on earth, betwixt whom there is a greater difference than between heaven and earth; and therefore in case they bid contrary things, they must prefer God before men, Christ before all men."[13] A wife "ought, like a true [mirror], faithfully to represent and return to her husband's heart, with a sweet and pleasing pliableness, the exact lineaments and proportions of all his honest desires and demands, and that without discontent, thwarting, or sourness. For her subjection in this kind should be as to Christ, sincere, hearty, and free."[14]

This Christ-church principle holds true even if a husband is a worthless man who does not know the Lord (1 Sam. 2:12; cf. 1 Cor. 7:12–13). Ambrose wrote, "A wife must be meek, mild, gentle, obedient, though she be matched with a crooked, perverse, profane, and wicked husband. She must in this case remove her eyes from the disposition of her husband's person to the condition of his place, and by virtue thereof (seeing he bears Christ's image) be subject unto him as unto Christ."[15] Her eye must ever be on Christ, who is above her husband and for whose sake she willingly submits to him, because this will enable her to fulfill her duty faithfully before the Lord who called her unto it.

Yet this principle also provides the *benefit* of submission. Christ as the head of His church protects and provides for it, so the husband as the head of the wife must protect and provide for his wife (vv. 23, 29). The wife submits to her husband for her own benefit so that she might enjoy his protection and provision. As his headship is one of responsibility so her submission is one of beneficence, and as his role reflects Christ's goodness so her role reflects the church's duty.[16]

So, how does this principle actually work in marriage? The husband should be mindful that his duty towards his wife is to represent and reflect the Savior's love for His church. Though a husband's love for his

---

13. Ambrose, 235–36.
14. Bolton, 279.
15. Ambrose, 235.
16. Gouge, 20–21.

wife will fall far short of Christ's love for His church, marriage is still meant to be an illustration of Christ's love for His church. A husband's love should be as pure as Christ's, not mixed with a wanton eye for other women, a lustful heart for other pleasures, or a selfish interest which quickly becomes dissatisfied. Rather, his love should be devoted entirely and only to her. His love should be as sincere as Christ's, not looking to her for wealth or family or talents, but to her as a person. His love should be as constant as Christ's, not like the passion of youth that quickly fades, but as an enduring and faithful love all her days. His love should be as sacrificial as Christ's, promoting not only her temporal but her spiritual interests, even at a cost to himself. Moreover, his love for his wife should be rendered in such a way as to endear himself to her and thereby make her submission easy. She should delight to be the wife of such a loving and caring husband and do all that is required of her by God towards him.

The husband should cherish and nourish his wife as Christ loves the church. He should not be harsh in his speech but speak words that comfort and build her up. He should not be careless in his manners but behave towards his wife with tenderness, softness, and the concern to please her and endear himself to her. He should speak highly and lovingly of her in her absence, making it clear to everyone that he cherishes her. He should be patient with her infirmities and seek to help her grow stronger in the Lord and be faithful in her duties to Him.

The husband's relationship with his wife points to Christ's place as the Head of His church, which is His body. So a husband should zealously strive to accurately represent Christ. He should care for his wife as for his own body since the two, by marriage, have become as one flesh (Eph. 5:28–31). This should be done with cheerfulness and willingness because of the honor placed upon him to show forth Christ in marriage.

Likewise, the wife should reflect the church's relationship to Christ by submitting to her husband. She should be enflamed with a desire, for Christ's sake, to honor her husband and submit to him in a manner that shows her own submission to Christ. Her husband is not _Christ_ to her, yet he is _as_ Christ to her within marriage. Christ regards her submission unto her husband as part of her submission unto Him since, as the apostle says, she is to submit "as unto the Lord" (v. 22). Her failure to submit to her husband in everything lawful is a sin because it is a failure to submit to Christ; it is rebellion against her Lord. Thus she should yield to her husband's leadership, depend upon his provision, and look to his protection of her, honoring the Lord who placed her husband over her.

It is important to understand that the submission to which the Lord calls her is not a matter of hierarchy but of *function*. God assigns the role of leadership to the husband not because he is better than his wife, but simply because He delegates this authority to him. John Robinson explained it this way: "God created man and woman spiritually equal, and when both fell into sin she did not become more degenerated than he from the primitive goodness. Yet in marriage one of the two must have final authority, since differences will arise, and so the one must give way and apply unto the other; this, God and nature lays upon the man."[17] Her submission is therefore not a servile subjection, but a God-honoring submission.

Can every member of a nation be king? Can all in a family be fathers? Can all be wives? Can all be everything? Of course not. There must necessarily be not only order but degrees of authority, submission, and rule. The godly wife will therefore look contentedly unto the hand of God which made her the wife and not the husband, the weaker vessel and not the stronger, to obey and not to rule. For her to rebel against her place would wrong God more than her husband; and for her to assume the reins of the family and govern in her husband's place would usurp authority rather than rule with authority. Whatever government she may enjoy in the family, she should enjoy it under her husband's headship and not contrary to it; she enjoys it with her husband's consent and with reference to his will over her (in the same way that the moon must refer its light to the sun's illumination). She enjoys it to administer her husband's honor and desires as wisely and carefully as she would administer his money or anything else entrusted to her.

Truly, a marriage in which God's order is observed and enjoyed is a *good* marriage. "In such a case, how great an honor is the wife's godly

---

17. Quoted in Ryken, *Worldly Saints*, 76.

government unto the husband, while he as king to command, yet with love as a husband, shall go in and out in the midst of his family, not fearing spoil, whether he be at home or abroad; nor needing unlawful spoils to maintain his estate? As also, how honorable a service is it in the wife, to depend upon his beck, to advise with her head, to lean upon his breast, and yet to [enjoy] the authority to do what she will [as long as] her will is honest, lawful, and to her husband's good?"[18]

Because her submission honors the Lord, the wife should render it willingly and cheerfully; for her subjection is not to be in word or deed only, but also done with heartfelt joy. Her husband should rejoice in how joyfully and quickly she honors him, serves him, and looks to him to be the head which God has appointed and called him to be. She should live in such a way as to endear herself to him and draw his love towards her. She should do her duty towards him in such a way that he can do his duty towards her with equal ease and delight. This means she must submit to him voluntarily. Her submission is not to be compelled any more than his love is to be forced. Rather, she is to render her submission as part of her obedience to Christ just as much as he is to render his affection as part of his obedience to Christ. Their marriage and therefore their roles are grounded upon the Christ-church principle. A wife's honor and freedom in Christ acknowledges her husband as her head and submits to him accordingly; and his honor and freedom in Christ acknowledges his wife as his own body and loves her accordingly.

But there is much more than mere motivation here. One might be motivated to do what is right but still be unable to do it. For believers, the Christ-church principle provides the enabling we need to do what God has called us to do. It is true that Christ is to be leaned on in every situation and His own holiness drawn upon in every station and duty. The apostle Paul said he could do all things through Christ who strengthened him (Phil. 4:13). If this is the case in all circumstances, then surely we can also expect Christ to enable us to be holy in marriage.

---

18. Ste. B., 49.

The Covenantal Principle

Flowing out of the Christ-church principle, which is the very reason for *duty*, is the second principle, the covenantal principle. Upon this principle both parties in a marriage freely and voluntarily consent to live according to the rules of marriage which God set when He solemnized the marriage of our first parents.[19] When a man and a woman enter into holy matrimony before the Lord, they promise to fulfill the duties of marriage without conditions and without reservations.

Two things are mentioned in Malachi 2:14 that underscore the solemnity of the vows made at the commencement of marriage. First is that this exchange of promises is a covenant. In verse 14 the Lord calls husbands to repentance for dealing treacherously with their wives by divorcing "thy companion, and the wife of thy covenant." In Proverbs 2:16–17, the adulteress is described as she who not only forsakes her husband but forgets "the covenant of her God," a reference to her marriage vows. Marriage is therefore a sacred bond. When a man and a woman exchange the vows of marriage, they are doing more than contracting to share a home and a bank account; they are entering into a covenant with each other with stipulations and responsibilities. As P. den Ouden observed, "for the Puritans it was not love but faithfulness which constituted the marriage. Even if the love would weaken... the partners remain under obligation to remain faithful to each other because of the marital oath."[20]

Marriage must be entered into as a covenant in which a husband and wife promise before God to perform the duties that God has assigned to each. The husband promises to faithfully love his wife as Christ loves His church, to serve her, comfort her, honor and cherish her, and forsaking all others keep faith with her as long as they both shall live. The wife promises to love her husband, comfort him, respect and submit to him as the church submits to Christ, and forsaking all others keep faith with him as long as they both shall live.

---

19. Cf. Chapter 1.
20. den Ouden, 45.

P. den Ouden therefore said, "Someone who does not wish to take on responsibilities does not understand the essence of marriage."[21] To define marriage in any way that ignores or negates its covenantal commitment of faithfulness to certain God-prescribed duties is to abandon its institution and foundation and redefine it in a man-centered way. Such marriages bring shame rather than honor upon the relationship of Christ with His church and therefore fail to experience the honor and blessings of marriage itself. Reyner wrote, "The duties of marriage are matters of religion, of conscience and obedience to the gospel, being fully prescribed and enjoined therein. And Christ will one day come in flaming fire to take vengeance on them that obey not the gospel, in the precepts of it, 2 Thess. 1:8."[22]

The second thing mentioned in Malachi 2:14 expressing the solemnity of the marriage vows is that the Lord Himself is a witness to the marriage covenant. Verse 14 says, "the LORD hath been witness between thee and the wife of thy youth, against whom thou hast dealt treacherously: yet is she thy companion, and the wife of thy covenant." In other words, marriage is not only concerned with the man and the woman being married. Marriage was instituted by God, blessed by God for those who honor Him in it, and is also witnessed by God. He hears the promises you make to each other, the vows which you utter. He is witness to your surrender to your spouse and He will hold you accountable to your own words. Scudder therefore advised married couples to "consider what you then did; you then entered into a near covenant with one another, indeed, into a *covenant with God* to be one another's, and to be faithful to each other…. So that if you break covenant with one another, you break covenant also with your God."[23] Marriage is not only a covenant between husband and wife; it is a covenant with God which He witnesses and seals.

Some think a good marriage is one in which a man secures the most beautiful woman for his bride. Some think a good marriage is one in which a woman lands the richest man to be her husband. Others

---

21. den Ouden, 42.
22. Reyner, 36.
23. Scudder, 71.

regard a marriage to be good if a husband and wife can enjoy a good measure of independence within the marriage and not feel tied down or restricted by it. Still others regard a good marriage as one in which the man finds a wife who will do whatever he tells her, or the woman finds a husband who will give her whatever she wants. All such marriages will prove disastrously disappointing because they fall far short of what God intends in marriage. Scudder advised unmarried persons to think about and prepare for the duties of marriage *before* they marry, for "God has in his Word told you what you must do when you are married."[24] Likewise, Reyner said, "For any to marry before they know their duty, or how to carry [themselves] therein, is like setting up before one has learned the trade; or like answering a matter before one hears it, which is folly and shame unto him, Prov. 18:13."[25]

To enjoy a marriage in which joy and peace reign, one Puritan gave the following counsel: "It stands not [upon] what man and wife shall [agree] upon, that there may be peace and quietness, but [upon] what order God has prescribed them, to be obeyed in their places; so that they must look unto God's wisdom, order, and polity, for [household] government, and not what may seem right and good in their own eyes.... Each must keep their place, their order, and heavenly polity, whereto God has called them. The husband is made the head and the wife resembled to the body. May the head of a natural body be turned [upside down]? Can the whole person so continue and live well in that estate? How unseemly is it? No more can a body [of household government] be in peaceable or blessed condition if the order is inverted."[26] Secker put it this way: "Our *ribs* were not ordained to be our *rulers*. They are not made of the head, to claim superiority; but out of the *side*, to be content with *equality*. They desert the *Author* of nature and invert the *order* of nature. The woman was made for the *man's comfort*, but the man was not made for the *woman's command*. Those shoulders aspire too high, that content not themselves with a room below their head...."

24. Scudder, 60.
25. Reyner, 35.
26. Ste. B., 41–43.

The body of that household can never make any good motion, whose bones are out of place."[27]

Richard Baxter gave similar counsel: "It is the subversion of all societies, and so of the world, that selfish, ungodly persons enter into all relations with a desire to serve themselves and fish out all that gratifies their flesh without any sense of the duty of their relation. They consider what honor, profit, or pleasure their relation will afford them, but not what God and man require or expect from them (Gen. 2:18; Prov. 18:22). All their thought is what they shall have, but not what they shall be and do. They are very sensible what others should be and do to them but not what they should be and do to others. Thus it is with magistrates and people, with too many pastors and their flocks, with husbands and wives, with parents and children, and all other relations. Our first care should be to know and perform the duties of our relations and please God in them and then to look for his blessing by way of encouraging reward. Study and do your parts, and God will certainly do his."[28]

Scudder counseled unmarried persons by saying, "It shall be your wisdom to be provident and wary how you enter into this estate; and that you foreknow and do thoroughly forethink and prepare for ability to do the duties and to bear the troubles which that estate will necessarily put upon you."[29] Would that such counsel was weighed today by those desiring to marry! Divorce would not be so common, especially among the people of God who should honor the covenant that they made to each other in front of God and other witnesses, and who should model their relationship after the example of Christ and the church.

Two caveats should be added here. First, since both husband and wife have obligations to fulfill in the marriage, neither is to wait for the other; instead, each must seek to be faithful before the Lord irrespective of the other. The husband is accountable to God for himself and cannot excuse himself of those duties if his wife fails in hers. If she neglects her duties, not only does she wrong her husband, but she also dishonors God who called her to those duties and in whose name she entered the

---

27. Secker, 256–57.
28. Baxter, 127.
29. Scudder, 65.

covenant of marriage. Likewise, a wife is not to withhold submitting to her husband saying that he is withholding his love from her. She is accountable to God to fulfill her duties as a wife regardless of her husband's behavior. She must persevere in submission and thereby not only endear herself to him, but also remind him of his own obligations to her before the Lord as her husband; for what should her submission to him recall but his own obligation to submit to the Lord as a husband?

Therefore both the husband and the wife should seek to do their duty first! Reflecting on Paul's words in Romans 12:10 ("in honour preferring one another") one Puritan wrote, "I wish that it might never grow to question of law between man and wife whose is the duty…to begin the work of household government; but [I wish] for them rather to strive, who should be most careful of each other's goods. The husband (in needful service) should not need to say, Good wife, help me herein…but the wife should [precede] him with, Good husband let me do it for you. Neither [should] the wife [need] to say (in like case), I pray husband do this for me; but he rather [should] take care to [precede] her desire…. Thus they should not strive, unless it were to give honor…and to do service, and by love to [precede] each other…. And surely where true love reigns indeed…or where…either of them are truly careful of each other's good, they shall not need to sue each other at the law for their right, or complain they have [been] wronged."[30]

Second, neither the husband nor the wife is to define his or her rights by the other's duties. The husband may be tempted to demand his wife's total submission and thereby behave as a tyrant, while the wife may be tempted to demand her husband's sacrificial love. Not only are such demands sinful in themselves, but the one who positions himself to think of his spouse's duties as his right has already neglected his own duties. Neglecting one's own duties is the *root* of the demand that your spouse fulfill hers. The only way to avoid this temptation is to zealously fulfill your own duties and to prayerfully allow your spouse to zealously pursue hers. When you do this, you will find the grace of God to faithfully perform what you are called to do. Happiness in marriage is

---

30. Ste. B., 53–54.

not bound up with what your spouse does but with fulfilling your own duties willingly and cheerfully because you do them as to the Lord.

Let it then be our chief concern to do *our own* duty. Though it is difficult to be married to a spouse who neglects his or her duty towards you, you can rejoice before the Lord when you fulfill your duty towards your spouse. As Gouge said, "to have others fail in duty to us may be a heavy cross, [but] for us to fail in our duty to others is a fearful curse."[31] Therefore if the husband will see that he rules with love and if the wife will see that she obeys with cheerfulness, and if they both will see that they remain content before the Lord with their own lot and portion, then the yoke of marriage will be both worn and pulled with ease.[32]

The following exhortation should encourage us as it encouraged the young married couple to whom it was written:

> I exhort you [Miss] to wise subjection, to loving, and Christian reverence, to faithful and dutiful obedience, which shall not only be your crown of glory amongst the godly wise, as it was Sarah's [1 Pet. 3:6]…but if you desire to rule and to be trusted with all your husband has, this is the way, and there is no other. If you thus say, Give me the sword, you shall have both it and all assistance to use it; but if you will strive to wrest it out of your husband's hand, you will not only miss your desire, but take hurt by striving. Thus your godly subjection shall gain you more liberty, ease, honor, and lawful government, than all the contention in the world can bring to pass. And hate both the name and nature of a contentious wife; remember she is as an incurable dripping, and intolerable. Besides, to rule the family with the husband's assignment is a great honor to the wife; but to bear sway against his will and favor, [there is] no greater shame….
>
> And you [Mister], as my dear friend, I counsel…know your wife to be a vessel, therefore necessary—I will not say, as one says, a necessary evil, for I trust she shall be that virtuous wife that shall do her husband good and not evil all the days of her life; but I doubt not to say, a necessary vessel for fruit unto God's glory; a vessel, when you are full of sorrows, to help bear them and ease you. A vessel to contain your counsels and instructions, and not to

---

31. Gouge, 96.
32. Ste. B., 92.

be plowed with, by any adversity, but as a faithful bulwark against adversaries. Yet being withal the weaker vessel, she must be treated accordingly. Our most precious vessels (whether glass or gold) are commonly the weakest…and those we most precisely [treat], not roughly or carelessly. To a virtuous woman, there is no vessel, no jewel comparable; count her therefore the chiefest vessel in your house that must contain yourself and all your treasures. Her price, says Solomon, is above the pearls; show not your rough and man-like courage (like Lamech) to your wife, but to your enemy. You are both one, therefore be as one. Look not so much [to] what is required of her, as what is due to her from yourself. You are the covering of her eyes, which must defend her, not oppress her. She is of godly, wise, and worshipful stock and parentage; her years have been seasoned hitherto with the salt of godly education; and therefore the fitter for your wisdom to work upon; make the work perfect and you shall have both the honor and the comfort of the work. To be brief, what is lacking in her…that may [take away] from the title of a virtuous wife?…You are both in the fittest time to begin an happy estate; lay therefore the foundation according to God's holy Word, and the building shall be glorious. Let that be the rule of both your duties, and know that God is most wise in directing both your states.

Thus while you both regard the duties of your several places, jointly towards the Lord first, then mutually towards one another, how easy will the burden of your family and callings be unto you? The equal [distribution] makes your burden light. What an example will [yours] be to servants, to children, to neighbors, to friends, yes to all men, to be followed and commended?…You shall be most happy first in this present life, and more happy above happiness in the life to come."[33]

May we be as moved to faithfulness in our marital duties as this young couple surely was by such a warm exhortation, and may we be brought to enjoy and preserve the honor of our marriages before God. Marriage is a tender flower planted by God. If we neglect our duties towards marriage, this flower will wither and die. If we treat marriage harshly, its beauty and life will be choked off and its blessing turned into a curse. But if we cultivate marriage according to God's instructions

---

33. Ste. B., 92–97.

and are thankful *to* Him and faithful *before* Him, we may preserve marriage's enduring beauty, fruitfulness, satisfaction, pleasure, and honor.

Study Questions

1. Explain the idea of mutual submission (Eph. 5:21). What does it mean practically?

2. How does the wife's submission to her husband parallel the church's submission to Christ (Eph. 5:22–24)?

3. What did Isaac Ambrose say should limit the submission of a wife? Provide some contemporary examples that illustrate this limitation.

4. How should the husband's love for his wife parallel Christ's love for the church (Eph. 5:25–27)?

5. According to William Gouge, how is a husband's love like "sugar" to his authority?

6. Read Malachi 2:14 and Proverbs 2:16–17. How would covenant loyalty protect and enrich a marriage?

7. Richard Baxter warned of "selfish ungodly persons" who "consider what honor, profit, or pleasure their relation will afford them." What does selfishness do to a marriage? What steps can you take in your marriage to limit the influence of selfishness?

8. Baxter contrasted the selfish to those who aim to "perform the duties of our relation and please God in them." If so, how is duty the path of love?

9. What is the danger of demanding your rights based on your spouse's duties?

10. In the lengthy exhortation quoted at the end of this chapter, what did you find most helpful or thought-provoking? Why?

The Mutual Duties of
Love and Chastity

The Puritans divided marital duties into three kinds: mutual duties, the duties of the wife, and the duties of the husband. Ambrose wrote, "The duties which the chief governor and his helper owe to one another are either common and mutual [or] proper and peculiar to each."[1] Having laid the foundation and explained the reason for all the duties of marriage in the previous chapter, we can now outline and explain the duties themselves. We will explore the mutual duties first.

Zechariah and Elizabeth are commended in Luke 1:6 because they walked blamelessly before the Lord in their marriage. Just because a marriage begins well does not guarantee it will continue well. The well-being of marriage must be cultivated and preserved, and that is done by striving faithfully before God in the strength of Christ in the duties of marriage. Hence Paul not only says that we must be married in the Lord (1 Cor. 7:39), but that we must also walk faithfully before the Lord in marriage (Col. 3:18–19). The mutual duties of marriage are what the husband and his wife owe to each other, and through which they enjoy and preserve the honor of their marriage before God. As Robert Bolton explained, the mutual duties of marriage are the first set of those marital duties by which we can secure "a comfortable continuance in the marriage state."[2]

---

1. Ambrose, 233.
2. Bolton, 265.

Among the dozens of Puritan authors researched for this book,[3] we found almost forty duties which they believed a husband and wife owe each other.[4] While some of these duties overlap (even in a single author's treatment), many were named so that every possible occasion of discord might be avoided and every possible occasion for enjoying the honor of marriage might be secured. Of this vast number, we will consider the five main points of mutual duty upon which the life, health, and honor of marriage depend. We will also consider the means to walk obediently in each duty.

Mutual Love

The first mutual duty is to love each other. According to the Puritans, love is the most significant and fundamental mutual duty. It is at the foundation of the whole marriage and as such undergirds and drives all other duties. It is the duty of both the husband (Col. 3:19) and the wife (Titus 2:4). A good marriage is therefore one in which husband and wife faithfully show love towards each other.

Consider first the *necessity* of this mutual love. Whately observed, "Love is the life and soul of marriage, without which it differs as much from itself, as a rotten apple from a sound [one] and as a carcass from a living body; yea, verily it is a most miserable and uncomfortable society, and no better than a very living death."[5] Likewise, Smith declared, "Unless there be a joining of heart and a knitting of affections together,

---

3. See the Abbreviations page for a full bibliography.

4. E.g., a strong love, care for one another's body, care for one another's name, care for one another's credit, care for one another's goods and estate, care for one another's family, care for one another's soul, conjugal honor, cohabitation, sexual intimacy, communion in worship, chastity, fidelity, bearing one another's burdens, avoid anger, assuage unruly passions, please each other in all things lawful, abhor adultery and all that tends to it, delight in each other, live in quietness and peace, edify each other in the things of God, be a helper in one another's Christian walk, patience, keeping one another's secrets, strive for peace, pray for and with each other, admonish each other for sin, exhort each other to grow in grace, procreation, build a godly family, family worship, satisfy each other, family government, faithfulness in temporal matters, court one another's happiness, prefer each other in kindness, counter one another's defects, helpfulness in one another's afflictions.

5. Whately, *A Bride-Bush*, 31.

it is not marriage in deed, but in show and name, and they shall dwell in a house like two poisons in a stomach, and one shall ever be sick of another."[6] Scudder therefore advised those who married to "love each other as [their] own souls with a Christian, pure, tender, abundant, natural, and matrimonial love."[7]

A marriage without love, noted Rogers, is nothing but a carcass void of life, since mutual love is "the vital spirit and heart blood of [marriage], causing a voluntary and practical union of two, without which [marriage] is but a forced necessity. For then has this ordinance her perfection when this solder of love being added thereto makes that union, which cannot be broken, to become such a *willing* one as... would not be broken."[8] Without this love, a husband and wife suffer the misery of a conjugal union without conjugal love. This love is to the marriage ordinance as the echo is to the voice; it is an answer in the heart to the consent of the mouth, so that the lovers who marry enter into a relationship which, as Rogers said, not only cannot be broken, but which they would not dare to break because of the love they enjoy in it. If this love could not be had in a marriage where the two become one flesh, then friendship is a better "one-ship" (i.e., intimate relationship) than marriage since friendship can easily be broken off when disturbed by hardship, whereas marriage is a bond for life. "Without the union of hearts," Swinnock wrote, "the union of bodies will be no benefit."[9] And Secker quipped, "Two joined together without love, are but two tied together to make one another miserable."[10] Mutual love is therefore a necessity in marriage.

Consider the peculiar *strength* of this mutual love. Marriage is the closest relationship and therefore requires the dearest affection. Who should be one in heart but those who share one bed, one table, and one house? This love is no common love; it is a love as unique as the marriage relationship itself and as singular as the spouse to whom it is

---

6. Smith, 1:22.
7. Scudder, 72.
8. Rogers, 138. Emphasis added.
9. Swinnock, 1:472.
10. Secker, 263.

given. Since it is based on the love between Christ and His church (a love so fervent that she is said to be sick with love for Him [Song 2:5] and so that He laid down His life for her [John 15:13]), this mutual love is the strongest of loves.[11] Because of it, a man and a woman are willing to leave their families and friends so they may cleave, as with glue, to each other (Gen. 2:24; 29:34). Their hearts are so joined together by this knot of affection that they cannot be separated. Trials tend to break relationships and divide acquaintances, which proves the weakness of those bonds; but mutual love is such a bond in marriage that whatever trials may threaten it, the love between a husband and wife will fill the breach with forgiveness and act as a sail by which they ride out the storm until the sun shines upon them again.

Consider as well the *nature* of this mutual love. Husband and wife are to love each other with a strong, fervent, and steady love; not with a love that waxes and wanes with the tide of beauty, dress, or riches, nor that fluctuates with emotions and lusts. This love, wrote Ambrose, is "a sweet, loving, and tender-hearted pouring out of their hearts, with much affectionate dearness, into each other's bosoms."[12] It is an *entire* love, a fulsome love, a love that pours itself out between spouses constantly and without reservation in a variety of expressions, gestures, looks, and actions. This marital love is not "raised suddenly in a pang of affection, ebbing and flowing…but a habited and settled love planted in them by God, whereby in a constant, equal, and cheerful consent of spirit they carry themselves [towards] each other."[13] Bolton therefore defined this duty of mutual love as "a drawing into action, and keeping in exercise, [the] *habit* of conjugal affection and matrimonial love."[14] If this mutual love is eclipsed for but a day or even an hour, said Baxter, the husband and wife are "as a bone out of joint; there is no ease, no order, no work well done till they are restored and set in joint again."[15]

---

11. Swinnock, 1:471–72.
12. Ambrose, 233.
13. Rogers, 137–38.
14. Bolton, 265. Emphasis added.
15. Baxter, 128.

Consider, too, the *universal benefit* of this love. This love makes everything in a marriage easy while its absence makes everything hard. When love is abundant in a marriage it will meet all other needs, and when it is lacking it makes all other duties no more than cold, lifeless acts. Whately said, "Love seasons and sweetens all estates; love breaks and composes all controversies; love overrules all passions; it squares all actions; it is, in a word, the King of the heart, which, in whom it prevails, to them [it] is marriage itself…a pleasing combination of two persons into one home, one purse, one heart, and one flesh."[16]

Love is therefore the sum of *all* the duties that a husband and wife owe to each other (Rom. 13:10). Being linked together by the bond of marital love, wrote Gouge, is "true wedlock."[17] Where love fills the hearts, the feet, hands, and lips move easily in the service of the one loved, but where love is lacking duties are either neglected or performed in a hypocritical, slothful, and careless manner. True-hearted love, wrote Steele, "will bring true contentment and constant comfort into [marriage], will make all counsels and reproofs acceptable, will keep out jealousy, that bane of marriage-comfort, will keep the thoughts fixed, and the heart chaste; for it is not the *having* a husband or wife, but the *loving* of them, that preserves from adultery. This will prevent or soon quiet storms within doors; as we see the mother that dearly loves her child, though it cry all night and disturb her quiet, yet love to it makes them very good friends in the morning."[18] Thus this love must be plentiful, large, and abundant; because if it is not, those who marry will lack what is required for the honorable fulfilling of all other marital duties. As love motivates the husband it rules to do all the good he can, so love stirs up the wife he loves to repay good for good. Love is like fire, "which is not only hot in itself, but also conveys heat from one to another."[19]

Consider further the mutual *contentment* that results from mutual love. This love will cause the husband to so settle his affections on his wife that he sees her as the fittest woman that the world could have

---

16. Whately, *A Bride-Bush*, 31.
17. Gouge, 163.
18. Steele, *Puritan Sermons*, 2:276. Emphasis added.
19. Gouge, 163.

afforded him; and the wife to so rest her heart upon her husband that she esteems him the most fit man for her of any under the sun. Love fills the heart with such contentment that the wife will not seek affection from another man, and the husband will not set his eyes upon another woman; rather they will love each other fervently, cheerfully, dotingly, and fulsomely.[20] Being motivated by this grace of love, the husband will overlook his wife's defects, cover her infirmities, supplement her weaknesses, and see her as his queen. Likewise the wife will overlook her husband's failures, cover his imperfections, and see him as her prince.

The Grounds for Mutual Love

Consider also the *grounds* for mutual love. Reyner identified several grounds of love between a husband and wife.[21] First is *donation*: they are special gifts bestowed by God upon each other. She is the wife fitted and fashioned by God's own hand to be her husband's helpmate (Prov. 18:22; 19:14). Likewise, he is the husband whom God has appointed to be her spiritual leader, guide, and protector in life. This ground endears them to each other and demands a love that excels all other loves.

The second ground is *propriety*, or the mutual interest a man and woman have in each other by marriage. Husband and wife belong to each other properly and peculiarly in a way that differs from how they belong to anyone else in the world. Peculiar or singular interest in a person is a strong ground for a special and singular love for that person (1 Cor. 7:3–4).

The third ground is *union*: a husband and wife are joined together in a way that makes them as one (Gen. 2:24). Marriage is a spiritual, legal, and sexual union of two persons into one flesh. It is the nearest relationship in the entire world, nearer than that between parents and children, and therefore demands the strongest love. Scudder wrote, "The foundation that must bear up this love and the spring which must feed and nourish this love, is not only, or chiefly, the commendable parts and endowments that are in each of you, but the near relation into which you are entered, being now no more two, but *one flesh*, and

---

20. Bolton, 263.
21. Reyner, 22–25.

bone of each other's bone; and that it is now from God that you are thus made one; and that it is His will and pleasure that it should be so."[22]

The fourth ground of love is *necessity*: a man and woman need each other. The husband and wife should look upon each other as a help and companion they cannot live without. Having been joined together by God, it is not good for either of them to be alone (Gen. 2:18). And this mutual necessity breeds mutual love (1 Sam. 1:8).

The fifth ground of love is *command*, for marital love commands that a man love his wife, not only or principally because she is beautiful, witty, housewifely, dutiful, loving, and every way well-conditioned; but chiefly because the Lord of heaven and earth, to whom all affections must yield, has said, "Husbands, love your wives." The wife also must love her husband, "not only because he is a man of good means or of good parentage, is kind to her, of good courage, and of good carriage in every respect; but because he is her husband, and God the Sovereign of all souls has told women that she ought to love her husband."[23] Thus, assuming we choose a spouse who is good and fit as outlined in chapter 3, we are *free* to marry whomever we love in the Lord, but we *must* also love the person we marry.

The Means of Preserving This Love

Gouge warned that if marital love is not mutual and reciprocal, "the end and right use of marriage will be perverted, and that estate made uncomfortable and very burdensome."[24] Likewise, Rogers wrote that "the most resolute love vanishes in a short time where the fuel of love fails"; and then asked his readers, "Do you think that this edge [of love] will hold without daily whetting?"[25] Ambrose also said to readers, "This mutual-melting-heartedness, being preserved fresh and fruitful, will infinitely sweeten and beautify the marriage state."[26]

How can mutual love be preserved and maintained in our marriages?

---

22. Scudder, 72.
23. Whately, 32.
24. Gouge, 163.
25. Rogers, 142.
26. Ambrose, 233.

First, we should regularly consider the command of God that husbands love their wives (Col. 3:19) and that wives love their husbands (Titus 2:4). The regular consideration of this chief ground of marriage will help preserve the fervency and constancy of the love we initially promised to each other in marriage. Bolton said the purpose of this command "should ever beat back and banish from both their hearts all heart-rising and bitterness, distaste and disaffection; all wicked wishes that they had never met together, that they had never seen one another's faces, etc.... Otherwise, so often as he sees a better, he will wish that he had his choice to make again, and so fall off from respect to this commandment."[27]

Second, as God is the Maker of souls, of marriages, and of affections, we should be in constant prayer that He would grow our love for the spouse that He first placed within our hearts, and that He would enable us to express that love in our speech and actions. God is gracious and gives what He commands, so we may look to Him both for the rule of our obedience in marriage and for obedience itself. Only by His grace and Spirit can we do His will in marriage (Phil. 2:13; John 15:4–5). We must pray that He will keep our hearts knit together, give us increasing satisfaction in each other, and help us delight in each other's person, smile, affection, touch, companionship, service, and time. We must pray that anything that would decrease, hinder, or withdraw our love from our spouses would be kept from us (Matt. 6:13).

Third, we should consider the compassion with which Christ and His church speak to each other in the Song of Solomon. Christ addresses His church in such terms as, "O thou fairest among women; my love; thou art all fair, my love; there is no spot in thee; thou has ravished my heart, my sister, my spouse; how much better is thy love than wine; my garden, my sister, my spouse; thine eyes...have overcome me; my dove, my undefiled is but one; O love, for delights." And we read of the church addressing Christ in like manner: "Thy love is better than wine; thou whom my soul loveth; my well-beloved; thou art fair, my beloved, yea, pleasant; I am sick [with] love; my beloved...the chiefest among ten

---

27. Bolton, 266.

thousand; he is altogether lovely."[28] If marital love is to reflect the fervent love between Christ and His church, then our marriages must also be bright with warm, heart-melting exchanges that powerfully enflame and preserve our love for one another. The mouth is the heart's vent; so if our hearts are filled with love for our spouses it should be expressed in loving conversations.

Fourth, we should spend considerable time together. The Puritans spoke much of cohabitation as a means of maintaining mutual love.[29] In Deuteronomy 24:5, God instructs that no Israelite should be called out to war during the first year of his marriage but should remain at home and "cheer up his wife which he hath taken." God wants a husband to enjoy the wife of his youth, be satisfied with her, and be ravished with her love (Prov. 5:18–19). In that time, He wanted their love to be firmly established by a year of protected cohabitation without the threat of being called off to war (cf. Gen. 2:24; Ps. 45:10; 1 Pet. 3:7; 1 Cor. 7:10, 12–13).

How then do couples expect to maintain the flame of their love when they live apart, eat apart, and sleep apart? Though two, they have been made by God to be but one flesh; therefore they must let one house, one table, and one bed hold them together. And they must not absent themselves from each other for any unnecessary purposes such as vanity or pleasure. Let them spend as much time together as their callings will permit. Let them be each other's best friend and closest confidant. Let them talk often together, be sorry together, and be happy together as they share their feelings with each other, for this will knit them more tightly together. Let them not allow any disagreement to settle itself between them and cause one of them to sleep apart from the other, for this is out of harmony with each other and with God (1 John 4:20–21). The sun should not go down on their anger (Eph. 4:26). Neither should their anger give the devil an opportunity to work against them and their affections (Eph. 4:27). Secker said a husband and wife "should be like two candles burning together, which make the house more lightsome; or like two fragrant flowers bound up in one nosegay, that augments its sweetness; or like two well-tuned instruments,

---

28. Cf. Song 1:8, 15; 4:7, 9, 10; 5:1; 6:5, 9; 7:6; and Song 1:2, 7, 13, 16; 5:8, 10, 16.
29. See e.g., Whately, *A Bride-Bush*, 42–54.

which sounding together, make the more melodious music. Husband and wife, what are they but as two springs meeting, and so joining their streams that they may make but one current? It is an unpleasing spectacle to view any contention in this conjunction."[30]

Fifth, mutual love is preserved and increased by religious exercises. Time spent together with God and in the worship of God will help preserve marital love. Let husband and wife pray together, said Whately, "let them confer with each other of their heavenly country, let them sing a Psalm together, and join in such religious exercises; so shall their hearts be knit together fast and firm to God first, and so to each other."[31] As they do so, continued Whately, "bright beams of God's image will shine forth, and show themselves in each of them, and that is lovely and alluring, and will make them amiable to each other. These will nourish the spirit of holiness in them, and that kindles love…. These will increase their faith in God, and faith will work by love; in these they shall feel themselves to have been spiritually profitable to each other; and to receive a spiritual benefit cannot but procure a spiritual affection. Here they shall perceive themselves strangers of one country, servants of one family, children of one parent, and members of one body, and this must needs increase their good will to each other."[32]

So critical is religious observance that no matter how fervent or strong a couple's love is for each other, if they fail to honor and obey God together they will soon feel a great distance between them. Many couples spend multiple hours together in worldly entertainment or vain pleasures only to see their passions cool towards each other and their hearts drawn towards others. Such hours can be a bane and a cancer to their marriage while time spent together in worship will increase their love for each other.

Sixth, we must strive to provoke the good rather than the evil in our spouses (Heb. 10:24). If we stir up the good in each other, the good will be more obvious than the evil and this will endear our spouses to us. "Draw out the fragrance of that which is good and delectable in them…

---

30. Secker, 259.
31. Whately, *A Bride-Bush*, 49.
32. Whately, *A Bride-Bush*, 49.

and then you shall find that even your faulty [spouse] will appear more amiable to you," said Baxter.[33] Focusing on their good will draw out our love towards them and the burial of their imperfections will quench any distaste we may be tempted to entertain towards them. On the other hand, if we daily stir up and provoke the sins of our spouse, then we will only have ourselves to thank for his or her failure. Therefore we must strive to overcome their imperfections with our love, not only to cause them to appear more lovely in our eyes, but to draw out their love towards us and to use them as an example of loveliness in our own behavior. Baxter said the best way to make a good and loving wife is to *be* a good and loving husband. Because of the love she has for her husband and her God, the husband's pattern of a wise, humble, loving, self-denying, patient, holy, and heavenly life will serve as a pattern towards which she will aim.[34]

In conclusion, let all who marry remember that their mutual love is a precious pearl that must be prized and protected; a flame in their bosoms that must be tended and fueled lest it go out; and a charge from God that they *must* fulfill. Hence, no one should marry without the grace of mutual love and, once married, none should go a single day without praying for the preservation, increase, and perfection of their marriage, because God is glorified when the mutual love of our marriages shows forth the mutual love between Christ and His church.

Chastity and Benevolence

The second mutual duty is a twofold duty: chastity—keeping oneself sexually pure within marriage—and what Paul calls "due benevolence," the cheerful giving of oneself sexually to one's spouse. In 1 Corinthians 7:2–3, Paul makes clear that this dual obligation is for both husband and wife. He says, "To avoid fornication, let every man have his own wife, and let every woman have her own husband. Let the husband render unto the wife due benevolence: and likewise also the wife unto the husband." On the one hand, Paul warns against sinful forms of sexual conduct; on the other, he sanctions sexual intercourse between a hus-

---

33. Baxter, 129.
34. Baxter, 129.

band and wife as "due," something they owe to each other as a matter of kindness or "benevolence." Similarly, in 1 Thessalonians 4:3–4, Paul charges us to "abstain from fornication: that every one of you should know how to possess his vessel in sanctification and honour." This advice is for married couples as well as single people.

It is important that we understand how this second duty is related to the first. As the foundational duty, love is the cement which binds couples together. Chastity characterizes the behavior that flows from this warm and settled affection. The chastity of husband and wife proves "that the heart loves entirely because the bodies are kept pure from pollution."[35] No one else is allowed to come between the husband and wife who freely give themselves to each other. For the married are bound by God, wrote Whately, "to afford to each other, a mutual enjoyment of each other, according as either of their needs shall require."[36] Their mutual love therefore *grounds* both the chastity of their marriage in that it is pure of defilement from without, and the "due benevolence" within marriage in that they freely and faithfully give themselves to each other.

So according to this twofold duty a man is forbidden to give himself sexually to anyone other than his own wife, and a woman is likewise forbidden to give herself to anyone other than her husband (because as Paul says, "let every man have his own wife, and let every woman have her own husband"). On the other hand, a husband and wife are obligated to give themselves sexually to each other (for Paul says it is their "*due* benevolence"). It is *due* because the covenant of marriage obligates them not to deprive one another of this conjugal right (1 Cor. 7:3–5), and is *benevolent* because it is an intimate expression of the love they have promised to show one another.

Think of it this way: in a chaste marriage the husband and his wife keep the door of their relationship tightly closed to all other persons because they are shut in to each other in marriage. Within the doors of their chastity, they turn to each other for the conjugal rights or "due benevolence." Likewise, a marriage in which husband and wife give each other their "due benevolence" is one in which sexual desire is

---

35. Rogers, 153.
36. Whately, *A Bride-Bush*, 14.

amply satisfied and chastity is preserved because the temptation to go outside the marriage is undercut.

Besides the scriptural mandate, there are many reasons for marital chastity. First, this duty flows out of the marriage covenant. When a man and a woman unite in marriage, they promise to be true and devoted to each other, forsaking all others. Such a covenant makes it utterly unlawful for them "upon any occasion, at any time…to give their bodies to any other in all the world, besides themselves; therefore the Scripture calls all others strange flesh" (Prov. 5:19–20).[37] This covenant obligates them to preserve marital chastity as long as the marriage continues.

Second, this duty flows out of the sacred union of a man and a woman who belong to each other. No one else has a right to what belongs to a married couple because it is theirs alone. Marriage is a relationship that gives a man his own wife and a woman her own husband. Paul says, "to avoid fornication, let every man have his own wife, and let every woman have her own husband" (1 Cor. 7:2). So much do the man and the woman become each other's that Paul goes on to say in verse 4, "The wife hath not power of her own body, but the husband: and likewise also the husband hath not power of his own body, but the wife."

Third, this duty flows out of the original institution of marriage. God *appointed* one man for one woman (Gen. 2:24). Had God intended a man to have more than one wife, He would have given Adam more than one wife. Had God intended a woman to have more than one husband, He would have married Eve to more than one husband. This ordinance was corrupted in the Old Testament church by polygamy, but its original institution and Christ's confirmation of it in Matthew 19 ("from the beginning it was not so," v. 8) make it clear that marriage binds one man to one woman.

Fourth, faithfulness in this duty can cover all other defects. A man may find weaknesses in his wife, but if she is faithful to him then he is able to overlook her defects. A woman could point out many shortcomings in her husband, but his singular devotion to her will bind her affection to him. Chastity is therefore to be prized and maintained for

---

37. Whately, *A Bride-Bush*, 3.

its ability to blind a person to whatever imperfections and infirmities may be found in a spouse.

Fifth, unfaithfulness in this duty is deadly. The marriage covenant binds spouses to a chaste and exclusive relationship. It is better to have no wife or husband at all than to have an adulterous one! All the blessings of marriage depend upon the chastity of a couple. Whatever honors, blessings, and benefits of marriage we might enjoy are nothing if chastity is violated. A woman might have the blessing of a rich husband, but what good is that to her if he is adulterous? A man might have a beautiful and amiable wife, but how can he treasure her if she gives herself to another?

Sixth, a chaste marriage enjoys the blessing of God everywhere. Whether in the sanctuary, in the home, in the bedroom, or in the womb, the blessing of God is upon that marriage in which the marriage bed, for His sake, is preserved and honored by "due benevolence" (1 Tim. 4:4–5; Titus 1:15; Heb. 13:4). Chastity not only brings God's blessing upon the womb (Ps. 128:3), but it also ensures the children born in a marriage are legitimate and therefore rightful heirs of the blessings of God upon a Christian marriage (Gen. 21:10; 1 Cor. 7:14).

Seventh, chastity is a cornerstone of marriage. A chaste spouse has eyes open, ears watching, and heart attending to the welfare of the family and home. Both husband and wife are ever mindful of family needs, home fellowship, family love, home obligations, and the need to be together. But an unchaste spouse will be absent from home and bed in spirit, and always wanting to escape in body.

Finally, chastity preserves the marriage from adultery. A lack of love makes a miserable marriage, but if chastity is lacking and adultery present, the way is open for divorce (Matt. 19:9) because unfaithfulness tears the very fabric of marriage. "Other failings disturb their comfort, but this unfaithfulness dissolves their covenant," wrote Swinnock.[38]

Adultery does not annul a marriage, but it strikes the root of it with such a blow of rottenness that it ceases to bear good fruit on any branch. Adultery is so contrary to the married bond, said Baxter, that "though

---

38. Swinnock, 1:476.

de facto ['as a matter of fact'] it does not actually dissolve the bond and nullify the marriage, yet it so far disobliges the wronged and innocent party that *de jure* ['as of right'] it is to such a sufficient ground to warrant a divorce."[39] If the delinquent party does not repent, the wronged party can in good conscience "seek in an orderly manner to be parted from a person living so disorderly."[40] Clearly marital chastity must be diligently maintained if the marriage itself is to remain intact.

This second duty is, according to Rogers, "the fairest flower, the richest jewel in the garland, the crown of marriage.... So essential an attribute...that the absence thereof quite destroys the being thereof."[41] By this mutual duty, a husband and a wife preserve and enjoy their marriage. But if one or both transgress the chastity of the marriage bed, "besides [suffering] a whole hell of spiritual miseries, they strike at the very sinew, heart, and life of the marriage knot."[42]

The Means of Preserving This Chastity

How can chastity be preserved in our marriages? "Due benevolence" is a primary means of preserving chastity, but the Puritans suggested several other ways as well.

First, we must guard our hearts against unbridled lust. "Keep thy heart with all diligence; for out of it are the issues of life," says Proverbs 4:23. Whatever is in our hearts will come out in our words and actions. If, by the sanctifying work of the Holy Spirit, our hearts are clean and pure, then our eyes and senses, bodies and members, will follow them in purity and not delight in adulterous temptations. We will be satisfied with the spouses of our youth and not be ravished by strangers (Prov. 5:18, 20). But if our hearts are vile and filled with lust, they will "betray the body to the eyes, ears, and company of the unclean, and Satan will play the proctor, soon bringing one unclean person to another."[43]

---

39. Baxter, 131.
40. Whately, *A Bride-Bush*, 6.
41. Rogers, 150.
42. Bolton, 267.
43. Rogers, 158.

Many people let their lustful thoughts and desires run loose and engage in immoral fantasizing as if it is harmless as long as they do not act upon them. Not only is this fantasy a form of committing adultery (Matt. 5:27–28), but it is also foolish. It is not innocent or harmless to let the mind wallow in such vile ditches; for the mind will soon take the heart and will along with it. James tells us that a man is enticed into sin by his own lust (James 1:14). By allowing ourselves to be led into vile, immoral, and adulterous thoughts, these desires may soon find a way to bring forth outward transgressions (v. 15). For at the first opportunity, the will seeks to seize the stolen waters that preoccupy the mind and heart (Prov. 9:17; cf. 5:15–20; Job 31:7). Such "contemplative filthiness," as Rogers called it, "sets the door open to outward actual defilement, which although providence restrains, yet…will break out in time."[44] Therefore, if chastity is to be preserved, we must pray to God that by His Holy Spirit He would make us chaste in heart and mind, for inward chastity is the core of outward chastity.

Second, we must preserve the inlets of our souls, or what John Bunyan once called Eyegate and Eargate,[45] since it is by these means that enticements to sin enter the mind. It is bad enough to have an evil heart to contend with in our battle for chastity; let us not add fuel to the fire by letting in temptations through our senses. David wisely prayed that the Lord would set a guard before his mouth and keep watch over the door of his lips (Ps. 141:3) because sinful words are so ready to escape from our evil hearts. But we must also pray that the Lord would set a guard over our eyes and ears and preserve us from outside temptations that so easily lead us astray. In addition to praying, we must take the necessary steps to prevent any unclean thing from appearing before our eyes (Ps. 101:2–4; Job 31:1–4) and any unclean speech from entering our ears (Eph. 5:3–8).

Many Christians confess they struggle with lust. They know how sinful and offensive to God it is and they have tried countless ways to overcome it, including reading books dedicated to the issue and getting counseling from mature Christians; yet they seem powerless

---

44. Rogers, 158.
45. Cf. *The Holy War*, by John Bunyan.

against lustful thoughts in public and are regularly tempted to visit pornographic sites on the Internet when in private. They abhor their sin before God, are ashamed of it, oppose it by fervent prayer, desire deliverance from it, and seek to quench it by Christian accountability and fellowship. But because they seem to lose the battle more often than they win, they begin to question their salvation and despair about whether or not they will be forgiven.

"My brethren, these things ought not so to be," says James 3:10. But how many people who struggle with lust have stopped to consider how they invited immorality into their hearts via their eyes and ears? And how many of those whose lustful thoughts and desires led to acts of fornication or adultery have stopped to consider their ways (Ps. 4:4) and admitted that they have indulged their senses with sexual immorality? A life of chastity is impossible for a person who feasts his eyes and ears on sexual immorality. A sensual diet will only enflame his lusts. Therefore such a person is led astray by his own heart. In submitting to his lusts, he brings defeat upon himself.

Indulging entertainment provided by Hollywood and television is like approaching the door of the adulteress's house, following the street near her corner, and taking the way to her house (Prov. 5:8; 7:8). We take a fire into our bosoms and walk on hot coals (Prov. 6:27–29). Prayers, books, accountability groups, church, and sermons are vain efforts toward chastity and purity so long as we're entertaining ourselves with the immoral scum offered on the screen and in books, by going to places of sin, by associating with sinful people, and by listening to those who are given up to sin. There is no preventing of this sin, Whately said,

> If a man will give himself leave to converse with such persons, and seek after such places and seasons, as may invite him to commit it.... The senses work vehemently in the presence of their objects, and by vehement working, do hinder the mind from bringing to remembrance that, that should prevent yielding. And if any man will tempt himself, by running to the place where he may sin, is it any wonder if God do punish his presumption, by giving him over to commit sin? [That man] turns from God to lust, that rushes upon the occasions of lust; and must not God then in justice turn away from him, and turn him over into the hands of lust? Shun

therefore with all diligence, all opportunities of this wickedness; especially shun…the company of a person apt to tempt, or to be tempted; and consider, that even cold water will become hot if it be set too near the fire.[46]

The ways many professing Christians entertain themselves differ little from those used by non-Christians. To be truly chaste, we must live lives of holiness, be consecrated unto God as a holy priesthood, and be filled with the Holy Spirit. We must, at all costs, set a guard upon our eyes and ears to open them only to those who build us up in our most holy faith. Consider this advice from Rogers: "I give to all who would shun this plague the counsel belonging to it: *soon, far,* and *slowly.* Get [away] from such occasions as *soon,* go from them as *far,* and return to them as *slowly* as you possibly can. If your eye, your right hand or foot causes you to offend, pluck them out and cut them off…and cast them from you; but make yourself a spiritual eunuch for the kingdom of God, and for chastity, using all contrary means of holding under your flesh and boxing it till it is black and blue [1 Cor. 9:27], if you would preserve your vessel in honor; indeed, count it all too little."[47]

Third, to preserve chastity in our marriages, we must abhor adultery and all temptations to be unfaithful to our spouses. We are surrounded today by immodesty, suggestiveness, and bad examples. The world bombards us with entertainment, magazines, novels, and advertisements that tell us fornication and adultery are sweet beyond measure. Unless we heed the warnings of Scripture, think God's thoughts on this as on all other issues, and are graciously overcome with love for our Savior, we will be deceived into thinking well of sin. As Steele wrote, "The least aberration herein (if it be not speedily and sincerely mortified) will strangely get ground and fester in the soul, and never rest till it come to plain adultery. And then the comfort of their lives, the quiet of their consciences, and the credit of their families, lie bleeding; and, without true repentance, their eternal happiness [is] shipwrecked."[48] We must take heed "of the causes of this odious sin and of all appear-

---

46. Whately, *A Bride-Bush*, 12.
47. Rogers, 160–61. Emphasis added.
48. Steele, *Puritan Sermons*, 2:276.

ances of it; do not suffer your eye or thought to go after a stranger or to begin a breach in your covenant and fidelity."[49]

Consider as well the *heinousness* of this sin. Gouge said he found "no sin throughout the whole Scripture so notoriously in the several colors thereof set forth" as adultery.[50] Besides being forbidden in the Ten Commandments, adultery is said to be a sin against each person of the Trinity, one's neighbor, and all the parties involved. As Gouge explained,[51] it is sin against the Father, because His law is broken; against the Son, because the adultery of members of His body defiles His body; and against the Spirit, because we are temples of the Holy Spirit and adultery pollutes these temples. It is sin against one's neighbor and that person's spouse; it is a sin against the children born from adultery, leaving them the stigma of being illegitimately born; it is a sin against the friends and family of the guilty parties, bringing disgrace into the midst of them and inciting vengeance; it is a sin against the community, city, and nation, who are all open to God's judgment because of the adultery of its inhabitants; it is a sin against the church of God which is thereby deprived of children legitimately born in the covenant; and it is a sin against the parties themselves, exposing their persons, possessions, and souls to the judgment of God (Heb. 13:4) which results in further troubles. A husband and wife are so alienated by adultery that their affections for one another can hardly recover. Adultery squanders their goods, whether money, time, affection, or concern, that should be used to build up a marriage and home. The wronged spouse may become so angry that he or she wishes the other were dead or gone. The adulterous spouse is racked by guilt, and without sincere repentance will acquire a hard heart and become consumed by sin (Rom. 1:18–32). How grievous is this sin of adultery!

Let us heed two warnings, the first offered by Scudder:

> You are to *satisfy yourselves* [Prov. 5:18–20] in the society and embraces each of your own husband and wife. Adultery is a most heinous sin, and most destructive of the marriage covenant. You

---

49. Baxter, 132.
50. Gouge, 159.
51. Gouge, 159–60.

cannot wrong one another in anything more, nor any way sooner wrong and *root out your posterity* [Job 31:12], nor bring a greater or more abominable and *everlasting blot* [Prov. 6:33] and infamy upon your name than by the embracing of a stranger. It will bring *destruction upon the soul* [Prov. 6:32], *for whoremongers and adulterers God will judge* [Heb. 13:4]. If any temptation or motion to that evil shall present itself, either from within or from without, repel it, with indignation, saying thus with yourself in like words to those of chaste *Joseph*, when he was tempted by the lewd mistress, Shall I wrong my [spouse]; shall I break my covenant that I made with God? *How can I commit this great wickedness, and sin against God?* [Gen. 39:9].[52]

The second warning is offered by Whately:

Let all married persons resolve upon it, as a chief part of their duty, that whatsoever their carriage has been before, yet after the making of this [marriage], they will never suffer any strength of desire or violence of allurement, to cast them into so deep a forgetfulness of the commandment of God, the Laws of their Country, the light of their conscience, the covenant of their marriage, the person of their yokefellow, the honor of their bodies, and the safety of their souls, as to offend God, disobey the Magistrate, scandalize the Church, wrong the yokefellow, pollute their bodies, and damn their souls; and all this for the attainment of a short, momentary, impure, brutish, and sensual pleasure; or for the satisfying of a foolish, sinful, shameful, unreasonable and unbridled passion, which will never so be satisfied; for always lust will prove the more tyrannical, by how much it is more yielded unto. This is a burning fire. O let no man, let no woman, go about to carry it in their bosom, and dream of not being burned. This is scorching coals, let no man venture to walk upon them in a false conceit of being safe from harm by any care that he shall use.[53]

Finally, we must delight in each other and give to each other "due benevolence." Gouge concluded, "One of the best remedies that can be prescribed to married persons (next to an awful fear of God, and a continual setting of Him before them, wheresoever they are) is that

---

52. Scudder, 76–78.
53. Whately, *A Bride-Bush*, 6–7.

husband and wife mutually delight in each other, and maintain a pure and fervent love betwixt themselves, yielding that *due benevolence* one to another which is warranted and sanctified by God's word, and ordained of God for this particular end. This due benevolence…is one of the most proper and essential acts of marriage, and necessary for the main and principal ends thereof; as for preservation of chastity…for increasing the world with a legitimate brood, and for linking the affections of the married couple more firmly together."[54]

That said, two things may prove helpful. One is that our love for our spouses should run much deeper and not depend on their appearances. Nevertheless, a spouse who neglects his or her appearance and gives no thought at all to being "presentable" can provide a foothold for Satan to tempt us to feel dissatisfied and for our own sinful heart to suggest that we deserve someone better. Two, while we must never seek to arouse lust in marriage by licentious behavior, dress, or speech, we can seek to be attractive to our spouses by giving due attention to our appearance and overall deportment. For if the marriage bed is to remain undefiled (Heb. 13:4) it must ever be a bed of *benevolence* and never become a bed of that sinful *lust* that sees our spouses only as means to our selfish, sexual satisfaction which differs little from the lust that drives the adulterer. For as Whately pointed out, "it is a principal means of living purely in this estate [of marriage], to enjoy it moderately and holily."[55]

Two extremes are to be avoided. The first extreme is when spouses unduly withhold themselves from each other. Gouge said this denies a due debt and gives Satan a great advantage.[56] Paul calls a husband and wife to give themselves to each other readily, willingly, cheerfully, and with all demonstrations of hearty affection. It is therefore sinful to withhold your body from your spouse. Paul says a period of abstinence may be observed by mutual consent for the purpose of prayer; but this should not last too long, lest Satan get a foothold (1 Cor. 7:5).

The second extreme is using the marriage bed excessively to the neglect of other responsibilities, or to the weariness of one's spouse.

---

54. Gouge, 161.
55. Whately, *A Bride-Bush*, 13.
56. Gouge, 161.

Though the marriage bed is undefiled and the sex of married couples is not sinful in itself, as with any other lawful activity or liberty it can become unlawful when it happens to excess. Food is good and necessary for the body, but gluttony is a sin. God gives His beloved sleep, but the sluggard sins against God. Likewise, those who use the marriage bed to the neglect of their work and their prayers abuse this gift by living a life of lust in marriage. Also, when the appetite for sex is so insatiable that it wearies and oppresses our spouses and is insisted upon despite physical weakness or sickness, it abuses the marriage bed and turns sex into an idol.

Study Questions

1. Why did the Puritans say that mutual love is the very life of a marriage?

2. George Swinnock said, "Without union of hearts, the union of bodies will be of no benefit." What implications does that have for sexuality in marriage?

3. What are the five grounds upon which spouses build their love for each other?

4. Of the six means to preserve and promote mutual love, which do you feel are strongest in your marriage? Which are weakest and most in need of attention?

5. Why are praying and worshiping together so beneficial to marital love? How could you encourage each other as spouses to do this more effectively in your marriage?

6. We have written, "In a chaste marriage the husband and his wife keep the door of their relationship tightly closed to all other persons because they are shut in to each other in marriage. Within the doors of their chastity, they turn to each other." How might someone see this as a negative image? How could it be a warm and beautiful image?

7. How would you summarize the reasons for marital chastity in addition to God's law?

8. Read Proverbs 4:23. Why is guarding the heart the first and most basic work of fighting against sexual temptation?

9. What does it mean to guard your "eyegate" and "eargate" against sexual temptation?

10. What did William Gouge say to show the heinousness of adultery?

The Mutual Duties of Help and Peace

The third mutual duty is helpfulness, or what the Puritans called *yoke-pulling*, because both husband and wife must put their shoulders together to bear their burdens and fulfill their callings. As Swinnock wrote, "Marriage is called…a yoke, because married persons should draw evenly and equally, and thereby the load would be carried the more lightly."[1] The idea here is that husband and wife are to help each other in what concerns them both, whether their bodies, their reputations, their family, their vocations, or their belongings.[2]

When the Lord created the woman, His first purpose was that the woman would be a help to her husband (Gen. 2:18),[3] enabling him to do what he could not do alone (Prov. 31:12–22). Likewise, he who received help was just as responsible to help his wife, since his obligation is to nourish and cherish his wife as his own flesh (Prov. 31:31; Eph. 5:28–29). We promise this help to each other in our marriage vows when we promise to be loving and faithful "in sickness and in health, in plenty and in want, in joy and in sorrow, as long as we both shall live."

---

1. Swinnock, 1:478.

2. According to the Puritans the greatest and primary concern of the mutual duty of helpfulness is with regard to each other's salvation. But we have chosen to deal with this as a separate section below.

3. Based on this text, many of the Puritans treated *helpfulness* under the duties of the wife; but then they would address helpfulness again as a mutual duty. We have chosen to follow their example. Helpfulness is treated at large here as a mutual duty simply because it is a "large duty" from which many particulars flow, particulars which obligate both husband and wife. It will be addressed again briefly under the wife's duties in a later chapter.

To begin, this duty includes the mutual care we have of each other's bodies, whether to prevent sickness or provide care and comfort during it. First, we are to avoid all things that may cause sickness or disease and practice things which maintain or restore good health such as a nutritious diet, necessary medicine, and physical exercise.[4]

Second, we are to comfort and support one another in times of difficulty. Days of sickness, adversity, sorrow, and loss must and will come. And when they do, a husband and wife must be a comfort and help to each other, doing all they can to assuage sorrow, ease pain, calm fears, settle hearts, and end misery.

Can a man fulfill this duty if he sees his wife burdened with sorrow and does not comfort her, or bent over with weakness and does not help her, or wearied with cares and does not relieve her? Can a woman fulfill this duty if she sees her husband sick and doesn't care for him, or in need and refuses to provide for him, or burdened and refuses to comfort him? Such behavior breaks the marriage vows, perverts one of the principal ends of marriage, and only makes the burden heavier, the grief more grievous, and the pain more piercing. Did it not break Job's heart that when his wife was most needed as a helpmate she was most cold and behaved as a stranger to him (Job 2:9–10; 19:17)?

Whately's counsel regarding this helpfulness in times of adversity is sobering. He wrote,

> Sickness and weakness are things of themselves sufficiently tedious, there needs not the addition of the husband's or wife's unkindness, disrespecting, grudging, to make the burden heavier. This is to add adversity to adversity and to [burden] one more that is already sinking under his load; a most barbarous and cruel unkindness! When the body faints, to make the heart faint also; when the limbs and joints are weak, to fill the soul with weakness, by grievous things being practiced from one so near, and [who owes] quite the contrary, this is verily murder in a high degree; like the kindness of men to their dogs, that when they be sick, will knock them on the head, and kill them out-right, to rid them of their pain. Wherefore let every husband or wife avoid or mend

---

4. Whately, *A Bride-Bush*, 66–67.

this fault, and look to their demeanor towards their yoke-fellow, especially in times of weakness, grief, and sickness.[5]

Such counsel may strike us as an overstatement. But Whately's comments appear right on target when we consider what John says in 1 John 3:14–18 about love for our brethren: "We know that we have passed from death unto life, because we love the brethren. He that loveth not his brother abideth in death. Whosoever hateth his brother is a murderer: and ye know that no murderer hath eternal life abiding in him. Hereby perceive we the love of God, because he laid down his life for us: and we ought to lay down our lives for the brethren. But whoso hath this world's good, and seeth his brother have need, and shutteth up his bowels of compassion from him, how dwelleth the love of God in him? My little children, let us not love in word, neither in tongue; but in deed and in truth." If we are to love one another in deed and in truth and thereby prove that the love and compassion of God dwells in us, then let our love and care be the medicine and ourselves the physician in the times of our spouse's sorrow and sickness.

Ambrose related what he called "a most memorable and famous pattern" of this loving helpfulness in times of adversity:

A young, tender, and beautiful Maid was matched…to a man stricken in years, whom after marriage she found to have a very fulsome and diseased body, full of many loathsome and contagious diseases. Yet notwithstanding, out of sense and convenience, that by God's providence she [had] become his wife, she most worthily digested all with incredible patience. Friends and Physicians advised her by no means to come near him, and for their parts they utterly forsook him; but she (passing by with a loving disdain those unkind dissuasions) becomes to him in their stead, Friend, Physician, Nurse, Mother, Sister, Daughter, Servant, everything, anything to do him good [in] any manner of way. At last by extraordinary expense and excessive charges about him she came to some want of some necessaries, whereupon she sold her ring, chains, richest attire, plates, and choicest jewels. And when he was dead, and friends came about her, rather to congratulate her happy riddance, than to bewail her widowhood, she not only

5. Whately, *A Bride-Bush*, 68–69.

abhorred all speeches tending that way, but protested [that] if it were possible, she would willingly redeem her husband's life.[6]

Hence it appears, wrote Ambrose, "that this worthy woman was wedded to her husband's soul, not to his body, seeing no infirmity or deformity thereof could cool or weaken the fervency of her love."[7]

Second, each spouse is to care for each other's name and reputation, both in their hearts as well as by what they say to others. In their hearts every married couple must nourish a good opinion of each other, believing in one another's faithfulness, honesty, purity, trustworthiness, loyalty, and love. If no ill report against a church elder is to be established except on the testimony of two or three witnesses (1 Tim. 5:19), then surely an ill report against one's spouse is not to be believed on any less. Rather, if a false report is heard against one of them, they should work together to be sure that they live rightly and with a clear conscience before God and man (2 Cor. 1:12), in Christian obedience and virtue (Eph. 4:25, 28–29).[8]

Also, to prevent being hurt by false reports and ensnared by jealousy, they should strive to nurture their love which covers a multitude of sins, mollifies and mitigates blows, and puts the most favorable construction on every circumstance, such that he or she hopes the best, believes the best, and will not easily give way to accusations to the contrary. For as the duty of helpfulness springs from love, it is also tenderly careful to believe the best about each other without proof to the contrary (1 Cor. 13:4–7). A jealous spirit is quick to find fault, condemn, assume, and suspect. Therefore this duty should make them hesitant to believe a bad report about each other and give no credit to ungrounded

---

6. Ambrose, *Works*, 236. Steele, *Puritan Sermons*, 2:292, referred to the same story in his sermon on marital duties and provided several details not related by Ambrose. The story was originally narrated by the Spanish humanist Joannes Ludovicus Vives. The woman's name was Clara Cerventa and her husband's name was Valdaura. The tender and loving care which Clara provided to her languishing husband lasted "ten long years." See Juan Luis Vives, *De Institutione Feminae Christianae, Liber Secundus et Liber Tertius*, ed. C. Fantazzi and C. Matheeussen, trans. C. Fantazzi, Selected Works of J. L. Vives VII (Leiden: Brill, 1998), 43–47.

7. Ambrose, *Works*, 236.

8. Gouge, 179–80.

accusations. A couple must defend each other's good name against a bad report from without and suspicions from within.

If jealousy enters the relationship they will find it difficult to keep from being infected with such mistaken notions about each other and, as Whately said, "they shall cease to be dear to each other."[9] Whately then advised,

> Therefore...of all those things which are apt to set quarrels betwixt the married couple, and to sow variance and discord, where [there] should be [the] most amity and good agreement; nothing in the world is more pestilently effectual...than jealousy. Having leavened the heart, it makes the speeches sharp and tart, the countenance sour and lowering, and the whole behavior, keen and untasteful. No good words, no good looks, no good gestures, no good actions can proceed out of a jealous man or woman's heart; but [only] nipping, girding, taunting, quarreling, reviling, raging, and all bitterness.... This evil weed must not be suffered to grow up in the garden of matrimony; for if it does, no good herb will prosper by it, it will overrun all that is commendable and suffer no praiseworthy thing to flourish. And therefore let all that have knit themselves together with this covenant, loathe and detest any motion of fancy that may arise within them of any unchastity, any unfaithfulness, any evil meaning or lewdness of their yoke-fellow...unless the proofs be so...manifest and triple plain, that no good construction can save them.[10]

Caring for each other's names and reputations will also help prevent each other from being ill thought of by others, which involves two things.[11] First, it requires that as much as possible husband and wife conceal each other's weaknesses from the eyes of others. Secker put it this way: "Who would trample upon a jewel because it is fallen in the dirt? or throw away a heap of wheat for a little chaff? or despise a golden wedge because it retains some dross? These roses [i.e., wives] have some prickles. Now husbands should spread a mantle of charity over their wives' infirmities.... Husbands and wives should provoke

---

9. Whately, *A Bride-Bush*, 72.
10. Whately, *A Bride-Bush*, 73–74.
11. Whately, *A Bride-Bush*, 76–81.

one another to love; and they should love one another notwithstanding of provocation."[12]

A husband must do his best to see that no one know his wife's faults but God and himself. He should be unwilling to voice them to anyone but God, asking that she may be pardoned for them and reformed from them. Likewise, a wife must do her best to keep her husband's struggles and sins to herself, as matters of prayer and not gossip. Neither spouse should be surprised by the sins of the other, for each of them is well aware of their own sins. Can it be helpful to uncover faults in public and fling mud in each other's faces? Will this help a husband reform or a wife repent? And which is more displayed in such a case, the spouse's faults and weaknesses or the gossip's unkindness, indiscretion, backbiting, and folly? Does not the family dog behave better than this when it barks at strangers but not at family?[13]

Moreover, if ill speech behind the back of an enemy is a sin, how much more grievous is ill speech behind the back of a spouse, who is as our own flesh? Whately said, "To hear a husband largely declaiming against his wife, and…aggravating her sins, as if he took delight in nothing so much as in branding her forehead with the black mark of infamy is a testimony of so much hatred, where there should be most love, and of so bitter unkindness, where nature itself requires most tender kindness, that no speeches almost can sound more harsh in the ears of wise men. So again for the woman to be clattering amongst her gossips what a foolish husband she has…and to be…making proclamation of his faults, as if she feared nothing but that they should not be known to people…is a most irksome and hateful folly and untrustworthiness."[14]

Love for each other must strive to cover sins much as bandages cover sores so they may heal. Swinnock said, "to procure a quiet life, the husband must be deaf, and the wife blind. Sure it is, the man must not hear to declare it abroad, nor the wife see to say it among her gossips whatever is amiss at home, if they would live in peace."[15] A breach

---

12. Secker, 263.
13. Whately, *A Bride-Bush*, 78.
14. Whately, *A Bride-Bush*, 77.
15. Swinnock, 1:476.

between a husband and wife is half reconciled when it is kept indoors where love and prayers can be repeatedly administered to it; but if it's announced outdoors to the ears of others, it will be like a festering sore that can hardly be healed.[16]

Therefore the common practice of publishing each other's faults must be put far away from a spouse; for it is a most treacherous evil and looks more like the hatred one might show to an enemy than the love demanded in a marriage. "What mutual love can there be in such?" asked Gouge. "Howsoever their hands have been joined together, surely their hearts were never united, so that it had been better [if] they had never known one another, unless the Lord do afterwards knit their hearts and unite their affections more nearly and firmly together."[17] In extreme cases, it may be necessary to acquaint a close and trusted friend with the faults of one's spouse for the purpose of prayer and sound counsel. But that is far different from publishing the little flaws and idiosyncrasies to any company and for no other purpose than murmuring, complaining, and gossiping. "Know therefore, and practice this duty, O husbands and wives," concluded Whately, "spit not in each other's faces, disclose not each other's faults, but conceal, hide, bury and cover them so much as truth and equity will allow."[18]

Second, caring for each other's name and reputation by keeping each other's secrets will prevent others from thinking ill of them. Scudder advised, "You must be so [yoked] to each other, that you may trust one another, and lock up yourselves in one another's breasts, keeping each other's secrets, never blazing abroad the faults or frailties of each. True love can, and *will cover a multitude of sins* (1 Pet. 4:8). You must do with them as you will do with the sores of your own bodies, never uncover them, but when a bandage is to be laid upon them."[19] A wife and husband should enjoy the assurance that what they have entrusted to each other is safely locked away from others. Whately said spouses should

---

16. Swinnock, 1:476.
17. Gouge, 182.
18. Whately, *A Bride-Bush*, 79–80.
19. Scudder, 78–79.

be "good secretaries to each other,"[20] faithful to keep hidden and under lock, as precious jewels, what they have shared between themselves.

Otherwise, how can a man ever trust his wife or a wife trust her husband? And how can they not live at odds with each other when one or the other gives away those "jewels" to strangers? Was not Samson angry when the men got his secret from his wife (Judg. 14:18)? And did not Delilah prove her heart was cold when she badgered Samson for the secret of his strength only to tell it to his enemies (Judg. 16:16–21)? Therefore let a husband and wife entrust themselves to each other with openness and honesty, knowing that whatever is shared between them is safe.

Third, helpfulness extends to a couple's family. If God graciously gives children to a couple, they must not only join together in giving thanks to the Lord but also in bringing those children up in the nurture and admonition of the Lord (Eph. 6:4). Secker wrote, "Children…are in a family as passengers in a boat; husband and wife, they are as a pair of oars to row them to their desired haven."[21]

Their first and most important duty must be to see that the living God is worshiped in their home and to pray that the knowledge and fear of Him and of His Word may be planted in the hearts of their children. Neither father nor mother can work salvation in the hearts of their children (John 3:5); only God does that. But He does expect parents to use the means He has appointed to fulfill the purposes of His election (Ps. 78:5–8; Deut. 6:7–9). Family worship is a mutual responsibility of both husband and wife. They must work together to build up a godly family because it requires their full attention and united devotion.

They are to do this, first, by regularly and habitually performing holy duties with their children. Whately wrote, "To this end, they must read the Scriptures, call upon the name of God amongst them [the children], and catechize them in the principles of true religion, that none under their roof may be ignorant of the fundamental truths of godliness, for want of their care to instruct them."[22] It is best if these duties are done together as a family and under the husband's spiritual lead-

---

20. Whately, *A Bride-Bush*, 81.
21. Secker, 260.
22. Whately, *A Bride-Bush*, 89.

ership; but in his absence the wife should lead in these duties (Esth. 4:12–16). To ensure that such holy exercises are done daily, the husband and wife need to work together to keep them high on their priority list and set aside time for them both for God's glory and for the family's spiritual and eternal welfare.

Bolton gave the following illustration of establishing Christ's kingdom in the home:

> As the two greater lights of heaven do govern this great world with their natural light, so let the husband and wife guide the little world of their family with the spiritual light of divine knowledge and discretion. When the sun is present in our firmament, the moon, out of a sense, as it were, of a natural reverence to the fountain of all her beauty and light, doth veil her splendor, and withdraw her beams. But when he is departed to the other hemisphere, she shows herself, and shines as a princess amongst the lesser lights. When the husband is at home, let the wife only, if need be, serve as a loving remembrance to him, to keep his turns and times of enlightening and informing the ignorant, dark, and earthly hearts of their people. But in his absence [she] comes her course, when her graces of knowledge and prayer ought to show forth themselves, and shine upon them, to preserve them from coldness, and that dreadful curse which hangs over the head of those that know not God, and shall certainly fall upon those families that call not on His name (Jer. 10:25).[23]

There will be many distractions and temptations to neglect family worship, so husband and wife will need to encourage each other to be faithful. We are naturally prone to be short on service towards God, but has He not been abundant in blessing and provision? Then we ought to abound in worshiping Him. Do we want godly children? Then we must constantly instruct our children in the things of God and be dedicated to Him.

Moreover, we must catechize our children in the Christian faith,[24] examining them after hearing sermons to give an account of what they

---

23. Bolton, 280–81.

24. Both the Heidelberg Catechism and the Westminster Larger and Shorter Catechisms are excellent tools for this purpose.

have learned, and charging them to walk in God's ways in the family (Gen. 18:19; Prov. 4:1–5; 1 Kings 2:1–2). For, as Whately observed,

> This is the fountain of most disorders in most families: where God is not feared, what can abound but profaneness and impiety in… the whole household; where people are not taught the knowledge and fear of God, how should they know or fear Him? Where these graces are absent, how should anything be found but rudeness, stubbornness, and undutifulness? Now therefore…let all husbands and wives that fear God be of one mind in the Lord, and let them not fail…[to establish] the exercises of religion in their houses.[25]

Family worship must also include weekly public worship. The Christian Sabbath is to be remembered and sanctified as the Lord's Day by the entire family (Ex. 20:8). That will require due preparation for it on Saturday, ordering all secular affairs so they do not encroach upon the Sabbath, and making whatever preparations might be necessary to ensure the Lord's Day is a day of rest from non-essential work and play (Ex. 20:9–10). Groceries may need to be purchased, laundry washed and folded, clothing ironed, and the car refueled. That will allow the Lord's Day to be a day wholly spent in the worship of God. On that day, participate in whatever Christian education classes are available at church and faithfully attend both of the worship services, not only to help your family sanctify the Sabbath but also to teach your children to do the same with future generations (Ps. 78:5–7).

In short, let every married couple work together to see that true religion is established and flourishes in their home so that they may have a church in their house (Rom 16:5; Ps. 101:2b). For it is better to have no family at all than to have one that is not dedicated to God and therefore is brought up in the service of sin and for no other end than the pleasures, achievements, and applause of this life. Secker said, "Take heed lest these flowers grow in the devil's garden. Though you bring them out in corruption, yet do not bring them up to damnation…. While these twigs are green and tender, they should be bowed towards God."[26]

---

25. Whately, *A Bride-Bush*, 93. Cf. Jer. 10:25.
26. Secker, 259–60.

Second, a husband and wife must help each other in the government of their home. "They must be helpful one to another," wrote Scudder, "in overseeing, guiding, governing, and well-ordering the ways of [their] family."[27] Baxter advises, "Those who have a joint interest and are one flesh must have a joint part in government, though their power is not equal, and one may oversee some business, and the other another business. Yet, in their places they must divide the care and help each other."[28] By faithfully striving in prayer and in the proper use of biblical discipline they must work together to cherish and encourage godliness as well as to suppress the sin in their children's behavior, especially at its first risings (Eph. 6:4; Job 11:14).

That this is the duty of both husband and wife is clear in Scripture. In Proverbs 31:27 the virtuous wife is commended for looking after the ways of her household; in 1 Timothy 5:14, young widows are told to manage their households. In 1 Samuel 3:13 God judges Eli's house because he fails to restrain the wickedness of his sons; in Genesis 18:19 God commends Abraham who would "command his children and his household after him, and they shall keep the way of the LORD, to do justice and judgment." Thus, to enjoy God's favor as Abraham did, a husband and wife must instruct their children in righteousness and restrain them from wickedness. The Lord promises that if they do so, their work will not be in vain, for He will bless it by building up their home (Job 8:6; 22:23).

Gouge said husbands and wives "may be very helpful one to another, and bring, by their mutual help in governing, much good to the family. The husband who helps his wife adds much authority to her, and so causes that she is not despised nor lightly esteemed. The wife by her help causes many things to be espied, and so redressed, which otherwise might never have been found out; for two eyes see more than one, especially when one of those is more at hand, and in presence, as the wife is in the house."[29]

---

27. Scudder, 80.
28. Baxter, 148.
29. Gouge, 186.

Finally, helpfulness extends to a couple's belongings. They are to work together to increase and care for their estate and possessions. Gouge wrote, "We see it requisite, yea a bounden duty, that husband and wife, even in a mutual regard one of another, be as provident as they can be with a good conscience in getting, keeping, and disposing competent goods and riches for the mutual good one of another."[30] In many marriages most things are either "his" or "hers" and very few things are "ours." But God created the woman and brought her to the man (Gen. 2:22) to be his helpmate, which implies that he is to be her helpmate as well, for they both are given to each other. In a marriage in which much of life, work, money, and vision are divided between spouses, the very purpose of helpfulness is thwarted. Such a marriage differs little from living together as roommates.

To honor God in marriage and enjoy the blessing that God crowns upon a faithful marriage, there should be one house, one bed, one table, one purse, and one estate. All things should be in common. If a man and woman bring their hearts together in marriage, should they not also bring their hands and goods together in married life? Can they not accomplish more, go farther, and be more successful in their pursuits with twice the hands, twice the eyes, twice the ears, and twice the minds working together and moving towards the same end? Swinnock wrote, "Husbands and wives should [be]...like two watermen in oars, that row and labor together on their several sides to get, through God's blessing, an honest and comfortable living. They are a pitiful pair that, like a pair of cards, are much together, but it is at play, not at work. A Christian couple, like the two hands, should both work to maintain the head and body, and not, like broken bones, be laying on the bed of idleness."[31]

Whately said mutual care for a couple's belongings requires three things of the husband, in which he must be helped by his wife: work, saving, and planning; or, as he put it, "painfulness in getting, discretion in saving, [and] providence in fore-seeing. These make up the virtue of good husbandry; and if any of these be wanting, so much is want-

---

30. Gouge, 182.
31. Swinnock, 1:475.

ing from the perfection of it, and so much shall be wanting from their comfort and prosperity."[32]

Now, whether or not the wife works some hours outside the home is a matter that requires much prayer, searching of Scripture, and godly counsel. But both husband and wife must give themselves to their work with all diligence and faithfulness, working together to acquire and maintain those things needed to live honorably before the Lord. It may be that his work is primarily out of the house and hers is within it, that his work is largely abroad while hers is at home, that his is largely taken up with acquiring and hers with maintaining. The point is still the same: they must unite their efforts, draw the yoke together, and be partners in this work.

Likewise, they are to help each other to save what money they can, both for their retirement and for the unforeseen expenses which naturally arise in the life of a family. They must live within their means, practicing thriftiness and guarding against lavishness and luxury. Savings will enable them to show mercy and hospitality to the needy and to the body of Christ as the Lord prescribes in Ephesians 4:28 (cf. 2 Cor. 9:11–12; 1 John 3:16–18). But how can they do so if the wife wastes what's brought into the home or the husband wastes it before it can be brought in? Would not this bring down the very house they desire to build up? Therefore they must refrain from needless or sinful expenses and use their money in a way that will enable them both to enjoy a good estate all their days and give a good account of themselves to the Lord as sharers with those in need.

Finally, they should jointly plan for future needs, prevent unnecessary losses, and faithfully bear all crosses. They must bring their minds and prayers together and plan for those seasons when provision may be sparse or when calamity may come. No one can foresee such things except the Lord, but prudence teaches us to anticipate such possibilities.

In closing, remember the spiritual aspect of mutual helpfulness. As helpfulness is a duty of married couples *before* the Lord, it is also a work to be done *unto* the Lord, that is, with an eye to His glory and in full

---

32. Whately, *A Bride-Bush*, 83–84.

dependence upon His grace. Baxter made this point well: "Another duty of husbands and wives is to be helpful to each other in their worldly business and estates…not for worldly ends or with a worldly mind but in obedience to God, who will have them labor, as well as pray, for their daily bread, and has determined that in the sweat of their brows they shall eat their bread and that in six days they shall labor and do all that they have to do and that he who will not work must not eat [1 Tim. 5:8; Gen. 3:19; Ex. 20:9; 1 Thess. 3:10]. The care of their affairs lies upon them both, and neither of them must cast it off and live in idleness."[33] And what a comfort it should be to every married couple that if they do their work as unto the Lord (Col. 3:23) they will surely be able to lean on Him for help in their work (1 Cor. 15:58) and trust Him to bestow His richest blessings upon them for Christ's sake (Pss. 84:11; 127:1). Let every marriage therefore seek to abound in the duty of helpfulness in temporal matters, as it concerns both of their bodies, their name and reputation, their family, and their belongings.

The Means of Performing This Duty

To be a help to each other, husbands and wives must guard against self-centeredness. In their marriage vows, both husband and wife promise to love, cherish, nourish, and care for each other, and to put each other first. Selfishness will stand in the way of this mutual helpfulness more than anything else.

According to Paul, marriage is giving away one's self and is the essence of self-denial (1 Cor. 7:4). Therefore a husband is to love his wife as his own body (Eph. 5:28) and a wife is to submit to her husband as to Christ (Eph. 5:22–23). Self-denial is necessary in marriage, especially regarding mutual helpfulness, in which both husband and wife join their mutual interests with head, heart, and hand, serving one another in love for Christ's sake. Let them pray for self-denial, a servant's heart, and greater understanding of the duty of mutual helpfulness.

---

33. Baxter, 147.

Helpfulness in Spiritual Matters

Mutual helpfulness is also a duty in spiritual matters. Husbands and wives should be the *most* helpful to each other in their efforts to promote each other's salvation and growth in grace. Gouge said the very best thing they can do for each other is "to be a means of helping forward [their] salvation."[34] Swinnock said the mutual duty of helpfulness "must principally appear in their care for each other's better part,"[35] that is, their souls. Baxter counseled that while husbands and wives are to faithfully help each other in all temporal matters, they are "especially to be helpers of each other's salvation."[36] Likewise, Ambrose called this helpfulness in spiritual matters "that *one necessary thing*, without which their family is but Satan's seminary and a nursery for hell."[37]

Establishing Christ's kingdom in their home is to be their mutual concern. Steele said, "For how do you know, wife, whether you will save your husband? Or how do you know, husband, whether you will save your wife? It is as if Paul said, 'This should be your chief design; and if you can attain this, though with trouble, you are made!'"[38] The greatest blessing is when your chief promoter and encourager in your walk with Christ is your own spouse with whom you share all of life's joys and trials that are ordered by God for your growth in grace.

The duty to be a help in spiritual matters is grounded upon the spiritual love a husband and wife are to have for each other. Spiritual love will seek a spiritual end for each other; a love which springs from God will seek, above all else, to help one's spouse live closer to God. Such a love values the soul above the body, piety above policy, and the inner beauty of godliness above the outward beauty of appearance, and does all it can for a spouse's spiritual welfare. Marital love is grounded not upon such things as affection, beauty, or riches, but upon God's commanding the husband to love his wife (Eph. 5:25) and the wife to love her husband (Titus 2:4).

---

34. Gouge, 172.
35. Swinnock, 1:479.
36. Baxter, *Works*, 4:234.
37. Ambrose, 236.
38. Steele, *Puritan Sermons*, 2:278–79.

If their marital love is *spiritual*, having an eye to God, resting upon His will for marriage, yielding to His authority, and resolving to obey Him, then their union will be lasting, durable, and most helpful in each other's spiritual and eternal welfare. Such love will take more pains to see that their souls are free from the dominion of sin and the wrath of God than that their bodies are free from poverty, sickness, or death. Indeed, such love will make them most careful to prepare for the endless eternity which follows their short marriage.

Consider the following thoughts from Baxter.[39] First, reflect on how inexplicable it would be to love each other and yet neglect each other's souls. A person's soul is his most treasured possession (Mark 8:36–37) and should therefore be the greatest concern in all our relationships. Can this be any truer than in marriage, where two have become one flesh? Of all people, husbands and wives have the greatest cause to make sure there is provision for their souls. If marital love does not include this most important matter, is it not worth very little? Can you love your spouse's body and not care for his soul? Can you love your wife and yet leave her in the darkness of unbelief? What would you do to relieve her if she were in bodily pain or misery; what would you not spare in order to comfort her? And yet would you do nothing to deliver her from eternal misery and help her heavenward? As Baxter said, "Never say you love them if you will not labor for their salvation.... It does not deserve the name of love if it can leave a soul to endless misery."[40]

What can be said of those who do nothing to forward the salvation of their spouses and, sometimes, do many things to hinder it (Gen. 3:6; 1 Kings 11:4; Job 2:9; Acts 5:2)? "If your love to your wife or husband tends to no greater matters than the pleasures of this life while the soul is left to perish in sin, seriously consider how little more kindness you show them than the Devil [does]," said Baxter. "The Devil himself scarcely does more against the saving of souls than ungodly husbands

---

39. Baxter, 138–40.
40. Baxter, 138–39.

and wives do against each other."[41] Steele wrote, "If you can suffer one another to be damned, where is your love?"[42]

Second, you will not fulfill the purpose for marriage if you do not help each other's souls. You are commanded to live together as heirs of the grace of life (1 Pet. 3:7). The husband in particular is appointed to love his wife so that he might present her acceptably to the Lord, having no spot or blemish (Eph. 5:25–27). If you only serve each other's bodily needs, how do you differ from the beasts of the field and birds of the air? If your greatest concern is to prepare your own soul for eternity, then the same concern should extend to the one whom you love as your own flesh.

Moreover, consider how painful it will be if you meet each other on judgment day having neglected to help each other to God. As Baxter said, how awful it will be to hear each other's accusations, such as "Oh, cruel husband! Oh, merciless, deceitful wife! You were commanded by God to warn me and tell me of my sin and misery and to never let me rest in it but to instruct and entreat me until I had come home by Christ that I might have escaped this place of torment. But you never spoke to me of God and my salvation unless you did it in jest! If the house had been on fire, you would have been more earnest to have quenched it than you were to save my soul from hell! You never told me of the misery of a natural and non-renewed state! Nor did you tell me the great necessity of regeneration and a holy life. Rather, morning and night your talk was nothing but of the world and the things of the world. We did not have one sober word of salvation. You never told me of this day or prayed with me or read the Scripture and good books to me. You never took pains to instruct me or humble my hardened heart or to save me from it or to draw me to the love of God and holiness by faith in Christ. You did not go before me with a good example. Rather, you led by an evil example, an ungodly, fleshly, worldly life. You neither cared for your own soul, nor for mine; nor I for yours or my own; and now we are justly condemned together because we would not live together

---

41. Baxter, 138–39.
42. Steele, *Puritan Sermons*, 2:279.

in holiness!"[43] Therefore let husbands and wives resolve without delay to live together as heirs of heaven and encourage each other's salvation!

A husband and wife are closer to each other than anyone else so they have the greatest opportunity to persuade and influence each other on all matters of life. This advantage is best used when they strive to help one another in matters of salvation. They do this by giving themselves to two main concerns: striving to warn each other against sin and stirring each other up to faith, love, and obedience in all good works. First, as husband and wife, they cannot help but see each other's sins. They should feel compelled by love to make every effort to persuade the other to repent of those sins. If they are to be faithful in this mutual duty, "there ought to be a mutual care in husbands and wives, both to prevent sin before it be committed, and also to make what redress they can after it is committed."[44] Though this pertains equally to the husband, Reyner said, "the wife should be a *second conscience* to her husband, a *bosom monitor*, to tell him privately of his faults, to amend them."[45]

They are to observe the "diet, temper, and constitution" of each other's souls until they learn what sins they are ensnared in or prone to; and having found them, Whately said, they must "diligently abstain from all things that may provoke them to evil and prove occasions of making them over-shoot themselves. And further, they must apply all means to weaken and enfeeble such corruptions, and to stop their over-flowing, that they may not proceed to any extremity, if they have begun to offend in some degrees."[46] Similarly, Smith said, "it is necessary to learn one another's natures, and one another's affections, and one another's infirmities, because you must be *helpers*, and you cannot help unless you know the disease."[47]

In other words, a couple must not foolishly provoke each other's weaknesses but join together in cutting off all occasions of temptation and adopt, wherever they can, words and actions fit to heal and miti-

---

43. Baxter, 140. Quotation abridged.
44. Gouge, 173.
45. Reyner, 27.
46. Whately, *A Bride-Bush*, 64.
47. Smith, 1.23. Emphasis added.

gate sin. If a husband is prone to anger, his wife should do everything she can to avoid provoking it and instead counter it with kindness and patience. If the wife is prone to fear, the husband should do what he can to prevent it and to bolster her faith in God's providence. In this way they are to be each other's watchman (Ezek. 3:17), each other's Aaron and Hur in the battle (Ex. 17:12), and each other's provocation to repentance and reformation (Heb. 10:24). For if sin is ignored in a marriage, it will choke the grace of the Spirit (Gal. 5:17) and put it out as quickly as water does the fire; and without repentance, it will bring the chastisements of God upon them both.

Gouge wrote, "If a husband should see his wife, or a wife her husband lying in the fire, or water, ready to be burnt or drowned and not afford their best help to pull them out, might they not justly be thought to hate them? But sin is as fire and water, which will burn and drown men in perdition."[48] If a husband is content to let his wife sleep in her sin and keep silence about it, is this not hateful and cold-hearted? Does this not betray the marriage vows and add sin to sin? Let every husband and wife therefore beware of failing in this duty to which the Lord has called them. "Woe unto such husbands or wives," said Whately, and "sorry help is it that they afford to their married companions, and miserable helpers are they; and God shall one day reckon with them for having done so little good where He appointed them to do all good; and so much hurt where He appointed them to do no hurt at all."[49]

Addressing sin in each other can be very difficult and so must be done with great care. For example, if the sin is anger, how can it be addressed without stirring it up? If it is the sin of pride, how can it be pointed out without suffering its blows? If it is the sin of unbelief, how can it be effectively removed? Consider therefore the following advice: let the *best time* be chosen to address it. Choose the time when your spouse appears to be most tender under the Spirit's preparatory hand and therefore most impressionable, approachable, and open to your counsel. Choose words that spring from humility and a sense of your own weaknesses, maybe even in the same area. *Precede* your gentle

---

48. Gouge, 175.
49. Whately, *A Bride-Bush*, 66.

reproofs with what positive affirmation and encouragement you can give. Likewise, *conclude* your reproofs by affirming, if you can, your assurance that your spouse had good intentions and motives and meant well in the effort. Above all else, pray to God for the wisdom to rightly see your spouse's weaknesses (as you must not be blind to the beam in your own eye), lovingly speak to them, and faithfully help to remedy them. As Reyner said, "Happy is that couple whom God makes…spiritual physicians one to another."[50]

If your efforts appear to be ineffective and your spouse seems to be hardened to reproof, seek the help of trusted and wise friends, and possibly even the leaders in your church. If your husband was sick and you could not cure him, you would call for a doctor and ask for medicine, if not surgery. Likewise, in addressing the sin of a spouse, you must seek the help of those who are spiritual before the matter worsens (cf. Gal. 6:1–2). Meanwhile, you must continue to wait and pray, referring the matter to God, the only Physician of the soul, who is able in due season to set all things right. Also, know that you have discharged your duty before God and can therefore enjoy the comfort of having been faithful to God and to your spouse, despite the outcome.[51]

Second, a couple must strive to provoke one another to godliness. They should be goads and spurs to one another, urging by tender entreaties and zealous example to draw from each other good works and spiritual duties. They should encourage each other in the faithful worship of God in public, in private, and as a family. They should behave as fellow pilgrims and travelers, walking hand in hand towards the Celestial City with that commitment to and love for each other which only a husband and wife can have.

For example, if the wife sees her husband is slack in generosity, she should strive to commend this duty to him and remind him of its excellence as a Christian virtue, the great reward God promises to the cheerful giver, and the example of their giving Savior. Likewise, if the husband sees his wife is backward in hospitality, he should stir her up to it by reminding her that Christ receives such labor as done unto Him-

---

50. Reyner, 27.
51. Whately, *A Bride-Bush*, 64–65.

self, and by helping her to prepare for hosting company as well as to clean up afterwards. All in all, they are to strive, Reyner wrote, "that they may be like Zacharias and Elisabeth, both righteous, walking in all the Commandments and ordinances of the Lord blameless, Luke 1:6; like Abraham and Sarah, both believers; like Elkanah and Hannah, both true worshippers of God; like Aquila and Priscilla, both helpers in the work of Christ, Rom. 16:3–4.... [For] such godly compeers make marriage itself honorable; and they will live and die with glory."[52]

Husbands and wives should also do all they can to increase the graces they see in each other. We are prone to wax cold and backslide, so the fires of grace must be continually stoked if the flame is to be maintained and rise higher. Spouses can help each other move forward in grace, said Gouge, by the following means. First, by taking notice of the beginning and smallest measure of grace and striving to stir it up to greater expressions. Second, by having frequent conversations about growing in grace and the specific ways in which their graces can be increased. Third, through mutual practice and example as patterns of piety to each other. Fourth, by faithfully performing those exercises of religion in the home which promote growth such as praying, singing psalms, reading and memorizing Scripture, meditating on the Word, listening to sermons, and reading good Christian literature. While the husband should take the lead in this, the wife should put him in mind of it and stir him up to it (2 Kings 4:9–10). And last, by stirring one another up to go to the house of God to hear the word preached, partake of the Lord's Supper, and consciously perform all the parts of God's public worship.[53]

Steele wrote, "Your work is to build-up one another in your most holy faith, and in all wisdom and holiness. And to that end, you ought carefully to watch over each other, lest at any time you fall into temptation; to study each other's dispositions, consider each other's snares, observe each other's decays in zeal and piety, that you may speedily supply remedies; and 'exhort one another daily, lest either of you be hardened through the deceitfulness of sin' [Heb. 3:13]. Your talk should

---

52. Reyner, 28.
53. Gouge, 175.

often be of God and of your eternal estate; and you should improve that analogy which is between Jesus Christ and His church and the married couple, to your comfort and direction. In short, you should in both your carriages declare plainly that you are going together to seek a country."[54]

The Means of Preserving This Duty

Baxter offered the following directions to husbands and wives so they might enjoy this greatest of blessings.[55] While some are repeated from above, they are spelled out in greater detail here and shown within the context of those practices that serve as mighty and effective goads to one another's growth in grace.

1. If you would help each other's souls, you must be sure that you care for your own and retain a deep and lively apprehension of those great and everlasting matters of which you are to speak to others. How can you rightly care for your spouse's soul if you neglect your own, and how can you take pains for the spiritual welfare of another when you take none for your own? How can you speak with any seriousness about those matters of which you are ignorant? Baxter wrote, "First see that you feel thoroughly that which you would speak profitably and that you are what you persuade another to be and that all your counsel may be perceived to arise from the bottom of your heart and that you speak of things that you are well acquainted with by experience."[56]

2. Speak to each other about the things of God and your salvation. Do not let your worldly business be all you talk about, but let God and your souls have the first and last and the freest and sweetest, if not the most, of your speech. When you have said enough about your common business, set it aside and talk together of the state and duty of your souls before God and of your hopes of heaven as those who consider these their greatest business in the world.

3. When one of you is speaking seriously about the things of God, see that the other does not extinguish the conversation. Cherish it by contributing to it and asking questions about it. You will extinguish it

---

54. Steele, *Puritan Sermons*, 2:279.
55. Baxter, 140–46.
56. Baxter, 141.

by a disinterested silence or disagreeable, argumentative, interruptive, or distracting speech.

4. Watch over the hearts and lives of each other to discern the state of each other's souls, the strength or weakness of each other's sins and graces, and each of your failings so that you can best help each other. You cannot cure unknown diseases or apply salve to an unknown wound.

5. Compliment each other but do not flatter each other through foolish love. Do not exasperate each other by passionate or contemptuous reproving. Do not be so blinded with affection that you can hardly see any wrong in each other nor be so critical that your reproofs are too bitter to stomach.

6. Keep loving each other and do not despise each other. Without love, you will despise each other's counsels and reproofs and be unable to take instruction.

7. Do not discourage instruction or reproof by taking it the wrong way or by rude responses or stubbornness. A person will be apt to give up when he is confronted with ingratitude and snappish retorts or when he perceives that his labor is in vain. Therefore you must always be willing to be corrected, especially by your spouse who sees and knows you more than any other.

8. Engage each other in reading spiritually enlightening books and especially the Word of God. Listen to the preached word together and engage in profitable conversation with holy persons.

9. Do not conceal the state of your souls or hide your faults from each other. You are as one flesh and should have one heart. As it is dangerous for a man not to know his own needs, so it is hurtful for a husband or wife not to know the other's needs.

10. As much as possible, avoid differences of opinion in religion lest you be tempted to despise and undervalue the help which you might receive from each other.

11. If you have differences, be sure that you deal with them with holiness, humility, love, and peace and not with pride, selfishness, or strife. Refer the matter to the Word of God as the divine arbiter and aim together for His glory and to do His will. Until a resolution is reached,

strive to outdo one another in humility and withhold none of the love which you owe to each other.

12. Do not be either blindly indulgent to each other's faults or too censorious of each other's state, lest Satan tempt you to alienate your affections from one another. Baxter said, "To make nothing of the faults of those whom you love is to love them foolishly, to their hurt, and to show that it is not for their virtues that you love them. To make too great a matter of one another's faults is to help the tempter to quench your love and turn your hearts from one another."[57]

13. If you are married to an unbeliever, keep loving that person for your marriage's sake. Though you cannot love this person as a Christian, you can love him as your husband, which you are bound to do (1 Cor. 7:12–13). The faults of your spouse do not discharge you from your duties towards him.

14. Join together in frequent prayer. Prayer forces the mind into sobriety and affects the heart with the presence and majesty of God. Pray also for each other when you are in secret that God may do that work that you desire most upon each other's hearts.

15. Help each other by living an exemplary life. Do what you expect of your spouse: excel in meekness, humility, charity, dutifulness, diligence, self-denial, and patience as much as you can. As Baxter said, "A life of genuine holiness, heavenliness, self-denial, meekness, love, and mortification is a powerful sermon that, if you are constantly preaching before those who are near you, will hardly miss having a good effect. Works are more clearly significant and persuasive than words alone."[58]

Striving for Peace and Happiness

The final mutual duty of marriage is to strive for peace and happiness in the home and to avoid occasions of anger and discord (cf. Eph. 4:3). Or, as Baxter put it, "Avoid all dissensions, and bear with those infirmities in each other which you cannot cure; assuage, and not provoke unruly passions; and, in lawful things, please each other."[59]

---

57. Baxter, 145.
58. Baxter, 146.
59. Baxter, *Works*, 4:234.

Pursue peace for the following reasons. First, husband and wife are in such a close relationship that peace is absolutely required. Division and discord are unbearable in a marriage. To allow anger to separate husband and wife is to allow "one flesh" to be at war with itself. Second, because of this close bond, discord will spill over into all other duties whether at work or play until it be mended. Third, dissension will cool their love for each other; and if it be allowed to fester, they will eventually be tormented by the marriage bond itself since it ties them to one with whom they have no desire to be joined. "As the difference between my heart and my prison is that I willingly and with delight dwell in the one but am unwillingly confined to the other, such will be the difference between a quiet and an unquiet life in your married state. It turns your dwelling and delight into a prison, where you are chained to those calamities that, in a free condition, you might overrun."[60] Fourth, it unfits spouses for the worship of God and for the spiritual help they owe to each other in the way to heaven. They cannot bring their hearts to their duties as long as they nurse anger and hatred within them. Fifth, dissension prevents them from rightly governing their families; their children will either follow their example and be at odds with each other or simply do as they want without reference to their parents. Moreover, they will refuse to bear their parents' reproofs when they see that their parents are guilty of the same or similar faults. Lastly, their dissensions will expose them to the malice of Satan and his many temptations. "You cannot foresee what abundance of sin you put yourselves in danger of."[61] Gouge concluded that "persons at variance are far better [to] be out of sight and place, than present together. [But] out of sight and place man and wife must not be, at peace therefore they must be."[62]

Striving for peace and happiness means an overall effort to be *pleasing* to each other. According to Whately, this "pleasingness" is "a disposition of the will and earnest desire of the heart to give all content [happiness] to each other, so far as they may possibly do it, without

---

60. Baxter, 134.
61. Baxter, 135.
62. Gouge, 165.

sinning against God."[63] If husband and wife perform this duty (which 1 Cor. 7:33–34 commends) with all diligence and faithfulness, then they will experience a great harvest of blessings to the whole family. No good or happiness can be enjoyed by that couple who live as enemies on the field when they are companions in one house and bed. Whately advised, "Next to the pleasing of God, make your main business to please each other."[64]

For example, in his attire, demeanor, speech, habits, hobbies, and even choice of company, let the husband keep his wife's desires in the forefront of his mind and work to please her. Let him deny himself, cross his own desires, lay aside his own interests, and strive to put his wife's before his own. As soon as he learns that something he does or wears or says is displeasing to her, let him make every effort to change it and consider her happiness and smile more precious than the thing he forfeits for her sake. Likewise, let the wife in her dress, cooking, speech, and all duties be ever mindful of those things which endear her to her husband and draw out his love towards her for giving such close attention to his every desire. Whatever it is, even if it seems at times unreasonable or peevish, let her avoid all murmuring and complaining and make every effort to do as he desires—short of sin and wickedness, knowing that the harder it is for her to do the more commendable it is, and the more it will please the Lord and therefore the more will He graciously reward it at the last.[65]

This mutual labor to please each other will accomplish two things. First, it will be easy for the pleased husband to please his wife and for the happy wife to strive with delight to make her husband happy. Secondly, it will also work so that they will be turned in on each other as it were, gladly giving and receiving contentment and satisfaction by each other's happiness. How effectively then will discord be prevented and, should it arise, how quickly will it be redressed! There should be a contest between them, Scudder wrote, as to "who should begin first to look cheerfully, and amiably, and show kindness one to another, that the

---

63. Whately, *A Bride-Bush*, 54.
64. Whately, *A Bride-Bush*, 59.
65. Whately, *A Bride-Bush*, 58.

breach may be prevented, or if any be, may be made up between yourselves. The wife, she out of duty, the husband, he out of wisdom, should begin first, which when it is done by the one, let not the other dare, but lovingly and readily to entertain it."[66] That marriage has a great blessing in it, said Reyner, "wherein the greatest contention between man and wife is who should love each other most and please one another best."[67]

Some might object that such advice will not work in their situations because they have spouses who are impossible to please and satisfy. But let them remember that while it is in no man's power to make another person be pleased with his actions, it is in every man's power to do all he can to see that his actions are pleasing; and the more he sees the other person is averse to it, the harder he should work at it (Rom. 12:14–21). We must be motivated by the resistance to pray more for our spouses and work harder still to please them. Whately wrote, "The husband that has a perverse wife, or [the] wife that has a perverse husband, must give more diligence to give [happiness]…and not carelessly cast off all, with saying that they be so cross and dogged that nothing will please them; verily, this is a painful work, but withal it is a possible work."[68] If after all your efforts to please your spouse he or she refuses to be pleased, encourage yourself by remembering that "if you cannot please your yoke-fellow as you desire (because he or she will misconstrue your actions and take them ever in the worst sense), yet you shall not fail to please God, who passing by your failings, will ever take them in the best [sense]."[69]

The Means of Fulfilling This Duty

There can be no peace with God where husband and wife do not strive to please each other and so nourish and create peace between them.[70] This is a duty to which God calls both the husband and the wife. Let no husband exempt himself on the ground that the wife is called to submit to him (Eph. 5:22), for his call to love his wife as Christ loves His church

---

66. Scudder, 86–87.
67. Reyner, 30.
68. Whately, *A Bride-Bush*, 56.
69. Whately, *A Bride-Bush*, 57.
70. Whately, *A Bride-Bush*, 57.

(Eph. 5:25) binds him to deny himself, humble himself, and please his wife with an eye to her being pleasing to God. Such a husband will get for himself a wife who delights to please her husband.

To this end, husband and wife must be patient with each other. Nothing is more intolerable, said Steele, than a civil war indoors.[71] No good can come of it, but rather all is ruined and wasted by it and all good is hindered from coming to fruition. "Let every man be swift to hear, slow to speak, slow to wrath: for the wrath of man worketh not the righteousness of God" (James 1:19–20). Patience is a fruit of the Spirit (Gal. 5:22). The exercise of this grace will help husband and wife bear each other's infirmities as Christ patiently bears them. It will help them support each other in those trials which befall them both and not seek to lay the blame on one another. It will also help them wait upon the Lord for the growth in grace for which they pray.

Reyner advised that spouses must remember and practice this rule: never be angry both at the same time. "The one should bear with the other's frowardness and passion; and for a time give way to it."[72] This is the way to overcome and quench anger in a spouse and afterwards to love each other better, when the one by his yielding actually conquers the other's heart. But to be angry at the same time and let hurtful and piercing speech fly is to add fuel to the fire, which will "dissolve the glue of affection that made them cleave together, and separate them, and make of one, two."[73]

Steele counseled married couples to withdraw from each other until anger is cooled, and *hold* their peace in order to *keep* the peace.[74] They must remember they are both sinful children of Adam; therefore infirmities, imperfections, and provocations must be expected.[75] They must deem it the greatest honor to be first in overtures of peace and never let angry passions rise. Moreover, what comfort can be had when a man gets into a fight with his wife who is his own flesh, or when a

---

71. Steele, *Puritan Sermons*, 2:278.
72. Reyner, 29.
73. Reyner, 29.
74. Steele, *Puritan Sermons*, 2:278.
75. Bolton, 268.

woman gets into an argument with her husband who is her own head? Would it not be better to bear a smaller offense from one's spouse in order to avoid a greater one by retaliating? It is better to give place to each other than to give the devil a foothold between them.[76]

A husband and wife must understand that great harm may result from anger between them. As Bolton wrote, "Well may they thereby become ridiculous to their servants, a by-word to their neighbors, table-talk to the country, troublers to their own house, and as a continual dripping one to another; but they shall never gain by their mutual hastiness, passions, and impatience."[77]

So take all occasions to avoid anger between yourselves. First, keep your love in constant fervor because a lively love will suppress anger. You cannot be angry at one whom you dearly love and neither can you speak harshly to one you labor to please. Second, both husband and wife must mortify their pride and pray for a meek and quiet spirit. A proud heart is easily provoked by every word or action that crosses it. A perverse mind is hasty and harsh in its judgments. Baxter wrote: "Once get the victory over yourselves, and get the cure of your own impatience, and you will easily keep peace with one another."[78] Third, remember that you are both diseased persons full of infirmities; therefore expect the fruit of those infirmities in each other. Do you realize that you married a sinner whose sins will cause you daily trials? If you could not bear her sins, then you should not have married her; and if you resolved that you would bear them, then you are obliged to do so. Fourth, remember that you are one flesh and therefore do not be angrier with your spouse over her failings than you would be over your own, but rather show her the same compassion and tenderness you would show yourself. Fifth, agree beforehand that when one of you loses your temper the other will quietly and patiently bear it until the storm is past. You are called to help and cure one another; so if one is under a fit of anger, the other must not tread upon him. Sixth, remember that you must live together until death and be companions in marriage all your days. It is absurd for

---

76. Steele, *Puritan Sermons*, 2:278.
77. Bolton, 269.
78. Baxter, 135.

you to vex one another. Seventh, as far as you are able, avoid all occasions of anger about things you cannot change. Eighth, if you cannot quench your anger at least rein in your tongue so that you do not speak words you may later regret. Silence will restore peace the sooner. Ninth, let the calm spouse try to speak words of sobriety and wisdom to calm the storm and revive reason and submission to the Lord. Lastly, confess your faults to each other when anger has prevailed between you. Ask forgiveness of each other and join in prayer to God for forgiveness and for grace not to behave so sinfully again.

Study Questions

1. How does a concerted effort and constant habit of being helpful to each other enrich a marriage?

2. Why is patient helpfulness in seasons of weakness, illness, or need such a powerful demonstration of love?

3. How should spouses work to protect each other's reputation and resist false accusations? How does this guard their marriage?

4. William Secker said, "Who would trample upon a jewel because it is fallen in the dirt?" What does this teach us about how we should view the weaknesses of our spouses?

5. How can husbands and wives help each other to manage their home and assets?

6. Read Mark 8:36–37. Why is helping each other spiritually the most important help of all?

7. Why do spouses have a unique opportunity to influence each other spiritually?

8. Of the fifteen means of being spiritual helps to each other, what is one that you believe you should practice more faithfully? How will you start?

9. William Whately said, "Next to the pleasing of God, make your main business to please each other." Is this right? Why or why not?

10. How would you summarize the ways to avoid anger breaking out in your home?

The Wife's Duties in Marriage

The Puritans divided the duties of marriage into three categories: duties mutual to both husband and wife, duties required of the husband, and duties required of the wife. Having spoken of mutual duties in the previous chapters, we now address the duties required of the wife and the husband respectively.

According to Ephesians 5:22 and Genesis 2:18, a wife is called to submit to her husband and to be his helpmate. Therefore these two, *submission* and *helpfulness*, are her fundamental and foundational duties, the duties that belong to her in her God-given role. These two duties are commanded by God for every wife. To refuse to give oneself to them is to rebel, not merely against one's husband but against the God of marriage.

Submission and helpfulness are so intrinsic to the wife's role that whatever else a wife may be, whether smart, rich, reputable, beautiful, house-wise, etc., if she is neither submissive nor helpful to her husband then all else is in vain and she is failing to perform her marriage vows. "Let her have never so much wisdom, learning, grace; yet if she do not reverence her husband, she cannot be a good wife," wrote Steele.[1]

Whatever else may be required of a wife, if she strives before God (who graciously gives what He commands, Ezek. 36:26–27; Phil. 2:13) to submit to her husband in the Lord and to be his helpmate in both temporal and spiritual matters, then all else will fall into place; every other duty which flows from these two will be done. As Steele wrote:

---

1. Steele, *Puritan Sermons*, 2:290.

"This principle must first be fixed in her heart…that it is neither agreeable to nature nor decency to set the head below, or no higher than, the rib. And when she is resolved in this, then will she with much delight and ease go through her duty. A wise God has ordered it thus; and therefore it is best."[2]

Therefore, however difficult these two foundational duties may seem to be and however contrary to her sinful nature, if she will but submit herself first to Christ as her Lord and heavenly Husband, and learn to be content with His will for her—being confident in His wisdom and His ways—then she will find herself cheerfully and freely submitting to her husband in the Lord and serving him in every way she can as his helpmate. In fact, until she does the former, she simply cannot do the latter acceptably to the Lord. Since her marital duties are prescribed to her *by God* and are therefore part and parcel of her obedience *to God*, she must first learn to submit to and obey God before she can submit to and obey her husband.[3] "The woman is first to subject herself to Christ, and in love to Him to subject herself to her husband," Manton said.[4] This order is necessitated by the fact that when a woman gives herself up to the Lord first, her heart can be purged of self and pride (which are the seeds of rebellion) and thereby made ready and fit for the duty of submitting to her husband as unto the Lord. Otherwise, if her outward submission to her husband begins before her inward submission to Christ, it will vanish like the light of a lamp for lack of oil.[5]

Of the wife's two duties, helpfulness has already been dealt with at length in the previous chapter. We therefore direct our attention in the reminder of this chapter to her duty of submission.

The submission required of a wife is decried by many in our day. But it is most often the case that what they decry is a caricature and not the biblical duty. They imagine that the Bible, and therefore Christianity, demands a slavish service from the wife; but that's not what the Bible means when it speaks of a wife submitting to her husband.

---

2. Steele, *Puritan Sermons*, 2:291.
3. den Ouden, 71–72.
4. Manton, 19:438.
5. Rogers, 239.

While God has invested the husband with headship and authority not given the wife, it is not "a tyrannical authority…to use them like slaves and menial servants; but as friends and companions in all the state of wedlock."[6] The submission of the wife to her husband is well defined by Gataker as "a faithful and careful, a constant and conscionable, performance of such duties as issue and flow from the inward acknowledgement of that superiority of power and place which God has given to the husband with regard to the wife."[7] These duties to which Gataker referred can be reduced to four kinds: reverence, obedience, assistance, and modesty. Let us look at each of these.

Reverence (Deep, Heartfelt Respect)

Steele called reverence "the great duty" of every wife, the duty which signalizes her and sets her apart because it is her peculiar qualification as a wife and distinguishes her as a *good* wife.[8] That this is her peculiar duty can be established at the outset in her creation. Eve was made *after* Adam (1 Tim. 2:13), she was made *out* of man (1 Cor. 11:8), and she was made *for* man (Gen. 2:18); all these show that, according to God's own appointment, a wife ought to reverence and esteem her husband as her head. This reverence is the wife's acknowledgement of God's ordinance in creation and God's appointment of him as her head. That we might understand this duty well, consider its nature and pattern.[9]

First, for the *nature* of this duty, Steele described it as true, cordial, and conjugal reverence, made up of honor, love, and respect. The wife ought to *honor* her husband, holding his person and everything about him in the highest esteem simply because there is no one so dear to her as he is. Surely she esteemed him when she consented to marry him and therefore she ought to still. If, for whatever reason, she finds herself no longer able to honor his person, then she is to honor his *place* over

---

6. *The New Whole Duty of Man*, 221.

7. Gataker, 190.

8. Steele, *Puritan Sermons*, 2:290.

9. Steele, *Puritan Sermons*, 2:291–99. Steele also spoke of the *effect* of reverence, which is an obedience in word and deed; but in keeping with Gataker's outline we will save this for the following section.

her since his place does not fluctuate though his character may. Baxter gave the same counsel: "Do not behave toward them with irreverence and contempt.... If the worth of their persons does not desire honor, yet their place does."[10] Whatever her husband is in himself and however others may regard him, if she properly reverences him, then to her he is what the Puritans called a *none-such*, a singular and distinct person, a person unequalled in excellence—because he is her husband. Hopkins said, "She must look upon him as that person whom God, out of all the numerous millions of mankind has particularly chosen and selected for her; and one, whom He saw fittest and best to be her head and guide."[11]

The wife's reverence of her husband also includes *love*. We have already seen that although love is the husband's foundational and sum-mary duty, it is required of the wife as well (Titus 2:4). She is to love him so completely and entirely that she will leave her father and her mother and her father's house and cleave to him as her head. She is to love him with that sincerity of heart and deep affection that will work in her heart the proper reverence she should have for him. Mere fondness will not do; neither will a doting upon his looks or strength. If she is to reverence her husband, she must really, deeply, and truly love him. Thus Baxter directed wives to "be especially loving to your husbands. Your natures give you the advantage in this, and love feeds love."[12] The wife who does not love her husband will find every part of her duty cumbersome and painful. Only a genuine love for him will sweeten her duties, making it more acceptable and delightful to reverence him as her husband.

As a third component of the wife's reverence for her husband, she is to *fear* or *respect* him (1 Peter 3:2). This part of the wife's duty is, to many, like a high pitch, painful to the ear; but this reaction says more about our sinful hearts than about the duty itself. The fear to which God calls the wife is not a servile or slavish fear, which would be inconsistent with love, but rather a free and generous fear, a fear, as Gataker said, "springing from love, and joined with love; consisting in a desire to do everything so as may please their husbands and give them content-

---

10. Baxter, 156.
11. Hopkins, 1:423.
12. Baxter, 155.

ment, and a care to shun and avoid whatsoever may displease them, or minister discontentment unto them."[13] When a wife fears her husband she does her utmost to please him, even if it means displeasing the whole world (1 Cor. 7:34). Out of her heart's desire to please him she endeavors in her speech, dress, behavior, and entire demeanor to endear herself to him as a most amiable and lovely wife. Therefore, a wife who pleases herself and does not care whether or not her husband is pleased or who purposely chooses those courses which cross her husband's will is both displeasing to the Lord and provokes the Lord, who commands that reverence and respect be paid to the husband as part of that reverence and respect which are due unto Himself.

Secondly, the *pattern* of the wife's duty is to submit to her husband as the church submits to Christ and as a body submits to its head (Eph. 5:22–24). In order for her submission to be patterned after the church's submission, two things are required. First, she is to submit to him "in every thing" (v. 24). Whether great or small matters, if there is nothing unlawful or sinful about his requests, then she is to comply. Second, she is to submit freely, willingly, constantly, and cheerfully. Her submission to her husband's will is to be so cheerfully and willingly done that it appears as though there is but one heart, one will, and one interest between them. Her respect or fear, said Swinnock, "must be like that of the church to Christ, an acknowledgement of his superiority over her, and an unwillingness to displease him in anything, and a dread lest she should offend him. When the judgment consents to the husband's authority, the will resolves to own it in all her actions, and the heart has a dread upon it, lest she should disown it; then she is said to fear him, and not before."[14] Otherwise, as Steele noted, "a contradicting and grudging spirit is very unsuitable to the religious wife, and ever leaves a sting in [her husband's] heart and guilt in hers; for usually it is a sign of unmortified pride and self-conceit.... If the husband's government be too heavy, yet it is better for you to leave him to answer for his severity, than for you to answer for your contempt."[15]

---

13. Gataker, 191.
14. Swinnock, 1:505.
15. Steele, *Puritan Sermons*, 2:293–94.

As the body does not teach the head which way to go but submits to the head's wisdom, so a wife is not to direct her husband but to follow his leading. Steele quipped, "It is preposterous for the head to go one way, and the rib another."[16] Rather than suffer any loss by following him, this is the very means by which she both engages her husband's sympathy and direction and increasingly endears herself to him. Her reverence of him will sooner draw out his love than anything else. "Indeed there is no better means to increase the husband's love than the wife's reverence, and *that* alone will make *this* sweet and easy."[17]

Obedience

Obedience is part of a wife's God-honoring submission to her husband, as is clear from Sara's example cited in 1 Peter 3:4–6 in which the apostle urges Christian women to adorn themselves with "a meek and quiet spirit…even as Sara obeyed Abraham, calling him lord." In Titus 2, Paul charges a young pastor to teach the saints to live in accord with sound doctrine (v. 1), teaching young women to be "obedient to their own husbands" (v. 5). So that rather than being a yoke to be cast off or a snare to be avoided, a wife's reverent obedience to her husband is an ornament to her beauty before God and the flowering of the doctrine of God in her marriage.

If it is to be acceptable to God, the wife's obedience should manifest itself in both words and deeds. Since the mouth speaks out of the abundance that fills the heart (Matt. 12:34), if she reverences her husband in her heart then it will manifest itself in her speech. She should refer to him with respect (1 Peter 3:6) and speak of him to others with respect (Song 5:16). She should guard against being argumentative or disagreeable, knowing that the Lord hears and she will give an account (Matt. 12:36). "No woman gets honor by the last word."[18] She will both win her husband's heart—if it can be won (1 Peter 3:1)—and get honor from the Lord by the imperishable beauty of a meek and quiet spirit (1 Peter 3:4–5). Thus Swinnock said, "a reverent wife may possibly make a reli-

---

16. Steele, *Puritan Sermons*, 2:294.
17. Steele, *Puritan Sermons*, 2:292.
18. Steele, *Puritan Sermons*, 2:295.

gious husband. The head may fare much better for the good temperature of the body. Fear in her may be instrumental to work faith in him."[19]

A wife shows her reverence in deeds by obeying her husband in all things lawful and harmonious with the Lord's greater headship over her (1 Peter 3:6; Eph. 5:24). Steele put it this way: "If he command her to do any thing that is sinful by the law of God (as if he should bid her to tell a lie, bear false witness, or the like), she must modestly and resolvedly refuse it. If he forbid her to do any thing that is by God's command made an indispensable duty unto her (as if he should absolutely forbid her to pray, to read the Scripture, to sanctify the Lord's Day, or the like), then she must 'rather obey God than man' [Acts 4:19–20]. But in all other cases, though she may respectfully persuade with him, yet if he insist upon it, her obedience will be her best sacrifice, and her compliance will be the means to make her yoke easy."[20]

The manner of her obedience is that it must be done "*as* unto the Lord." She obeys her husband with the intent of not only pleasing him but also pleasing the Lord because she sees the Lord's authority in her husband's, even when the thing required by him has no other argument for doing it than that it pleases him. "Then it will appear, that though there be no necessity in what is required [by her husband], yet there is a necessity she should perform what is required"[21] if she is to please the Lord.

Her reverence to her husband should also be evident in her submission to her husband's counsel and reproof. In Scripture we see that godly women submitted to their husband's counsels. When the Shunammite woman wanted to make a room for Elisha in the house she consulted with her husband (2 Kings 4:9–10). Whether it be how she dresses, how she behaves, the company she keeps, or how she manages the home, the wife should look to her husband as her guide so that she might both honor his place and please his person as well as prove to be a daughter of "the holy women" of old (1 Peter 3:5–6).

---

19. Swinnock, 1:505.
20. Steele, *Puritan Sermons*, 2:296.
21. Hopkins, 1:422.

Let every husband hereby take note of his great duty to be a guide and counselor to his wife. If your wife is to *submit* to your counsel as unto the Lord's, then you must be ready to *give* the Lord's counsel. You must be ready to govern both yourself (as an example to your wife) and your household by the Word of God. You must therefore be acquainted with seeking the Lord's will and discerning between right and wrong (Rom. 12:2). You must know how to consult God in prayer and discern His will from Scripture (2 Tim. 3:16–17) if you expect to be faithful to your leadership and encourage your wife to be faithful in submission and obedience.

To her obedience to her husband's counsels, the wife must add obedience to his reproofs. This will be her hardest task and a bitter pill to flesh and blood, especially where she harbors a proud and contentious spirit within; but she must lovingly and thankfully bear his reproofs.[22] Let her consider that since none is as close to her as her husband, so none is more able and more obliged to speak to her about her sins. Moreover, since the two of them are one flesh, whatever sins beset her beset the relationship itself and pain them both. Likewise, whatever sins are repented of and cut off in either of them will bring healing and joy to the both of them. If she reverences him as she should and believes that he reproves her in love, desiring only her increase in holiness, then she can digest the pill and, by God's blessing, bring forth repentance.[23]

Gataker's counsel is very helpful. The wife, he said, is to be

> willing to reform and amend what he admonishes her of as amiss. Not ready to return a snappish answer, and to give one angry word for another; nor to be pouting and lowering upon it... for a long time together, as if [she] would make him weary of admonishing ought any more; but hearing it with mildness, and hearkening to it with meekness, remembering that when the husband admonishes, God admonishes in him; and hearkening to him, she hearkens to God in him; as on the other side, contemning him, she contemns God, and God's ordinance in him. Yea, though the husband should chance to blame and find fault without cause (as even the best and the wisest sometimes may do), it shall be a wise

---

22. Steele, *Puritan Sermons*, 2:298.
23. Steele, *Puritan Sermons*, 2:298.

and discreet woman's part rather to take it quietly and patiently, as if there were just cause of it, than to give any unkind or uncomely language [in return], remembering that *it is*, as one says well, *the property of an ingenuous disposition, to acknowledge a fault sometimes, even where there is none, not by lying or dissembling (for that is altogether unlawful)*, but by patient bearing and forbearing, being as ready to alter what is done, as if it had been done otherwise than it ought.[24]

This is not to suppose, said Gataker, that the wife may not, on appropriate occasions, counsel or reprove the husband.[25] But the wise and submissive wife will seek to do so in such a way that she aims to do him "good and not evil all the days of her life" (Prov. 31:12). When she must reprove him, she should offer the admonition so seasonably and with such loving respect to his person and place, that he will receive it, as it were, from her heart rather than from her lips, as medicinal rather than abrasive, and as from one who seeks his good rather than to usurp his place. Likewise her advice to him should be complemented with such a readiness to obey his leading and a willingness to let him decide the matter that he will gladly take up her idea, where he sees it to be good, and ratify and seal it with his authority and blessing as the best course of action. Thus Swinnock said, "If a woman answer her husband, it must be with modesty; if she would advise him, it must be with lenity; and if she admonish him, with much humility. If she speak of him, it must be respectfully; if she speak to him, it must be reverently."[26]

Though this duty of obedience may seem hard, and no doubt will at times be hard to the flesh, that wife who obeys her husband *as unto* the Lord because she obeys her husband *for* the Lord's sake will gain favor with God, comfort to her own soul, love from her husband, and a good report before others. Therefore, dear wife, see that you regard not so much what your husband deserves as what God requires of you towards your husband. If there were none over you but your husband, then you might well disregard his government if it did not please you; but the Lord

---

24. Gataker, 191–92.
25. Gataker, 192.
26. Swinnock, 1:506.

is over you and His government of you is administered through and in your husband. Your obedience is not subject to the question of what your husband deserves in himself or whether or not he does his duty with regard to you. These matters must be left, prayerfully, to the Lord. Your duty must be done as unto the Lord, for the Lord, and out of conscience to the headship of Jesus Christ over you, whom you serve and who sees your faithfulness and will graciously reward it, both in this life and in the life to come, for that is His promise (1 Tim. 4:8; Col. 3:23–24).

Assistance

The third aspect of a wife's submission to her husband is assistance, or helpfulness. "The woman is not man's guide, but his help…his helper and partner in the cares of the family," noted Manton.[27] We treated this duty in an earlier chapter because of the great obligation which rests upon the husband to be helpful to his wife—a duty forgotten by too many husbands—and because of the largeness of this duty when considered mutually. There is therefore no need to repeat it here. Instead, after a quick summary, we want to take a brief look at Proverbs 31 to see what it teaches us about the helpful wife.

Reyner summarized this well when he said her helpfulness should be "in everything: in his body to cherish that; in his soul to tender that; in his family to order that; in his estate to get, at least to save and to dispose that aright, not to spend and waste the same; in his calling and affairs to promote them; in his name and credit to preserve that; in his secrets to lock them up in her bosom. She ought to be a help to him in everything, a hindrance in nothing, else she is *a woman, but not a wife*, and he that finds her does not find a good thing (Prov. 18:22)."[28] Manton gave a similar summary: "The woman is to be a help, not a hindrance; not the governor, for the right is originally in the man, but a help in government, to ease him in part of his burden and cares; a help every way, for the comfort of society, for assistance in governing the family, for the increasing and for the propagation and continuance of posterity; [since] for these uses was the woman created, and intended

---

27. Manton, 19:441.
28. Reyner, 17.

by God."[29] To make clear how suitable a helpful wife is to her husband, Reyner drew the following analogy between a garment, which can be neither worn with comfort nor liked with contentment *unless it fits.* Reyner said, "A wife is like a garment: though the cloth it's made of be very good, yet if it does not fit us, it will not please us, it will be uneasy or uncomely [and] we take no delight to wear it. Conveniency causes contentment. If the wife be no [suitable] help shaped and cut out, as it were, on purpose for the man, to fit and suit him every way in his disposition, conversation, and occasions, [then] she will not sit close to the man, as a garment [sits close] to the body that fits it, but [she will] hang loose, or be ready to fall off and rather hinder than further him and not be an ornament to him."[30]

A wife is therefore to *help* her husband in everything. With regard to his soul, she is to help him cultivate his graces and lovingly urge him to his duties before the Lord, especially those duties incumbent on him as the spiritual leader in the home. Indeed, her own godly conduct as well as her meek and quiet spirit may well serve to both bring him to Christ and provoke him to grow in godliness (1 Peter 3:1–2; 1 Cor. 7:16). With regard to his body, she is to cherish it and tenderly care for it both in sickness and in health. She should cherish her husband as the greater part of herself since she was made by God to be his helpmate. Out of the love she has for him she should tend to the needs of his body as well as she tends to her own. With regard to his name and reputation, she is to endeavor to protect and preserve it from slander by speaking well of him both at home and abroad. With regard to his estate, if she does not add to it by her own work, yet she is to strive before the Lord to be a faithful manager of all that he provides for her and the family. What a comfort it is to the husband to have a helpful wife! Surely he who "findeth [such] a wife findeth a good thing, and obtaineth favour of the LORD" (Prov. 18:22)!

The Puritans called Proverbs 31:10–31 a mirror in which all good wives should dress themselves, a pattern to imitate, and a rule to walk

---

29. Manton, 19:440.
30. Reyner, 17–18.

by every day.[31] This passage sets forth the ways and means by which a wife proves to be a choice helpmate to her husband.[32] First it declares her value: "her price is far above rubies," that is, she is worth far more than rare and costly gemstones (v. 10). She is of inestimable worth to the man who has her. Second, and more fully, this passage sets forth her virtues. She is prudent, knowing when to speak and what to say (v. 26). She is full of charity and generosity, freely giving what she has to the needs of others (v. 20). She is pious, clothed with grace in life because she is filled with grace in heart (v. 25). She fears the Lord (v. 30), as can be seen by both the praise of her holiness (v. 31) and the praise of her husband (v. 28). Swinnock wrote: "While other [wives] have but the black beauty-spots of sin to set them forth, pride compasses them about as a chain, and atheism covers them as a garment; grace is her glory, and godliness is her comeliness. Religion builds her such an honorable monument, that neither age nor hell can ever pull it down."[33] She is faithful, worthy of her husband's confident trust since nothing he entrusts to her is lost or squandered but is prudently employed (v. 11). She is diligent and zealous in her management of the home (vv. 17–19, 27), seeing that all in her house have food (vv. 14–15) and clothing (v. 21). As a way of encompassing all that the godly wife is, we read that she is good, and not harmful, to her husband all the days of her life (v. 12). She will do her husband good by faithfully performing all the duties of her place, by honoring his person, and by submitting to his leadership of her, all the days of her life. Her goodness to him will not be like the bright morning sun which is soon hidden behind a cloud and continues all the day unseen; but rather in all changes and circumstances she will cleave to him with good like ivy to a wall and will sooner cease to live than to remove her goodness from him.

Modesty

The fourth duty of the wife is modesty in apparel. In 1 Timothy 2:9–10, Paul directs that "women [should] adorn themselves in modest apparel,

---

31. E.g. Reyner, 18; Swinnock, 1:512.
32. Swinnock, 1:512–16.
33. Swinnock, 1:503.

with shamefacedness and sobriety; not with broided hair, or gold, or pearls, or costly array; but (which becometh women professing godliness) with good works." In 1 Peter 3:3–4, Peter lays down the same rule for Christian women: "Whose adorning let it not be that outward adorning of plaiting the hair, and of wearing of gold, or of putting on of apparel; but let it be the hidden man of the heart, in that which is not corruptible, even the ornament of a meek and quiet spirit, which is in the sight of God of great price." Modesty is therefore a biblical mandate for all women and especially for married women.

All outward adornment and show is *useless* if a woman's heart is not right before God, and *sinful* if it displays a rebellious heart towards her husband's headship. If she neglects to furnish her heart with grace and dresses to be seen by men, then she is neither a blessing to her husband nor faithful to her duty before God. This, then, is a wife's best, most precious, and therefore most coveted adornment: the adornment of her spirit with grace before God, resulting in the adornment of her life with good works before men (1 Tim. 2:10), beginning with her husband (1 Peter 3:5).

Reyner said this duty of modesty with regard to a woman's apparel is not to be understood to *prevent* the wearing of gold, jewels, and precious things by a woman, but is to set or *limit* their use within certain boundaries.[34] These boundaries include the following. First, she should wear that which does not exceed responsible financial stewardship. Second, she should not wear clothing which manifests wastefulness, wantonness, or desire for the newest fashions. Third, she should not dress vainly, excessively, or with pride, as if her clothes make her better or more than she is before God. Fourth, she should strive above all else to adorn herself inwardly rather than outwardly, striving to be more precious for her graces and good works than for her garments, and endeavoring that whatever she wears before men shows that she herself prizes her inner Christlikeness far above her outer beauty.

Modesty therefore begins as a desire in a woman's heart that the beauty of Christ would so thoroughly penetrate and determinatively

---

34. Reyner, 19–20.

adorn her heart and spirit that her outward apparel, adornment, and grooming would befit and reflect that inward beauty. In other words, it is the Christian woman's aim to dress in keeping with her pursuit of practical godliness (Matt. 5:16). To such a woman, it would be grievous to think that her manner of dressing in any way obscured or contradicted her relationship to Christ.

But more needs to be said. So far we have spoken of modesty as it relates to Paul's and Peter's prescription for clothing and grooming. What about the duty of modesty as it relates to the seventh commandment? A woman's duty before God—and before her husband, if she is married—is to dress in such a way that she expresses an inner chastity and purity and, so far as lies in her, not tempt others to lust. Is not dressing modestly included in the Lord's charge that we "possess [our] vessel[s] in sanctification and honour" (1 Thess. 4:4) and implied in the Lord's commandment that we "not commit adultery" (Ex. 20:14)?

Consider what William Perkins and Vincent Alsop had to say regarding modesty itself. Perkins taught that modesty is one of the two virtues (sobriety being the other) necessary to fence in and preserve the chastity of soul and body required by the seventh commandment.[35] Modesty, said Perkins, preserves chastity by "working a holy decorum" in the countenance and eyes, in the speech, and in the apparel.[36]

A modest countenance or look, he explained, is when the eyes of a person neither express nor excite the lusts of the heart. Job exercised modesty in this sense when he made a covenant with his eyes not to look lustfully upon a woman (Job 31:1). He had resolved not to use his eyes as outlets for the lusts of his heart. In contrast, the daughters of Zion are rebuked in Isaiah 3:16 because they walked with "wanton eyes." Their eyes were lasciviously used in such a way as to incite men to lust after them. Peter warns of wicked men who have "eyes full of adultery" (2 Peter 2:14) and Solomon describes the "impudent face" of the harlot who catches and kisses her prey (Prov. 7:13). If chastity is to be preserved, the countenance must portray and invite pure and chaste thoughts.

---

35. Cf. Chapter 5.
36. Perkins, 60–61.

Modest speech refrains from the use of the filthy, foolish, jesting talk typical of an adulterous heart. "But fornication, and all uncleanness, or covetousness, let it not be once named among you, as becometh saints; neither filthiness, nor foolish talking, nor jesting, which are not convenient: but rather giving of thanks" (Eph. 5:3–4). Why? "For this ye know, that no whoremonger, nor unclean person, nor covetous man, who is an idolater, hath any inheritance in the kingdom of Christ and of God" (v. 5). Our speech must therefore be conducive to pure thoughts, in keeping with a holy walk. There is no place among God's people for flirtatious, sexually suggestive, or seductive talk because, as the apostle says, no unclean person has any inheritance in heaven.

Modesty also preserves chastity by "working a holy decorum" in the way we dress. The pure fire of chastity which burns upon the altar of a holy heart, said Alsop, "must flame out and shine in [chaste] words, actions, clothing, and adorning."[37] This means that whereas immodest apparel tends to express and stir up the sin of lust, modest apparel seeks to express the sincerity, godliness, and temperance of the heart.[38]

As a help to preserve our own and others' chastity, our naked bodies need to be covered.[39] Indeed, God commands this very thing in the seventh commandment when He forbids adultery, since to forbid adultery is to command chastity. And when God commands chastity, noted Alsop, "He commands whatever may feed and nourish it, manifest and declare it. And He forbids whatever may endanger it, wound, weaken, blemish, or impair it."[40]

This silences the objection of those who argue that the problem with immodest clothing is not in the clothing itself but in the sinful mind of the beholder. Such objectors shift the blame for immodesty from the revealing clothing and the party wearing it to the party look-

37. Alsop, 120.
38. Perkins, 61.
39. This is not to suggest that the covering of Adam and Eve with the skin of an animal had no relation to their need for and God's provision of a covering for their overall sinfulness. The garments provided by God showed them that He alone could cover their guilt and that from Him alone we must seek our garments of salvation and a robe of righteousness for acceptance with Him.
40. Alsop, 120.

ing upon it lustfully. But according to the positive requirement of the seventh commandment, God requires a chastity and a purity that show themselves in how we talk, behave, and dress. If we dress to *promote* sexual immorality or solicit the lust of others, then it is *we* who are sinning. There are certain styles of clothing and certain ways of dressing that are immodest and therefore sinful. It therefore matters very much what we wear and how we dress. Christians are duty-bound before God to "abstain from all appearance of evil" (1 Thess. 5:22), that is, "to avoid all approaches towards it, and deny themselves the use of such ornaments, and forbear such gestures, which give ground of suspicion to the censurer, or whereby they themselves may be tempted to pride, or their admirers to the lusts of the flesh."[41]

Likewise, Paul tells us in 1 Thessalonians 4:3 that God's will for us is to "abstain from fornication." This abstinence, Paul says, means exercising strict self-control and keeping our bodies, or "vessels," in sanctification and honor, rather than "in the lust of concupiscence, even as the Gentiles which know not God" (v. 5). Thus, as Alsop counseled, "Godly fear must be placed as a severe sentinel to keep strict guard over the heart so that nothing is admitted that may defile our own hearts, [and] nothing steal out which may defile another's. We must keep a watch over our own hearts and other men's eyes; neither lay a snare for the chastity of another, nor a bait for our own."[42]

The Puritans believed that while any given culture will have something to say about how we dress and what is modest or immodest dress, it is God's Word which must have the final authority. Culture may help us in applying Scripture to our specific context, but Scripture may never be trumped by culture. Moreover, where culture will at times push the limits of what is morally acceptable, it is our wisdom as Christians not to seek to live on the edge of those limits but to strive to ever keep far away from them, well within the bounds of Scripture and consistent with holiness.

Therefore we can take our cues for dressing from the culture only in so far as they agree with and do not contradict the law of God to pre-

---

41. *The New Whole Duty of Man*, 396.
42. Alsop, 121.

serve our own and others' chastity, the commands of Scripture to dress modestly as a reflection of pure thoughts and intentions of the heart, and the general directions of Scripture for our conduct regarding our abstaining from sexual immorality, fleeing all appearances of evil, and not purposely putting a stumbling block in another's path.

Given that today's fashions are unabashedly driven by an effort to show as much of one's nakedness as the public will allow (whether by too little clothing, tight-fitting clothing, or see-through clothing); and given that today's culture is making a last-ditch effort to throw off all sense of shame by glorying in the display of its nakedness; and given that today's dress codes are set, not by the rule of Scripture, but by one's own lustful desires to both express and excite lust; it should go without saying that, if we ever expect to dress modestly and thereby preserve our own and others' chastity, we cannot take our cues from the world but must return to Scripture, bringing the motives behind what we wear, our wardrobes themselves, and the reasons we choose to wear certain things all under the dominion of Christ's Lordship. What changes would take place in your wardrobe if you took this aspect of the seventh commandment seriously?

Are there any guidelines from Scripture for modest apparel? First, Alsop noted that whatever is inconsistent with modesty, gravity, sobriety, and godliness is inappropriate. According to 1 Peter 3:2-5, the holy women of the Old Testament who trusted in God are the standard for imitation. "Not a painting Jezebel, nor a dancing Dinah, nor a flaunting Bernice, but a holy Sarah, a godly Rebecca, and a prudent Abigail."[43] Second, whatever violates the distinction God has put between the sexes is inappropriate (Deut. 22:5). When God made man He clearly distinguished between male and female and our clothing should honor His wisdom by observing that distinction. Third, whatever clothing that fails to serve the purpose for all apparel, i.e. to cover one's nakedness, is inappropriate (Isa. 47:2-3). The Puritans stressed that it does not matter if a society has degenerated so far that certain parts of a woman's (or a man's) body are no longer considered parts of their "nakedness"

---

43. Alsop, 121.

and therefore not inappropriate to leave uncovered. Nor does it matter if women who expose much of themselves through immodest clothing no longer find or feel shame in doing so. Nor does it matter if an entire society has determined that a particular fashion or style of immodest clothing is acceptable. None of these is determinative of what is morally right before God. What matters is that God has given clothing to cover nakedness (Gen. 3:21), the seventh commandment to govern clothing (Ex. 20:14), and holy women of old as a pattern for modest apparel (1 Peter 3:3–6). Therefore once the light of God's truth has illumined our minds and taught us the truth as it is in Jesus, we are accountable to bring and should desire to bring our dress code into agreement with biblical truth (Eph. 4:17–21; cf. 1 Cor. 6:9–11). Fourth, a safe rule of dress is to strive for a kind of golden mean which Alsop described as "below envy and above contempt".[44] Fifth, 1 Timothy 2:9–10 provides "a divine [mirror] wherein [women] may contemplate…their glory."[45] Their glory consists first in being adorned with modest apparel: their outer clothing should reveal inner chastity rather than inner uncleanness. Second, in a modest countenance: a face that befits the modest heart and modest clothing. Third, in being adorned with sobriety: self-control that manifests itself in their choice of apparel. They do not dress to turn heads; they do not dress to be an object of lust; they do not dress to express their sexual desires; instead, they dress with sobriety and a bridle over their own passions. Fourth, their glory consists in being adorned with good works "which becometh women professing godliness." "Godliness must be…your tailor and seamstress for the back; godliness must be consulted as what to buy, how to make up what you have bought, and how, when, and where to wear what you have made up."[46] In the end, "Let the inward garb of your souls, the frame of your hearts, be such as may approve it to God. Let the outward garb and deportment of your bodies be such as may have a good report from good men."[47]

---

44. Alsop, 129.
45. Alsop, 138–39.
46. Alsop, 139.
47. Alsop, 143.

Finally, Alsop provided several helpful directions with regard to clothing.[48]

1. Do not be ambitious to appear first in any fashion. "When custom has made that which is strange [to be] familiar, when time has mellowed the harshness, and common usage has taken off the edge of novelty, a good Christian may safely venture a little nearer, provided he does not leap over those bounds prescribed by God, nature, and decency.... A modest Christian, in conscience as well as in courtesy, will not think it unwise to let others go before him."[49]

2. Do not strive to come up to the height of fashion. Stay back from the limits and well within safe ground.

3. Follow no fashion so fast or so far as to run your finances into ruin. "Advise first with conscience what is lawful, then with your purse what is practical."[50] We cannot always do what we would like to do.

4. If you determine to follow lawful fashions, then keep in step with those who are your equals in religion and holiness, having them as your pattern. Your equals are those who are heirs together with you of the grace of life (1 Peter 3:7), partakers with you of the same precious faith (2 Peter 1:1), and have the same hopes as you of a common salvation (Jude 3). We should not dress as if we were at home in this fallen world which lies in the power of the evil one (1 John 5:19) when we are but sojourners here and citizens of a kingdom whose builder and maker is God (Heb. 11:10, 16).

5. Do not come near those fashions whose numerous implements, trinkets, and tackling require much time in dressing and undressing. How much time is lost in adorning the body of flesh with such clothing that could be spent on adorning the soul by using the means of grace?

6. Suit your apparel to the day of God's providence and to the day of His ordinances. That is to say: in a day of mourning, dress for mourning; in a day of joy, dress for rejoicing; in a day of worship, dress for worship; and see that there is never a day of immorality to dress immodestly.

---

48. Alsop, 151–59.
49. Alsop, 152.
50. Alsop, 152.

7. In all apparel, stay a little above contempt and somewhat more below envy. Virtue commonly lies in the middle between extreme vices, and decency of apparel lies in the middle between the height of fashion and merely opposing it.

8. Let the ornament of the inward woman be your rule for adorning the outward woman. "Take [the] measure of your bodies by your soul, that is, consider what graces, excellencies, and virtues will adorn a soul; and let something [analogous to that] be made the trimming for the body."[51]

9. Get the heart mortified and that will mortify the clothing. Once grace circumcises its lust and pride, the heart will proceed to circumcise the clothing of all its lasciviousness and vanity (Matt. 12:33; 23:26).

10. Avoid in your own dress whatever fashions of apparel you have found to be a temptation to your own soul when worn by others. All sinners have the same seeds of sin in their hearts, and that which awakens pride or lust in you will most probably awaken the same corruption in others.

11. Let all your indifferences be brought under the government and guidance of religion. "Consult with God's glory as to what you should eat, what you should drink, and what you should put on; that will teach us to deny ourselves in some particulars of Christian liberty"[52] (1 Cor. 10:31; Col. 3:17).

12. Use all these indifferent things with an indifferent affection for them and an indifferent concern for them and about them. Clothes will not commend us to God so we should not place stock in them as if they will. Moreover, we should remember that God and the world usually do not agree, and that which is highly esteemed among men is oftentimes an abomination in the sight of God (Luke 16:15).

13. Seek above all else that honor which comes from God alone. Our absolution or condemnation will be from Him, not from the world (Rom. 14:4). Let us so dress that it may be clear that we seek His honor and His commendation, not the honor and approval of an evil world from whom He has separated us unto Himself (2 Cor. 6:14–7:1).

---

51. Alsop, 156.
52. Alsop, 158.

It should now be clear how all four of these duties rest upon and express the wife's summary duty of submission. It should also be clear how dependent upon God's grace a wife is to be faithful in these duties. She must know herself to stand in need of God's grace to subdue her natural pride and selfishness and transform her into a woman that fears the Lord and therefore departs from evil and runs in the way of His commandments. She must see her own emptiness and seek, by God's grace, to live on Christ's fullness. She must pray for *sincerity* that she might heartily and wholly seek to be faithful in her duties; for *love* that she might really and truly love her husband, delighting to please him and wanting in nothing to displease him; and for *selflessness* that she might cheerfully, readily, willingly, and fully serve him, striving in all things to be his helpmate, bringing him comfort here and eternal joy hereafter. Above all else, she must pray *to be filled with the Holy Spirit* who alone can empower her to put to death the misdeeds of the flesh and work in her to will and to do for God's good pleasure for her as a wife.

Study Questions

1. What are the two fundamental duties of a wife? Prove them from Scripture.

2. How should a wife's esteem for her husband be shaped by:

   • Honor for his person and position?

   • Love for him above all other earthly relations?

   • Respect for his wishes and desire to please him?

3. Where does the Scripture command wives to be obedient to their husbands?

4. What does it mean for a wife to obey her husband "as unto the Lord"?

5. Can a wife reprove her husband yet remain submissive? How?

6. What extended passage of Scripture is a picture of a wife who helps her husband? Summarize it.

7. How should a wife's modesty in dress reflect her heart toward God and her husband?

8. Which of the guidelines for modesty do you find most helpful?

9. Do you disagree with anything presented in this chapter? On what biblical grounds?

The Husband's
Duty of Love

Based on Ephesians 5:23, 25–30, the Puritans taught that a husband's two foundational duties are *authority* and *love*. The husband is the authoritative head to whom his wife is to submit herself just as the church submits to Christ (v. 23), and the husband is to love his wife just as Christ loves the church (vv. 25–30). Thus Ambrose wrote that the husband's *whole duty* towards his wife lies in these two things: he must dearly love his wife and he must wisely maintain and manage his authority over her.[1]

Man's sinfulness being what it is, a husband may be tempted to exercise an austere authority void of love or an indulgent love that abdicates authority, but a husband's obedience to God requires the exercise of *both* these duties. Consider this direction to husbands from Baxter: "The husband must so unite authority and love that neither of them may be omitted or concealed, but both will be exercised and maintained. Love must not be exercised so imprudently as to destroy the exercise of authority; and authority must not be exercised over a wife so magisterially and imperiously as to destroy the exercise of love. As your love must be a governing love, so your commands must be loving commands."[2] Similarly, Steele taught that a husband's authority is so directly connected with his love that it is one of the *effects* of his love.[3] It is an act of the husband's love, said Steele, to wisely keep and mildly

1. Ambrose, 234.
2. Baxter, 152.
3. Steele, *Puritan Sermons*, 2:289.

use his authority. "If his rule be too imperious, his love is destroyed; if his love be not discreetly expressed, his sceptre is lost, and then he is disabled from doing God service, or his family good."[4]

The Puritans therefore saw the two duties as intricately intertwined. As goes the one so goes the other. Gouge wrote that a husband's authority is a *branch* of his love.[5] Scudder advised that a husband is, *with love*, to both keep his place and use his authority.[6] Boston said the husband's love is to temper his authority.[7] And Rogers urged that it was the husband's duty to walk before his wife, as her head, with such understanding—which is the fruit of love—"that he may sweetly strike into his wife's spirit a due reverential love and esteem of his person and headship, for the virtues of a husband."[8]

Therefore just as the wife's helpfulness is part of her primary duty of submission, so a husband's authority should be seen as a part of his primary duty of love. Though the Apostle states in verse 23 that the husband is the wife's head, when he comes to the husband's duty in verse 25, rather than telling them to "rule" he tells them to "love" their wives. The husband is to be a loving head, a ruling lover. Just as her submission is to inform her helpfulness, so his love is to inform his authority.

"Men Ought to Love Their Wives"

The call to love his wife comprehends all others duties a husband owes her before God. If his love is active, he will do for her all that he should, say to her all that he should, treat her as he should, feel towards her as he should, and tincture all his deeds and words towards her with the kindness, gentleness, and understanding which make up *love* and stand contrary to *bitterness* (Col. 3:19). For love, said Steele, is "the great wheel which, by its [own] motion, carries about all the other wheels of the affections that are within us and the actions that are without us."[9]

4. Steele, *Puritan Sermons*, 2:290.
5. Gouge, 254.
6. Scudder, 88.
7. Boston, 4:213.
8. Rogers, 186.
9. Steele, *Puritan Sermons*, 2:282.

Thus Byfield said love so makes up and comprehends the husband's duties that this is his word, which he is to write on his heart and ever have in his eye.[10] Steele said love is the great duty of every husband, since it comprehends all the others.[11] To understand what it is for a husband to love his wife, consider three aspects of a husband's love: its ground, its pattern, and its fruitfulness.

The *ground* of a husband's love is fivefold. First, God requires it. Colossians 3:19 says, "Husbands, love your wives," and this command is repeated no less than three times in Ephesians 5 (vv. 25, 28, 33). When all else fluctuates, this remains the same; when all else fails, this remains sure; when all else is shaken, this remains intact. If his wife is not congenial, he still must love her; if he does not feel like it, he still must love her; if she hurts and wrongs him, he still must love her.

Second, his own vows require it. If God's command binds him from above, his marital vows bind him from below. His marriage to his wife is a covenant before God (Mal. 2:14) in which he has promised to love and cherish her, not because of anything in her but because she is his wife, for love is far more than a warm feeling. It is a commitment carried out daily with heart and hand, in word and deed.

Third, her nearness to him requires it. There is none so near to a husband as his wife and therefore there is none who has as much right to his love—or the right to as much of his love—as she does. A man is commanded to love his neighbor as himself (Lev. 19:18); and is there a neighbor more near to him than his wife? She shares his home, his table, his bed, and his children. For her he has left father and mother, to her he has inseparably cleaved, and with her he has become one flesh (Gen. 2:24). Moreover, if he is to love his neighbor *as* he loves himself, how much greater must that love be which he has for his wife when to love her truly is to love himself (Eph. 5:28). The natural bond between parents and their children is deep and strong, but the bond between husband and wife so far exceeds it that it justly severs it, as it were (Gen. 2:24). Gataker wrote, "Parents are as a fountain or the body of a river; children as streams derived from it, and flowing apart; [whereas] man

---

10. Byfield, *Colossians*, 353.
11. Steele, *Puritan Sermons*, 2:282.

and wife are as two springs meeting and so joining their streams, that they make but one current, and run both in one channel, that the water of the one and the other cannot be severed.... Man and wife are as those *two branches* in the Prophet's hand [Ezek. 37:17], enclosed in one bark, and so closing together that they make but one piece, and the same fruit comes of either."[12]

Fourth, his comfort and happiness depend upon his loving his wife. Hopkins wrote that since it is love which first makes the marriage knot, so it is love alone that can make married life easy: "No other respect whatsoever can keep it from wringing and galling us. And, although want of love cannot dissolve the bond, yet it does [dissolve] the joy and comfort of a married state."[13] The truth of this point led Taylor to declare that all the commandments of God which bind a man to love his wife are "nothing but so many necessities and capacities of joy. *She that is loved is safe*, and *he that loves is joyful*. Love is a union of all things excellent; it contains in it proportion and satisfaction, and rest and confidence."[14]

Finally, a husband's other duties require it. All his other duties must flow out of love, or they cannot be done well (1 Cor. 16:14). His wife should see and feel his love in all he does. That is to say, she must be able to distinguish his care from all others, his instruction from all others, his reproof from all others, his authority from all others, and his protection from all others by the love which marks them all as his.

How important it is, then, that men not marry women whom they do not and cannot sincerely and faithfully love. Given the great variety of choices in women provided by God, it is drunken folly, said Steele, "to choose where a man cannot love, and the greatest injury possible to the wife, to ensnare her heart, and bind her to one that shall afterwards say, he cannot love her."[15] The happiness of marriage depends on being able to love each other completely and faithfully. The comforts of the married estate depend on being able to work together, communi-

---

12. Gataker, 200–201.
13. Hopkins, 1:414.
14. Taylor, 27.
15. Steele, *Puritan Sermons*, 2:283.

cate clearly and honestly, and serve each other cheerfully. Let men and women therefore be admonished, Gataker said, to "*look ere they leap*; and…remember that *one had need to deliberate long, and advise well on that which but once can be determined*."[16]

Consider as well how hard it is for men who married for the wrong reasons and must now, with difficulty, force their affections and beg God for the grace to love and serve their wives as He requires. Gataker wrote, "He that is free, may frame his choice to his mind; but he that has chosen must frame his mind to his choice. Before he might conform his actions to his affections; [but] now he must endeavor to frame his affections to his action."[17] Or as another Puritan put it, "No law obliges a man to marry; but he is obliged to love the woman he has taken in marriage."[18]

The second aspect of a husband's love is its *pattern*. Once a man has entered into marriage he is duty-bound before God to love her in the twofold manner which God has prescribed for him. First, he must love his wife *as* Christ loves His church. This love is outlined clearly for us in Ephesians 5:25–29.[19]

Acording to verse 25, Christ loves the church *sacrificially*. He gave Himself up for her. "Greater love hath no man than this," Christ says, "that a man lay down his life for his friends" (John 15:13) as Christ did for His church. He spared no expense to purchase her, but paid the greatest possible price—His own life. Therefore a husband must love his wife sacrificially, sparing no cost to himself in order to do her good. He is to lay down his life for her, preferring her to himself, putting her interests before his own, working for her good, and feeding her with his own sustenance, as it were.

Christ loves the church *heartily*. He loves her with a sincere and real love. His is not a love in word only, a superficial and external love, but it is a hearty love, a love in deed and in truth, a love tested by our needs and proven by His deeds. If a husband would follow this pattern,

---

16. Gataker, 202.
17. Gataker, 202.
18. *The New Whole Duty of Man*, 228.
19. Cf. the Christ-church principle in chapter 4.

his love must be a hearty love without hypocrisy. His love must not be "from the teeth forwards," as the Puritans used to say, but must be a love so deep and real that if his heart were opened, his wife's name would be seen written on it.[20]

Christ loves the church *freely*. In other words, His love sought nothing from her, preceded hers, and sought only to give to her the fruits of His free love. Christ's love arose wholly and solely from Himself and is freely given to the church (Deut. 7:7–8; 1 John 4:19). There was nothing in the church to warrant His love in the first place and nothing in the church to sustain it after it was given. Therefore a husband is to love his wife freely. His love is to be set upon her simply because she is his wife. He is not to love her for what she gives him or does for him, but rather because he has promised to love her. Being freely given, his love looks more for what he can do for her than what she can do for him.

According to verse 26 Christ loves the church *holily*. His is a love which seeks the church's sanctification, a love which moves Him to cleanse her by the washing of water with the Word. His love flows from His holy heart and works to accomplish her holiness. So must a husband's love be. As it flows out of his own heart, it must be a love undefiled by lust and undivided by hypocrisy; and as it flows towards her, it must be a love which seeks her spiritual welfare. To be sure, a husband, even by the best of loves, cannot love his wife as holily as Christ does His church; but he can seek to be an instrument in Christ's hands for his wife's growth in grace and to put nothing in her way that would hinder that growth.

According to verse 27, Christ loves the church *enduringly*, that is, through all her struggles and setbacks, until He presents her to the Father as a glorious church without spot or wrinkle. His love will be fully realized in her final perfection, and so it never fails (John 13:1). He is not put off from His intentions by His church's shameful coldness, stubborn hard-heartedness, or perpetual backwardness to His ways. Though she often behaves as such, He does not cast her off as incorrigible and hopeless, but steadily and purposefully perseveres in

---

20. Steele, *Puritan Sermons*, 2:284.

loving her and doing for her according to her needs and His covenant commitments to her (2 Sam. 7:15). More than that, He *delights* to show her mercy and to manifest the perfections of His love in her weaknesses (Isa. 30:18; Jer. 31:20; 2 Cor. 12:9). If a husband is to follow this pattern he must love his wife consistently and unalterably through all her struggles and failures. His love must be a love which flows every day the same, not fervently today and coldly tomorrow, freely today and meagerly tomorrow, or cheerfully today and begrudgingly tomorrow. His love must be a love which no provocation can alter and which bears all her infirmities with patience, understanding, and sympathy, endeavoring in love first to overcome evil with good and then to correct what he can and accept what he cannot.[21]

Lastly, according to verse 29, Christ loves the church *fruitfully*, for He nourishes and cherishes it. He takes note of what she lacks and supplies it from His own store (Phil. 4:19). He takes note when she is in trouble and delivers her from it or protects her in it (Mark 4:38–39). He takes note of when she is ready to sink under affliction and saves her from ruin for His own name's sake (Isa. 43:1–5). His love is one which addresses her present needs, a love which never leaves His church empty-handed or in doubt of His affection for her. And so it must be with a husband's love. He must take note of his wife's needs and do what he can to supply them, of her pains and do what he can to relieve them, and of her concerns and do what he can to resolve them. He must be better than a friend to her when she needs support and encouragement, and better than a nurse to her when she's bedridden with sickness. His love must actively benefit her and so prosper her that she is better for it and would be worse without it. She must be able to say of all she enjoys as a wife that they are all tokens of her husband's love for her.

But the pattern of a husband's love is *twofold*. Not only is he to love his wife as Christ loves the church, but he is to love his wife as he loves himself. Paul says, "So ought men to love their wives as their own bodies. He that loveth his wife loveth himself. For no man ever yet hated his own flesh; but nourisheth and cherisheth it" (vv. 28–29).

---

21. Ambrose, 235.

Christ's example is so perfect and complete in every way that nothing can be added unto it. A husband can do no better and, practically speaking, need do no more than love his wife as Christ loves His church. However, as Gouge pointed out, the pattern of loving one's wife as he loves himself is added because of the difficulty we have in fully comprehending and therefore suitably imitating Christ's example.[22]

To read in Paul's letter that a husband is to love his wife as Christ loves the church requires of us to think through the height, depth, length, and breadth of Christ's love if we expect to fashion our love after His. But when Paul says a man ought to love his wife as he loves his own body, nothing more needs to be explained. We know the love we have for ourselves and how naturally we feel and express it.

Two things are to be gathered from this pattern by the husband for his imitation: tenderness and cheerfulness.[23] A man loves himself *tenderly*. If he is hurt or uncomfortable, no one is more tender towards him than he is towards himself. He nurses his wounds with the tenderest care, excuses himself from anything that will cause him more pain, and does all he can to relieve himself or make himself more comfortable. As Paul says, he nourishes and cherishes himself. He bears patiently with his own infirmities and weaknesses. He labors long to acquire a new skill or to improve his proficiency. He perseveres in the face of failures and repeats the same lessons to himself again and again with little or no complaint. What man speaks harshly with himself, fights with himself, gives up on himself, or refuses himself? And if he ever disappoints himself, how soon he is reconciled to himself and ready to try again! A husband is to love his wife with the same tenderness with which he loves himself.

Secondly, a man loves himself *cheerfully*. There is no need to convince a man to care or provide for himself. He does this gladly and cheerfully. He is always ready to serve himself. Even in the most difficult or dangerous of circumstances, he will readily put his shoulder to the burden and endanger himself to serve his own interests. And so must the husband love his wife in this way. His ear, hand, and heart

---

22. Gouge, 303.
23. Gouge, 303–4; Steele, *Puritan Sermons*, 2:285–86.

should be as open and ready to gratify her needs as they are to gratify his own.[24] He ought to serve her more cheerfully than he serves his parents, his friends, and his children, because he serves her as cheerfully as he serves himself. He ought to be as eager, forward, and solicitous in doing for her as he is in doing for himself. Thus a man's natural interest in his own self is in every way to dictate his interest in his wife who, by the union of marriage, is as his other self. The twofold pattern, then, for a husband's love is the fulsome love of Christ for the church and the natural love a man has for his own body.

The final aspect of a husband's love is its *fruitfulness*. Steele said a husband's love to his wife is the foundation of all his duties, is mixed with them all, and is the epitome of them all. He said if this love were but fixed in the heart, it would "teach a man, yea, it [would] enforce a man, to all that tenderness, honor, care, and kindness, that is required of him. These are but the beams from that sun…the fruits from that root of real love that is within."[25] Swinnock said, "Love is the key that opens the door into every duty; love is the fulfilling of the whole law."[26]

What are some of the fruits produced when a husband loves his wife? First, it will make a man find great joy and delight in his wife (Prov. 5:18–19). Just as love causes Christ to be satisfied in His church (Isa. 53:11), delight in her (Prov. 8:31), and cling to her (John 10:28), so it will cause a husband to be satisfied in his wife, delight in her, and cling to her. He will delight in her company more than in that of any other, having no desire to be separated from her any more or any longer than necessary, because he enjoys his time with her (Eccl. 9:9). When away from her he feels he has lost half of himself and when restored to her he feels himself whole again. In love, he counts her to be his dearest confidant and closest friend. He takes the greatest pleasure in her embrace, feels his heart warmed by her smile, rejoices in her laughter, and persists in being well satisfied with her, ravished with her love, and completely fulfilled in his sexual intimacy with her. His affections are wholly, singly, persistently, and ardently for his wife. For the love he has

---

24. Steele, *Puritan Sermons*, 2:286.
25. Steele, *Puritan Sermons*, 2:282
26. Swinnock, 1:489.

for her, and for the delight and joy he finds in her, all other women are counted as strangers to him and cannot capture his affections (Prov. 5:20), "for it is not the having a wife, but the loving a wife, [that] will make a chaste husband."[27]

Secondly, it will make a man speak affectionately to his wife (Col. 3:19). The tongue, James says, is an unruly evil, a world of iniquity, often set on fire by hell (James 3:6–8) for which we desperately need the mortifying and sanctifying grace of God. A husband's tongue is no different. In fact, the closer we are to someone, the deeper our words can penetrate and the more hurt they can do. A spouse's ill speech may be the most painful of all. The author of Psalm 55 prophetically laments in verses 12–14 that Judas's wounding of Christ is exacerbated by his nearness as a friend (cf. Matt. 26:49–50).

To a soft and tender wife who is easily melted by her husband's tender and gentle speech, how crushing are harsh and cruel words from the lips she loves to kiss? How painful is it when he rebukes her with sharp and stinging words? How hard it is to bear up patiently and quietly under the bitter and demeaning speech of her bedfellow and dearest companion! How hard it is to lovingly respond to his demanding and impatient tones! Where is the loving man she married?

Love will cause a man to put away all bitterness and cruel speech (Eph. 4:31; Col. 3:19) and speak kindly and affectionately to his wife because there is nothing more contrary to love than bitterness. Love sweetens a man's heart towards his wife which in turn will sweeten his speech towards her (Matt. 15:19). Not wanting to hurt so dear and near a one as his wife, a husband's love will cause him to admonish her with gentleness, to advise her with sympathy, and to correct her with sweetness and tenderness, conducting himself carefully in these things just as he desires that others would do for him. Besides that, because his love will open his eyes to see her good deeds, his heart to appreciate them, and his hands to enjoy them, so it will easily open his lips to praise them (Prov. 31:28).

---

27. Swinnock, 1:492.

Hopkins made the following observation about a husband's ill speech: "That is a wretched family, where those, who are joined in the same yoke, spurn and kick at one another. If the wife be careful in performing her duty, there belongs to her a kind and loving acceptation of it, and praise and commendation for it; or, if she sometimes should fail, she ought not to be rebuked with bitterness; but with meekness, and in such a way as the reproof should show more of sorrow than of anger. But perpetual brawlings and contentions, besides that they wholly embitter this state of life and eat out all the comfort of it, instead of preventing offenses for the future, do usually provoke and exasperate to more."[28] Therefore in summary, love will cause a husband to speak to his wife in such a way that she never doubts his love for her, but ever feels his love to be the soil from which his speech springs, the sieve through which it passes before she hears it, and the stream by which it flows unto her, all of which will motivate her to return her love to him.

Thirdly, it will cause a man to live openheartedly with his wife (Song 1:7). He will not treat her as a stranger from whom he keeps secrets and whom he ever holds in suspicion. Rather, he will pour his heart into hers and they will live together as bosom friends who share their thoughts, hopes, fears, desires, and dreams with one another. He will welcome her into his mind and be glad to know hers. He will seek her insight and wisdom in making decisions and forming plans.

Fourthly, love will cause him to live tenderly with his wife's weaknesses (1 Peter 3:7). Steele said, "his whole carriage to her should be *full* of tenderness, and composed of love and [compassion]."[29] Therefore he will not demand of her what she can never give and will wait patiently for that which she cannot give at the present time. When she labors all the day over the home, children, and shopping, he will see that she gets the rest, support, and assistance she needs and will not behave as if her work is no work at all, but will live with her in an understanding way.

Moreover, love will cause him to be a signal comfort to his wife in all her trials. None is nearer to her than he and therefore no presence is as welcome as his, no touch as soothing as his, no words as pleasant

---

28. Hopkins, 1:417–18.
29. Steele, *Puritan Sermons*, 2:288. Emphasis added.

as his, no aid as comforting and effective as his. A husband's love will therefore comfort her under her crosses, sympathize with her in her sufferings, and cheer her as best he can in the face of all difficulties.[30] In a word, out of love for his wife, a husband will show her that tenderness for which he himself humbly looks and ever receives from Christ. Christ's tenderness as *his* Husband will serve as the model and rule of the way he carries himself towards his wife as *hers*.[31]

Fifthly, love will cause him to do everything in his power to protect his wife from all danger and harm which he sees threatening her. When David's wives were captured by the Amalekites (1 Sam. 30), he raised his voice in weeping until he had no more strength to weep (v. 4), and he pursued the enemy with six hundred men and rescued them all (v. 18). Thus a husband's love will enflame his strength and cause him to put himself between his wife and danger. He will spread his cloak of protection over her as Boaz did for Ruth (Ruth 3:9) and as the Lord does for His people (Ruth 2:12; Ezek. 16:8). He will do everything he can to protect her reputation and guard her purity and sincerity (Ruth 3:14). He will be a hedge of protection about her so that whatever is aimed at her will strike him first.

A wife is compared in Scripture to a fruitful vine clinging to the side of a house for protection and support (Ps. 128:3). Hopkins wrote, "Now a vine is a weak tender plant, and requires support, and the husband should be as the houseside for her stay and support; and therefore woman was at first made of a rib taken from under the man's arm: the office of the arm is to repel and keep off injuries; which signifies unto us, that the husband ought to defend his wife from all wrong and injuries that she may be exposed unto."[32] Therefore out of love for his wife, a husband should be eager to "protect her soul from temptation, her body from harm, her name from reproach, and her person from contempt either of children, servants, or others, forasmuch as she has

---

30. Swinnock, 1:489.
31. Rogers, 221.
32. Hopkins, 1:416.

forsaken all her friends, and cast herself upon his care and kindness; and it would be unpardonable cruelty in him to desert or betray her."[33]

Sixthly, love will move him to provide faithfully for his wife's needs (Ex. 21:10). Husbands, Manton wrote, must provide "all things necessary for them that conduce to health, food and raiment, and that according to the decency and decorum of their estate; for herein they imitate the care and providence of Christ, who has provided all things for His spouse; food for their souls, garments of salvation to cover their nakedness, healing grace to cure their distempers. So must the husband do for his wife."[34] If a man fails to provide for his aging mother, Paul declares him to be worse than an unbeliever (1 Tim. 5:8). How much greater denunciation is therefore due to the Christian husband who fails to provide for his wife! Unless he would be charged as having neither the love of a husband, nor the faith of a Christian, nor the nature of a man, he must provide for his wife, giving her not only the comfort, nurture, and love she requires, but also the simple necessities and, where he justly can, the easing comforts of life (Eph. 5:29).

When a woman is married to her husband, she leaves behind the provision of her father, the nurture of her mother, and all the comfort of her friends; will he not provide for her? To whom else is she to turn if she cannot find all this provision in her husband? And does she not have every right to seek and find these things in him (Gen. 2:24; Ex. 21:10; Ruth 1:9)? A loving husband will "provide her that assistance and attendance, which is [suitable] for one who chooses to be [and] do all for [his] sake."[35] Moreover, he will do what he can, as God enables him, to provide for her a suitable maintenance when he is gone. "The love of a husband to his wife must outlast [his] life. He must not, when dying, so much remember that he is a father, as to forget that he is a husband, but [must] mind the root before the branches."[36]

---

33. Steele, *Puritan Sermons*, 2:288.
34. Manton 19:472.
35. Rogers, 227.
36. Swinnock, 1:496.

Finally, love will cause a husband to promote his wife's spiritual welfare (1 Cor. 7:16; cf. 1 Peter 3:1).[37] Though mentioned last, this must be first and primary among the husband's desires because if this is lost, all is for naught; but if this is gained, or at least sincerely and prayerfully pursued, then all the preceding is within reach and, with God's blessing, will be in hand. Christ, Paul says, came to sanctify and cleanse the church in order that He might present her to Himself as a glorious church without spot, wrinkle, or blemish, but holy (Eph. 5:26–27). Therefore as this was Christ's primary aim, so it must be the husband's (v. 28).

In his wedding sermon, Greenham charged the groom with this duty:

> You, brother, must learn hereby so to love your wife, as Christ Jesus loved His spouse His Church. That is to say, even as our Savior Christ is very patient towards it, and by little and little purges, washes, and cleanses away the corruption of it, so must you in like manner in all wisdom use the means (and with a patient mind wait for the amendment of any thing that you shall find to be amiss in your wife) that the graces of God's spirit may daily increase in her. Therefore, I charge you in the sight of God and his angels, and as you will answer unto me and the parents of this my sister, before the judgment seat of Christ, that as you receive her a virgin from her parents, so you neglect no duty whereby her salvation may be furthered, that you may present her pure and blameless, as much as in you lies, unto Jesus Christ when He shall call you to account.[38]

A husband must have his wife's spiritual welfare in his mind's eye as a compass and rule for all that he does for her. This compass is the only safe guide for the rest of his duties and to aim primarily at this is a sure way to preserve the honor of his marriage and not fall short in any of his duties. Therefore the loving husband will strive that his marriage is seen to be a Christian marriage by aiming that he and his wife walk together as fellow heirs of salvation whose primary and constant aim it is to honor God in their marriage. He will strive to see that they walk

---

37. Cf. chapter 5.
38. Greenham, 281.

together, by God's grace, as partners in grace here so that they may walk together as co-heirs of glory hereafter.[39] In this regard, the loving husband will see that he is a good example to his wife (Prov. 2:17). He will lead her in piety, charity, wisdom, and goodness, which will be the most constant and effectual lecture he can provide to her. His discourses will direct hers, wrote Steele, "his prayers will teach her to pray; his justice, temperance, and charity will be a law, a rule, a motive to make her just, sober, and charitable. If he be an atheist, an epicure, a Pharisee, it undoes her. He is to go before her; and usually she follows him either to hell or heaven."[40]

If the *ground*, the *pattern*, and the *fruitfulness* of a husband's love are as we have described and if marriage obligates a man to so fulsome a duty as love has been shown to be, then, without doubt, no man is sufficient of himself for these things. Any man who would seek to be married must first be certain that he is married to God, in whom alone is a husband's sufficiency (John 15:5), from whom he can be sure to receive it (Ezek. 36:27; Phil. 2:13; 4:19), and upon whose blessing he is entirely dependent for fruitfulness and effectiveness (Deut. 28:8–14).[41] Therefore let every man who would preserve the honor of marriage refuse to marry until he is absolutely convinced before God that he can holily, completely, singly, fervently, and enduringly love the woman of his choosing as his wife. Let every man who takes a woman in marriage see that he entirely withdraws his affections from loving anyone but her since the love required of a husband is so great and fulsome that it cannot be given to more than one. And let every man who has a wife see that he loves her not as *men* do, which falls so far short of the patterns prescribed by God, but as *Christians* should and, by God's grace, do. For the testimony of a good conscience, the veracity of his profession of faith, the delights and comforts of his marriage (which surpass all other earthly delights and comforts a man can enjoy), the honor of his marriage, and his eternal welfare, all depend upon it.

---

39. Gataker, 208.
40. Steele, *Puritan Sermons*, 2:288.
41. Cf. chapter 3.

Study Questions

1. What are the two fundamental duties of a husband? Prove them from Scripture.

2. What are the five grounds for a husband's love?

3. Which of these grounds is most persuasive to you? Why?

4. In what ways is Christ's love a pattern for a husband's love?

5. We summarize the Puritans as affirming that a husband should "seek to be an instrument in Christ's hands for his wife's growth in grace." How can he become such an instrument?

6. What can a husband learn from the way that he loves himself about how to love his wife?

7. Why are harsh words so painful when spoken from a husband to a wife?

8. What are the fruits of a husband's love?

9. Which of the fruits of a husband's love are most evident in your marriage?

10. Which of the fruits of a husband's love require the most improvement?

The Husband's Duty
of Authority

That the husband has authority over the wife is clear from Paul's directions to wives in Ephesians 5:22–24, "Wives, submit yourselves unto your own husbands, as unto the Lord. For the husband is the head of the wife, even as Christ is the head of the church: and he is the saviour of the body. Therefore as the church is subject unto Christ, so let the wives be to their own husbands in every thing." Wives are charged to submit to their husbands as those who have been given authority over them by God. Husbands are commanded by God to exercise authority over their wives as a matter of stewardship.

Sadly, however, this stewardship—or responsibility of headship—entrusted to husbands has long fallen on hard times. On the one hand, it suffers from abuse. Some husbands turn their authority into tyranny, ruling over their wives with harsh and cruel words, with threats and curses, with yelling and screaming, and even with physical abuse. God gives a husband authority to do his wife good, but these husbands pervert that authority by using it to do their wives evil. On the other hand, headship suffers from neglect. Some husbands abdicate their post and neglect their stewardship, leaving their wives unloved, unprotected, and without leadership like a body left without a head. They may know the duty expected of them but defer to their wives and neglect their high calling. Therefore, for the good of our marriages and the honor of He who joins men and women together as husbands and wives, it is vitally important that we recover a biblical understanding of the husband's headship. That recovery will be greatly furthered by an understanding of four things about the husband's authority: what it is, how it is to be maintained, its purpose, and how it is to be exercised.

What Is the Authority Entrusted to the Husband?

It is noteworthy that Ephesians 5 says nothing about a husband needing to *acquire* authority over his wife. His headship is inseparable from his status as a husband. The moment he enters into the covenant of marriage and commits himself to the role of husband, he becomes his wife's head.

Headship is therefore inseparable from marriage, but not because it originates with it. Rather, the headship possessed by a husband in marriage originates with God, who instituted marriage and assigned to both husband and wife their respective roles and responsibilities. Indeed, all authority is from God and can in no way be assumed by a creature unless delegated by God to exercise it. In Romans 13:1–2, 7, Paul says, "Let every soul be subject unto the higher powers. For there is no power but of God: the powers that be are ordained of God. Whosoever therefore resisteth the power, resisteth the ordinance of God.... Render therefore to all their dues: tribute to whom tribute is due; custom to whom custom; fear to whom fear; honour to whom honour."

Thus a husband's authority over his wife is actually God's own authority committed to the husband as God's vicegerent. The wife is charged to submit to her husband "as unto the Lord" because her submission to her husband is part of her submission to the Lord. For the wife to repudiate her husband's lawful authority is to repudiate God's authority. The husband may abdicate his authority, he may neglect it, he may abuse it, he may defile it, but he is absolutely powerless to release himself from it since it is part of what it means to be a husband. He must be faithful to exercise it or be held accountable by God for his unfaithfulness, for he has been entrusted by God with the responsibility for the woman given to him as his wife.

This divine entrustment to the husband has several implications for understanding a husband's authority. First, his authority is a *stewardship* and he is not left free to determine its outworking. As God alone can delegate such authority, so God alone has the right to determine how it will look, what it will encompass, and the manner in which it will be exercised. He has been called by God and must act for God, exercising his authority in a way that makes it clear to his wife that he too is under authority. Secondly, his authority is a *responsibility* and a man will be held accountable for how he fulfills it. "The Lord in His Word has entitled him by the name of head, wherefore he must not stand lower than the shoulders…without question it is a sin for a man to come lower than God has set him," wrote Whately.[1] On the day of judgment, when a husband stands before God to give an account of the talents entrusted to him, a large (if not the largest) part of his account will be how he behaved himself as his wife's head. Thirdly, his authority is a *trust* from God Himself. God has entrusted him with one of His own children as a wife and has authorized him to protect her, provide for her, and lead her. God has given him to her that he might be an instrument in His own hands towards her sanctification. He must care for her as an emblem of Christ's care for her, to be to her such a head that she can better see and appreciate Christ's headship over her. What a trust! Thus, the husband's authority over his wife is a stewardship, a responsibility, and a trust given to him by God who is both the Original and Exemplar of the authority he is to exercise and the one to whom the husband is directly accountable for his calling.

How Is the Husband to Maintain His Authority?

If a husband has authority over his wife and it is incumbent upon him to faithfully and honorably exercise it, then it is necessary that he behave in such a way that he not lose his authority—not that he could lose it before God, but he could lose it before his wife by causing it to be despised by her.

If the husband fails to carry himself as he should, he may lose his wife's respect, esteem, and willingness to submit herself to his headship. If he behaves as a fool she will despise him and hold herself to be wiser and better than he. If he behaves as a monster she will likewise despise him; and though she may cower in his presence, this slavish fear is not

---

1. Whately, *A Bride-Bush*, 98.

the submission required of her and beneficial to him. It is necessary to understand how a husband is to behave as head to maintain the authority entrusted to him. For only then will he enjoy a clear conscience before God in the exercise of it, and the comfortable and beneficial submission of his wife unto him for the Lord's sake. As Rogers said, "A husband, who would save the stake of his own honor, should set down that for his maxim: let not your wife despise you; for if once the woman's heart despises her husband, the whole frame of marriage is loosed."[2]

According to 1 Peter 3:7, the maintenance of a husband's authority begins with his living with his wife as a man of *understanding*—"according to knowledge"—which answers the duty of submission required of his wife. As she is to live with him in a submissive way (Eph. 5:22) so he is to live with her in a knowing and understanding way. Rogers said that the husband is "so to behave himself that he may sweetly strike into his wife's spirit a due reverential love and esteem of his person and headship, for the virtues of a husband; such [a man] as may satisfy her to be a meet guide of her life, by his gravity, stayedness, and prudence of carriage, [so] that her heart may tell her in secret, my husband is indeed a man of understanding."[3] If he walks in the pride of his heart, with an insulting and domineering spirit, he shows that he lacks the wisdom to rule himself, and she will conclude that he is ill-equipped to rule her.

Therefore the husband must dwell with his wife in such a way as to draw out her ready and willing submission to his rule, his instruction, and his leadership (Prov. 17:27).[4] First, he must renounce his own wisdom and abase himself before God in recognition of his natural inability and incapacity to manage his marriage honorably before God. He must confess the bankruptcy of his own wisdom (Prov. 30:2) and the defects and disproportion of his own abilities to be a husband and instead look to the Lord. Consider how it will endear his wife to him. Will she not more readily and gladly submit to a man whom she sees depending entirely upon God to lead her and be her head? Will she not feel herself greatly prized by him when he refuses to follow his own

---

2. Rogers, 186.
3. Rogers, 186.
4. Rogers, 189–90.

wisdom in his marriage, and looks instead to the Lord for grace to fulfill so great a responsibility and stewardship over her?

Secondly, he must submit to Christ's headship over him. He must understand that he, too, is under authority and that he must give an account of his headship over his wife to the One who is Head over him. Though he is his wife's head, he is also the servant of Christ. His wife is his equal in regards to bearing the image of God and being an heir of salvation and the grace of life (1 Peter 3:7). And will this not make the yoke of marriage easy to his wife, when she sees that her husband bears the same yoke of submission to Christ?

Thirdly, he must not neglect the responsibilities of marriage over its privileges. He should be thankful for the blessing of his marriage and for the many comforts and honors which God affords him within it, but he must zealously give himself to the duties laid upon him, and, in this regard, to promoting his wife's spiritual welfare. He must lead her and direct her to Christ who alone can sanctify her by His power (Ps. 110:3). What wife will not readily follow her husband when she sees that her spiritual welfare is his greatest interest and when she sees him giving himself diligently to so great a work?

Fourthly, he must be a man of God through and through, being guided by God's Word and filled with the Spirit manifesting the holiness of the Spirit in all his conduct. "Such a [man] first orders his own personal way of religion, conscience before God, conversation in tongue, dealings, and example before men. Then, next, he walks before his wife as a wise man ought, and he attempts not to rule others before he has the upper hand of himself. But, having begun (as physicians do sometimes) to try conclusions upon himself, then he prescribes to others."[5]

Whately's counsel on this matter is very helpful. Whately said there are two things related to a husband's headship in the home that are required of him: he is to maintain it properly and he is to use it honorably.[6] To discourage the tendency of many husbands to "yell louder" and use a heavy hand to rule over their wives, Whately began by forbidding husbands from using any force or violence, and charged them

---

5. Rogers, 190.
6. Whately, *A Bride-Bush*, 97.

instead to use wisdom and skill. He wrote, "Know therefore all you husbands, that the way to maintain authority in this society [of marriage], is not to use violence, but skill. Not by main force and by strong hand must a husband hold his own, against his wife's undutifulness; but by a more mild, gentle, and wise proceeding. Here we must take up the words of Solomon: *the excellency of a thing is wisdom*. We wish not any man to use big looks, great words, and a fierce behavior (as it were of a mankind mastiff over some silly little cur [a huge male dog over some weaker, small dog]), but we advise you to a more easy, certain, and [skillful] course."[7] Whately advised husbands to get more grace and avoid three chief faults.

First, he must endeavor to be garnished with all commendable virtues and to exceed his wife as much in goodness as he does in place.[8] Hopkins put it this way: "The right and most effectual way of keeping up this authority, is by prudence and gravity, by soberness and piety, and a [respectable], exemplary and strict life. This will cause a reverent esteem and veneration in the wife, and in the whole family."[9] Whately's argument is convincing:

> Let his wife see in him such humility, godliness, [and] wisdom, as may cause her very heart to confess that there is in him some worth and dignity, something that deserves to be stooped unto. Let him walk uprightly, Christianly, soberly, religiously, in his family, and give a good example to all in the household. Then shall the wife willingly give him the better place, when she cannot but see him to be the better person. No inferior can choose but in his soul [to] stoop to that superior in whom grace and God's image do appear according to his place. A virtuous man shall be regarded in the conscience of the worst woman, yea in the behavior also of any that is not monstrous and void of all womanhood. To be worthy [of] esteem will make one [to be] esteemed. It is no burden to any to yield themselves to such a one, as is apparently better than themselves. A godly wise carriage will draw on good respect and allure to willing subjection. Neither can any man produce an example of a husband thus qualified, that is trodden down in con-

---

7. Whately, *A Bride-Bush*, 99–100.

8. Whately, *A Bride-Bush*, 100.

9. Hopkins, 1:419.

tempt [by his wife]. If a Prince commend a coward to the place of a Captain, his soldiers soon [discover] it, and scorn him; but if he has courage and sufficiency for the charge, though they may be mutinous, yet he shall hold his respect amongst them. It is true, that (in a mad fit) the wife of the best husband may fling forth and be undutiful; but when that fit shall be past, and she is returned to herself again, [she] shall condemn herself and justify him; and so instead of losing his authority, he recovers his own with good advantage. Be you therefore all assured, that you shall find virtuous and good carriage [to be] the best preservatives of good account. These awe the heart, these command reverence, these offer themselves to the mind with an honorable kind of gravity, and will not suffer the man (in whom they be) to be long spurned at. Take pains to make yourself [godly] and that is the most compendious way to make yourself reverenced.[10]

Thus the first thing required of a husband is that he get more grace from God to walk faithfully as a husband and therefore be worthy of his wife's esteem and submission. To be sure, the Lord requires her submission *regardless* of how well or faithfully he behaves himself as head;[11] but it should be the husband's desire to make her submission easy by walking worthy of it and faithfully in it. He should labor that his wife should not only submit to him in body, but in spirit and with all cheer, just as the church should submit to Christ. Majesty, authority, and venerableness, said Bolton, "is not any ways more lessened or sooner lost [by the husband] than by light behavior, personal worthlessness, or unworthy deportment in his place. Whereas true worth, goodness, grace, shining from within, do beget a more loving reverence and reverent love, than all outward forms of pomp and state, than any boisterous or big looks can possibly produce."[12] And Hopkins adds: "Where there is an excellent mixture of prudence and piety together, the one to be a guide, and the other to be an example, these will make a man truly aweful and reverend; and induce the wife and the whole family to esteem and imitate him."[13]

---

10. Whately, *A Bride-Bush*, 100–1.
11. Cf. chapter 7.
12. Bolton, 270.
13. Hopkins, 1:419.

Secondly, Whately said the husband must shun and abandon three disgraceful evils that always cause a man to appear base and vile in the eyes of others.[14] These three evils are bitterness, unthriftiness, and levity. The husband must put off those sins which, in his wife's estimation, lower him from his place and cast his mantle in the mud, and instead put on those Christian virtues which draw out her ready and hearty submission to him as one whom she delights to follow and to whom she delights to entrust herself for protection and provision.

The first of these evils, from Colossians 3:19, is *bitterness*. Paul charges husbands that they "be not bitter" with their wives because it stands opposed to the love charged upon them. "He must never imagine that a rude insolence, or perpetual bitterness, is either the way to keep or use his authority aright."[15] Bitterness is marked by sharp, sour, and hurtful behavior as well as railing, reviling, rebuking, and furious speech. Bitter words cut and wound the heart; bitter words carry anger and hatred along with them; bitterness taints the touch with resentment and leaves behind a trail of contempt; and bitterness separates and makes enemies of friends. Such bitterness in a husband will invite contempt for him and his rule and undermine his authority because his wife will grow weary of his painful headship.[16] The husband's authority becomes unbearable.[17] Therefore he must put away all bitterness towards his wife and remember that she is as his own self and that no one ever hated his own self (Eph. 5:28–29).

The second evil to be avoided is *prodigality* or *unthriftiness*. Whately had in mind that despicable vice found in the fool so often described in Proverbs, which leads a person to waste and squander the things entrusted to him. This is a vice in any man, but especially in a husband upon whose prudent management and thrift his family depends. The unthriftiness that a husband must shun includes drunkenness, gambling, and bad company. By drunkenness a husband drowns his wit and banishes his reason. He clouds his own mind and blurs his vision

---

14. Whately, *A Bride-Bush*, 101.
15. Steele, *Puritan Sermons*, 2:290.
16. Whately, *A Bride-Bush*, 102.
17. Ambrose, 235.

of the pathway set for his feet in Scripture. How can a husband lead and rule his wife honorably and faithfully without his reason? By gambling a husband consumes his wealth and depletes his provision. He throws away what God gave him for the good of his wife and family, spending it riotously as did the prodigal son (Luke 15). How can a husband protect his wife from harm and want and provide for her according to his marriage vows without his wealth and estate? By keeping bad company a husband loses his good name and sullies his good character (1 Cor. 15:33). Moreover, by inviting their counsel into his heart and mind, he will soon be so convinced of their ways and values that he will settle himself comfortably in their paths (Ps. 1:1). How can a husband instruct his wife in good or correct his wife's evil actions when his judgment is blinded, his conscience is seared, his character is vilified, and he himself stands in need of instruction and correction? (1 Cor. 14:35; Heb. 5:12)? Therefore, Whately wrote,

> He that follows [this vice] must needs forfeit at once his wit, his wealth, and his estimation. Contempt will come upon him as swiftly and irresistibly as poverty that ruinates at once his soul, body, name, family, posterity, by seeking to please his inordinate appetite and burying his reason in sensuality. Never did unthrift keep his place [any] more than his money. Honor and wealth run from him both at once; for who can regard him that will needs make himself worth nothing? Our English calls thriftiness good husbandry, and a thrifty husband a good husband, as if it were the chief part…of a good husband's duty to be thrifty. Wherefore away with drinking, gambling, and following riotous companions, if you would not be cast at once out of the hearts of all your family, and all your neighbors, and of your wife also, both for love and reverence.[18]

The third and final evil to be avoided by the husband is *levity*. Whately had in mind a kind of puerile behavior that always wants to play and seems to care little for work and personal responsibilities. Of course, recreation is warranted by Scripture as necessary to refresh both the body and the mind. We all need time to relax and refresh our-

---

18. Whately, *A Bride-Bush*, 103–4.

selves, but when recreation encroaches on the time we should give to our daily work and to "good husbanding" (Eph. 5:15–16), we become guilty of this sin of levity, or failing to take our responsibilities seriously. Whately concluded his warning against bitterness, prodigality, and levity with these words: "Such men will soon displace themselves, though no man strive to undermine them. But let every godly man abhor and cast from him all these base evils, and strive for holiness and gravity of conversation, [so that] he may be indeed a governor, and that his superiority (supported by such pillars) may stand upright and unshaken, and not be cast down flat into the dust of contempt and dis-reverence."[19]

What Is the Purpose of the Husband's Authority?

Why is the husband entrusted by God with authority over his wife? Is the wife incapable of ruling herself? It is critical that we understand this point. Both the husband's proper use of his authority and the wife's proper submission to him depend largely on the answers to these questions.

To put it simply, the husband's authority is *for his wife's good* and not for any lack of good in her. The woman is not a lesser or inferior person. She is made in the same image of God as the man (Gen. 1:27) and is a joint-heir with him of eternal life (1 Peter 3:7). Manton observed, "Though Christianity does not abolish those distinctions which are between master and servant, and the distinction of the one sex above the other, yet they all have the same communion in the merits and grace of Christ. They make up one mystical spiritual body, whereof Christ is the head and husband, as being heirs of the same grace of life (1 Peter 3:7). Because of their equality in partaking in spiritual and eternal privileges, the wife is no less dear to God than [husbands] themselves are."[20]

To be sure, we may rightly argue for the husband's headship from: the order of creation (that Adam was made first, 1 Tim. 2:13), the means of creation (woman was made from man, 1 Cor. 11:8), the occasion of creation (woman was made for man, Gen. 2:18; 1 Cor. 11:9), and the

---

19. Whately, *A Bride-Bush*, 104.
20. Manton, 19:469.

deception of Eve in the fall when she behaved *independently* of both her God and her husband (Gen. 3:4–5; 1 Tim. 2:14), because all of these are biblical reasons for a husband's headship over his wife. But we cannot argue for the husband's headship from any inequality between a man and a woman. Therefore we do well to answer all objections and prevent rebellion with the simple fact that it has pleased God to establish the husband as head over his wife (Gen 3.16; 1 Cor. 11:3). If it pleases God for the husband to rule over his wife with authority as her head, then how can it not please the husband and the wife who want nothing more than to do the will of God and enjoy that happiness which He has inseparably tied to obedience and enjoy that honor which He placed upon marriage?

But our gracious God has been pleased to pull back the curtain on His ways and tell us why it pleases Him and why it should also please us: because it is for the wife's good. When God, in His infinite wisdom and immeasurable kindness, was determined to do the wife good, He placed her under her husband's authority and charged her to submit to him as unto the Lord in everything (Eph. 5:24). The purpose or end of the husband's authority, Whately said, is "the good of his wife…the making her better, and helping her to [enjoy] comfort here, and salvation hereafter; even in [a] better manner than she could be helped to without a husband."[21]

What this means in regards to our opening question is very simple. Since Christ uses His headship as the Savior of His church to do her eternal good, the husband must therefore use his Christlike headship to do his wife all the good he can.

Moreover, according to the husband's charge from God in Ephesians 5:25–29, whatever headship he has is defined by and shut up within the boundaries of love. Rather than charging the husband to rule over his wife, Paul charges him to love his wife. Paul is bridling the husband's authority with the bit of love, lest it break out of bounds in sin, by showing him that there is no place for tyranny, oppression, or cruelty. His headship is for her good and it is in the very exercise of it,

---

21. Whately, *A Bride-Bush*, 109.

and not in contradiction to it, that he expresses his love for her. Thus she should be better for his headship and leadership, not worse. The headship of the man, wrote Rogers, "is given him not to discourage or destroy, but to direct, benefit, and build up the wife."[22] The power and authority entrusted to the husband is what Manton called "a great servitude"[23] because it is of so great a benefit to his wife.

Whately commented on the great benefit of a husband's rule:

> All governors have their power from God, rather for the benefit of them whom they govern, than for their own ease, pleasure, profit, or for the fulfilling of their own desires. The King rules that the people may enjoy more happiness by his scepter than they could without it. And every Magistrate keeps his place for the safety and welfare of the subjects under him.... So the Minister exercises spiritual jurisdiction...for the spiritual commodity of his flock.... The not knowing why they govern makes husbands govern amiss and so become burdens to themselves and their wives. He that shoots at a wrong mark cannot but shoot awry from the right; and he must needs take a wrong way that mistakes the town to which he should travel.... Wherefore a husband should often demand of himself, saying: "Why am I the chief in this household? and why does the government lie on my shoulders? Is it that I should live at more ease than any in my family? that I should fulfill my own wishes? and have what I would? and that every one should care for me, and I for none? No; for the head in the body was not created for its own sake; and I would count him an evil Magistrate and Minister that should bewray such a conceit in his place. But here I am the chief, that all may fare the better for me, that by my using more wisdom, and taking more pains, and showing more virtues than any of the family, all the family may live more orderly and comfortably (and especially my wife) may enjoy more quiet, and get more grace, than could be attained, if I were away. The fruit of my ruling my wife must be her comfort and happiness; neither must I account any happiness to myself, wherein she has not her portion." So by often informing himself to what purpose he rules, he shall exceedingly help himself to rule well.[24]

---

22. Rogers, 218–19.
23. Manton, 19:430.
24. Whately, *A Bride-Bush*, 109–11.

This beneficial service of a husband to his wife as her head has already been laid out above under the consideration of the pattern and fruitfulness of a husband's love, so we need not repeat its details here. Because love and authority are so intertwined that a husband's love is a governing love and his authority is a loving governance, whether we speak of the reaches and outlets of a husband's love or of the reaches and outlets of the husband's authority, we arrive at the same point.

Yet we would note this: whereas a husband's love *compels* him to do his wife good, a husband's authority *enables* him to. In a sense, his headship empowers his love; it puts hands and feet, as it were, on the love he has for his wife. Gouge therefore described the husband's authority as a branch of his love.[25] He therefore wrote that "if then a husband relinquishes his authority, he disables himself from doing that good, and showing those fruits of love which otherwise he might. If he abuse his authority, he turns the edge and point of his sword amiss; instead of holding it over his wife for her protection, he turns it into her bowels to her destruction, and so manifests thereby more hatred than love."[26] The husband's authoritative headship is the means by which God enables a husband to love his wife according to His command. Therefore it is *after* appointing the husband as the wife's head (Eph. 5:24) that the Scripture calls upon the husband to love his wife (v. 25). Without authority over his wife a man cannot be faithful to the duties incumbent upon him as a husband, duties summed up in the charge to *love* her as Christ loves His church. Thankfully, the Lord has linked authority and love together, graciously joining the enabling and the calling in one husband.

How Is the Husband to Exercise His Authority?

In addition to what has been said so far, the Puritans universally recognized another dimension of the husband's authority which needs to be addressed in order to help husbands be faithful to their duties before God and thereby preserve the honor of their marriages. That dimension was how the husband was to lovingly and yet faithfully exercise his authority over his wife. Surely his wife is not to be treated as a child or a

---

25. Gouge, 254.
26. Gouge, 254.

servant and yet he clearly has responsibility over her before God as her head. If a husband is to love his wife as Christ loves His church, then it must involve guiding her into the paths of righteousness and keeping her out of the paths of wickedness. But *how* is this to be done? The Puritan answer to this question is a twofold duty of *directing* and *recompensing*.

Before we unfold this duty it is important to see that this was addressed in the husband's duties as a way of providing the necessary counterpart to the wife's responsibility before God to submit to her husband *in everything* (Eph. 5:24; Col. 3:18). If the wife is to submit in everything then the husband's authority covers everything. But may he then command anything he wants without regard to the Lord's commandments, and would she be bound to obey? Does his position give him free reign to direct her according to his heart's desires without regard to the Lord's headship over him? On the other hand, if his headship encompasses her spiritual wellbeing, then can he stand idle and say nothing when she goes astray? If God will hold him accountable to do what he can to see that those committed to his charge walk in His ways, then should he say nothing to her and not lovingly correct her when she turns into the ways of sin? Furthermore, should he not commend her and lovingly encourage her when she does well?

These are the sorts of questions that the Puritans addressed with this duty. On the one hand, they wanted to guard against the husband's abuse of his authority. If he has the authority to command his wife then he must do so to the glory of God. On the other hand, they wanted to equip the husband to be the kind of domestic governor and head that actually benefits a wife by guiding her into and strengthening her in the practice of all virtue, as well as by directing her away from and helping her in the reformation of all vices.

Whately wrote more extensively about this matter than did any other Puritan. He described the Puritans' intention behind this duty when he wrote: "We will direct husbands how they shall rule, so as to weaken every corruption and strengthen every virtue they shall meet with in their wives, and to make their lives ten times more holy and happy than else they could be, and to give them just cause (which is the most desirable thing that can be in government) of hearty praising the name of God for their meeting together in marriage."[27] If we can keep this commendable intention in mind in what follows then we will not only appreciate this contribution of the Puritans to the husband's duties but we will put ourselves in a far more likely position to apply their counsel to our own marriages and reap the benefits which countless marriages before us have enjoyed by applying it.

Consider therefore the first part of this duty, *directing* or *commanding*. There are three things with regard to a husband's authority to direct his wife. First, the husband must learn to direct his wife not as the chief and absolute commander over her, but as one who himself stands under God's power—a power to which he owes far more subjection than his wife owes to him. Therefore he has no right to command his wife to do things that are contrary to what God's government over him authorizes him to do, for this would be an abuse of his authority. "Where God commands, he must not forbid; what God forbids, he must not command."[28] He has no right to expect her to yield to his demands when he has exceeded his commission and the bounds of his place by requiring of her that which God forbids. In such a case he shows himself to be a foolish husband to his wife and a rebellious head under his God. "Let no husband therefore forget that the Lord in heaven, and the public Magistrate on earth, are above both him and his wife, and that they both ought equally to be subject to both these; and therefore let him never set his private authority against these authorities that are stronger than his; nor make his wife undutiful to either of these, by a false claim of duty to himself."[29]

If a husband commands his wife to lie in order to protect his own reputation, or to break the Lord's Day for his monetary gain, or to participate in fraud and deceit for his financial advancement, he has transgressed the limits of his place and if his wife yields to him then she shares in his guilt. Likewise, if a husband forbids his wife to pray, or to attend upon the Word and Sacraments on the Lord's Day, or to read her Bible, he abuses his authority over her. Whately concluded this first

---

27. Whately, *A Bride-Bush*, 112.
28. Whately, *A Bride-Bush*, 114.
29. Whately, *A Bride-Bush*, 115.

point with the following charge: "See then (all you husbands) that your words to your wives hold agreement with the Laws of God…else you govern not, but tyrannize. And to disobey you is the best obedience; or rather to withdraw one's self from following your ill ordered directions is not to deny subjection to your place, power, and persons, but to your sins, lusts, and corruptions."[30]

Second, the husband must exercise his authority with wisdom from above, a main part of which is to conform his exercise to his wife's disposition. To do this he must be thoroughly acquainted with his wife's temperament and constitution (1 Peter 3:7). For example, if his wife is easily provoked and quickly overcome with anger then it would behoove him to do what he can to avoid provoking her. If his wife tends to be easily overwhelmed by the burden of the week's demands at home and with the children, then it would be wise for the husband to do what he can on the weekend to relieve his wife. All in all, the intent is to know his wife so well that he dwells with her in an understanding way, doing what he can to moderate and accommodate his government according to her nature. "While most men will do as their neighbors do, and look that their wives should do as their neighbors' wives [do], they fill their houses with contention. Yea, many, while they follow their own passions and run as their present mood drives them forward, do utterly overthrow the peace of their families, because they will not do and speak what is fittest for their wives' estate, but what holds most agreement to their own [desires]."[31] Bolton therefore charged husbands to dwell with their wives according to knowledge "by a wise discovery at the first, and timely acquainting himself with her disposition, affections, infirmities, passions, imperfections."[32]

Third, the husband must be careful *not* to exercise his authority in hurtful ways. One, he must not micromanage trivial and inconsequential things as if his own hand needs to be at the helm in every little matter in the home. Many matters should be and are best committed to the wife's care and charge. She has been given to him to be his helpmate

---

30. Whately, *A Bride-Bush*, 116.
31. Whately, *A Bride-Bush*, 132.
32. Bolton, 273.

(Gen. 2:18) and it is demeaning to her and harmful to himself if he does not let her be that help, especially in the home where many of her gifts come to beautiful fruition. If he will be both husband and housewife, said Whately, "and be dealing with brewing and baking, and washing, and the particularities of these and the like business; it will come to pass that his wife can be helpful in nothing, because he engrosses all things into his own hand."[33] Whately continued, "In these things therefore, he should permit his wife to rule under him, and give her leave to know more than himself, who has weightier matters…more nearly touching the welfare of his household, to exercise his knowledge in. And if in any of these matters he shall meet with any disorder, it were a part of wisdom in him to advise and counsel rather than to charge and command."[34]

Two, he must not command things that are unreasonable and ridiculous. Rather, he must use his authority in a way that shows him to be prudent and thoughtful. It is true that the wife's desire to submit to her husband in everything as unto the Lord (Eph. 5:22–24) should make her willing to do whatever pleases her husband so long as it is lawful before God; but it is also true that the husband should not command her to do things for no other reason than to prove himself to be her head. To exercise his authority in this way would show that he cares little to possess his wife's heart and only cares to govern her body. On the other hand, if the things he commands are not only reasonable to his wife but carry with them the authority of God, to whom they are both subject, then she will be most willing to do it.

Lest this counsel be misunderstood, two words of caution are in order. The first caution, said Whately, is that the commanding part of a husband's government should be *rarely used*. "A garment that comes upon a man's back every day will soon be threadbare; so will a man's authority be worn out with overmuch use. Wherefore, let it be kept in, till due occasions of using it do call it forth."[35] Furthermore, when he feels that he must command or forbid an action, let him see that his authority is not exercised in a way that it calls his love into question, but

---

33. Whately, *A Bride-Bush*, 151.
34. Whately, *A Bride-Bush*, 151–52.
35. Whately, *A Bride-Bush*, 154.

rather that his love will be most on display, even if his wife only realizes it later when she is of a better mind. Be very seldom in laying any command upon your wife, said Scudder; "an intimation of what you would have done is enough between a husband and a wife; entreaties of a wife do not unbecome a husband…and usually they do more prevail than flat commands. Frequency and imperiousness in commands of one so near in equality will make your authority burdensome and grievous unto her and will much abate in her (do what she can) of that honor and reverence which she should and would give unto you."[36]

The second caution is this: the husband must avoid all severity and sternness in his commanding and ever unite his commands with the Christlike virtue of *mildness*. Mildness, or gentleness, Whately said, is "the sweet sauce of this government, which causes, that it shall not prove over-tart and sour for the wife's palate. This is the soft lining of this yoke, which keeps the hardness thereof from being felt; and without which it will be insupportable. No woman can endure her husband's government with comfort, if gentleness does not temper it."[37] If pastors are to correct their opponents with gentleness (2 Tim. 2:24–25) then surely husbands are to govern their wives, with whom they are one flesh, with gentleness. And if we are commanded to be gentle with all men (Titus 3:2), then how much more ought husbands to be gentle with their wives?

Consider how this mildness relates to both the matter and manner of the husband's commanding. With regard to the *matter*, his mildness should be manifest in two ways. First, he must not extend the use of his commanding authority too far. Out of confidence in his wife's gifts, strengths, and love for him, a husband is to show himself to be "of a kind and free nature, not rigorously taking upon him to command all he may, but willingly gratifying his wife in some, in many, in most things, that she may less unwillingly, yea, and with more cheerfulness, be subject unto him in other things."[38]

---

36. Scudder, 94–95.
37. Whately, *A Bride-Bush*, 156.
38. Whately, *A Bride-Bush*, 157–58.

The more willing he is to allow her to govern those matters entrusted to her, the more willing she will be to submit to him in those matters entrusted to him as her head. "A man should find his wife ten times more [obedient] if he would be but easy in exacting duty, than any rigor could make her. And much more quietly will she obey, when she sees herself not pressed to a kind of unmeasurable obedience, than otherwise she can bring her heart unto."[39] In conclusion, said Whately, "Let not a husband be like churlish [rude] Nabal to his wife, but rather follow…holy patterns of husbandly mildness, which will beget at once both love and reverence, [and will] both testify kindness and procure it. He that will be Lord in everything stretches the string of his authority so high that it is…in danger of breaking, and causing that at length he shall be Lord in nothing."[40]

Second, the husband must show mildness by not demanding of his wife those things which he knows are hard and difficult for her to do. He finds, even with himself, that while there are things required of him which he delights to do and does with ease because they come so naturally to him, there are some things which are so hard and painful to do that he is almost unwilling to do them and will sometimes plead to be exempted from those tasks. Likewise, there are things that he himself simply cannot do and therefore needs others to do them for him. With that in mind, if he would exercise his authority over his wife with mildness and gentleness, he must refrain from requiring and insisting upon those things which he knows she finds very difficult to do or which he knows she cannot do. "You must not put her upon anything, but according to her strength and abilities; you must support her weakness by your strength, and supply her defects by your wisdom," charged Scudder.[41] "A good husband must take heed of breaking the back of his wife's obedience, with requiring hard things at her hand [which] she cannot without much ado perform."[42]

---

39. Whately, *A Bride-Bush*, 158.
40. Whately, *A Bride-Bush*, 159.
41. Scudder, 91.
42. Whately, *A Bride-Bush*, 160.

With regard to the *manner* of his commanding, the husband must see that if and when he must command things of his wife that he does so not arrogantly and in a domineering manner, but entreatingly and tenderly. He must so lovingly and kindly lay his commands upon his wife that she feels nothing of their weight upon her *shoulders* but only their gentle tug at her *heart*. "When need requires that some commandment be given," said Whately, "it must not be imperiously prescribed, in the heat and extremity of charging and enforcing words, but with a sweet instinct of kindness...with loving persuasions and familiar requests."[43]

Now it may be that his wife is prone to be stubborn and disagreeable and submits begrudgingly to the things he must require of her. In such a case a husband may be tempted to "yell louder" and "slam more doors" in order to assert his authority. However, the chances are good that he will find more happiness and greater effectiveness in overcoming his wife's anger and resistance by a mild and tender authority, for "the quieter way is more comfortable [to her], and the more husbandlike."[44] It prevents her resistance, Whately said, when he requests when he might have enjoined. "There is nothing to strive for, when a man does not (as it were) vaunt...his authority; things are also best done when the will is allured, rather than the body compelled. If you stand upon it highly, and come with, 'You shall, and I will make you,'...and the like big words, the heart will go against that which the hand performs; and you shall be inwardly disliked, though obeyed in show. And if [her] obedience come not from the heart, how can it last long? The way then to prevail with least burden to [the wife], and toil to [the husband], is with mild words to wish this or that, rather than with imperious phrases to enjoin it."[45] Unless absolute necessity requires an insistence, let him see that he uses mildness in his commands and fills his mouth with such words as, "Good wife, I pray you, let it be so; I entreat you, do me the kindness to do this or this,"[46] for this will procure him a more happy home, marriage, and wife.

---

43. Whately, *A Bride-Bush*, 161.
44. Whately, *A Bride-Bush*, 162.
45. Whately, *A Bride-Bush*, 162–63.
46. Whately, *A Bride-Bush*, 163.

The second part of this important duty is *recompensing*. There are two sides to recompensing: the positive side in which the husband commends his wife for well doing, and the negative side in which the husband lovingly reproves his wife when she does amiss. First, the husband must see that good deeds are recompensed with praise and gratitude. In Proverbs 31, we read that the exemplary wife is not only praised by her husband for her good works (vv. 28–29), but also in the gates where the townsfolk meet and converse (v. 31). Of course the glory for her works must be given to God who works in her to will and to do for His good pleasure, enabling her to walk in the good works which He prepared beforehand (Phil. 2:13; Eph. 2:10); but it takes nothing from the Lord her God when her husband recognizes and commends her for her faithfulness and kindness to him as the wife given him by God to do him good (Gen. 2:18).

How else is she to know whether or not she pleases him if he never commends her or shows his appreciation for her? How else is she to know the good he seeks from her if he never marks it by his happy recognition? Therefore the husband must make a point of praising her when she pleases him. Not only will this commendation be a blessing to his wife to see that she brings her husband the good which God intended for him, but it will encourage her all the more to do good to him. In fact, she may find herself seeking out ways to do him more good than he ever asked for or imagined. His commendation will nourish and cultivate her dutiful service and submission before the Lord and encourage her to be that excellent wife who surpasses all others by the effect her fear of God has on her marriage (Prov. 31:29–30).

Whately described the duty in this way: "A man must give his wife to understand, by words of comfortable approbation, what good contentment he takes in her good and dutiful behavior. He must animate and encourage her to a perpetuity of pleasing and loyal [conduct] by some special courtesies, as gifts or the like, in which he knows that she will most delight; for the cheerful countenance, amiableness, affableness, and liberality of the husband is to the good wife a cause of as great a contentment as anything in the world, next to the favor of God."[47]

Moreover, when the husband is to recompense his wife for the good she has done, he must see that he not ruin the gift given by the manner in which he gives it. For example, if his praises are given coldly and his gifts are given begrudgingly then she will see less of his kindness than she feels of his coldness, and whatever good his recompensing may have done for their relationship, the manner in which he gave it will cause the opposite to occur. Whately therefore warned husbands, "Let not the distemper of your passions overthrow the fruit of your kindness; and make not things sweet in themselves to become bitter by mixing your gall and [bad temper] with them."[48]

On the negative side of the husband's recompensing, the husband must lovingly reprove his wife when she has done amiss. At first this may seem out of place. Is it even healthy in a marriage? Should not the great love he has for her overlook all her faults and leave her in the hands of God who alone can work in her heart and bring about change? These objections sound plausible, but they miss an important element of the love of a husband which they presume to be advocating. According to Matthew 18, it is because of Christ's love for His people that He leaves the ninety-nine and goes after the one who went astray (vv. 10–14); and it is because of love for our brother that we go to him when he wrongs us and tell him his fault in order that he might repent and our fellowship might be restored (v. 15). The point is clear: love does not leave a brother in sin. Love pursues the loved one with a heart of forgiveness; love seeks to recover, restore, and redeem. To leave a brother in sin, to see a brother go astray and say nothing, to see a brother harm himself with transgression and not try to recover him, or to see a brother in danger because of his sin and do nothing to prevent it is not to love him, but to hate him.

John declares in 1 John 3:14–18, "We know that we have passed from death unto life, because we love the brethren. He that loveth not his brother abideth in death. Whosoever hateth his brother is a mur-

---

47. Whately, *A Bride-Bush*, 125.
48. Whately, *A Bride-Bush*, 164.

derer: and ye know that no murderer hath eternal life abiding in him. Hereby perceive we the love of God, because he laid down his life for us: and we ought to lay down our lives for the brethren. But whoso hath this world's good, and seeth his brother have need, and shutteth up his bowels of compassion from him, how dwelleth the love of God in him? My little children, let us not love in word, neither in tongue; but in deed and in truth." Christian love exercised towards a sinning brother reflects Christ's Good Shepherd and Good Samaritan love which He exercises towards His sinning sheep. It pursues the fallen with a heart of compassion. It extends a helping hand in an effort to lift him up from his sin (Jude 23). It refuses to forsake the fallen. Love treats the brother's sin as sin and calls it what it is, urging him to forsake it, but it also treats the brother as a brother, doing what it can to facilitate and be instrumental in his recovery and return (Matt. 18:15–17, 21–22).

Now if this is the case between brothers, then how much more should this be the case between husband and wife, who are closer than brothers ever could be? The two of them have become one flesh. When a husband loves his wife he loves himself (Eph. 5:28–29). If a brother may not let another brother go astray, then neither may a husband let his wife go astray. Rather, he must love her as Christ loves His church whom He relentlessly and tirelessly pursues when she goes astray (Hos. 2:5–7, 14–15). Therefore it is not a question of *whether* the husband has this authority and responsibility; rather, as with his directing, it is a question of *how* he is to exercise it. Bolton therefore directed the husband to "with all holy discretion, apply and address himself in a fair and loving manner to rectify and reform all he can, and to bear the rest with patience, passing by it without passion and impatience, still waiting upon God by prayer, in His good time, for a further and more full redress and conformity."[49]

The Puritans were very sensitive to the proper exercise of this duty and offered five guidelines. First of all, the husband must not reprove where there is no fault. The whole purpose of correction is to help the offender see and reform her offense. "No good surgeon will lay a [ban-

---

49. Bolton, 273.

dage] upon a sound place. That [is] always a needless labor [and] most times dangerous, for some medicines will make the sound flesh sore. So neither must a husband find fault where no fault is, for fear of making a fault where none else would be,"[50] said Whately. He may indeed reprove where God has been dishonored, but he has no authority to reprove where no wrong has been done. Scudder strongly warned husbands to "be sure that there be a fault, and a great fault in her, else reprove her not—lesser failings may be healed and amended, either of themselves, or by a bare [reminding] her of them; many failings you are not to take notice of, and are to bear with in her, as she must do the like with you."[51]

Second, he must not reprove his wife for that which she has already reformed. A fault reformed should be forgiven and treated as no fault at all since it has been amended and, as it were, annihilated. It is harmful to the marriage if the husband reproves or corrects when his wife has already been cured by amendment, repentance, and reformation. When a sin is left off and repented of, Whately explained,

> It is dead and buried. Why then should any man go about to poison himself and another, with raking the dead carcass out of the dead sepulchre? Indeed former faults may justly be alleged, to aggravate the same offense reiterated or fallen into again; but if the wife do not repeat her sin in committing, the husband shall deal exceedingly unjustly if he repeat it in reproving. God promises that if the sinful man do cast away his sinful deeds, he will also blot them out of his remembrance and bury them as in the bottom of the sea. Why should man remember what God has forgotten? Doubtless therefore it is an ill memory that will recall those things, which God would have buried in deepest silence, and repeat that which He promises not once to mention. To hit a penitent sinner in the teeth is a manifest iniquity.[52]

Third, he must measure his reproof by the offense. The husband who measures his reproofs by his mood, his anger, by the loss suffered, or by the pain caused wrongs his wife and forgets the purpose of his reproofs. Just as the bandage must be fitted to the wound and the medi-

---

50. Whately, *A Bride-Bush*, 120.
51. Scudder, 95–96.
52. Whately, *A Bride-Bush*, 121–22.

cine measured by the sickness, so his reproof and correction must be fitted to the sin committed. A sin of ignorance is not to be reproved as if it were a sin of blatant rebellion. A sin of weakness is not to be reproved as if it were a sin of resistance—in some cases, a sin may even need to be passed over in silence. Neither is a sin of arrogant rebellion to be ignored as if it were an excusable weakness.

Whately offered the following advice: "if any man would know a sure rule for the compounding of this medicine, let him take this.... A small sin must be lightly passed over, though it bring a great loss with it; a great sin must have more sharpness, though instead of loss it procured profit. As the cause of reproving must be the breach of God's commandment, not the crossing of the husband in pleasure or profit, or the like; so the measure of earnestness and sharpness therein must be taken from the measure of the sin against God."[53] Baxter put it this way: "the husband must be strongest in family patience, bearing with the weakness and passions of the wife, not to make light of any sin against God, but so as not to make a great matter of any frailty against him, and so to preserve the love and peace that is the natural temper of their relation."[54] In short, where no sin has been committed, no reproof can be given; but where a sin has been committed and reproof must be given, let it be measured by God's account of the sin and not man's.[55]

Fourth, when the husband feels that he must reprove his wife and urge her to return to the ways of truth and righteousness, he must wisely and carefully choose a *fit time* and a *fit place*. There are times which are unsuitable and unseasonable for reproving. We have all appreciated the love of that parent or brother who wisely sought out and patiently waited for the right time to reprove us for our sins. We all remember the pain caused by an untimely reproof which someone brought to us or which we brought to another. A husband must therefore carefully and prayerfully seek out a seasonable time and seasonable place for reproving lest his efforts to heal the wound serve only to aggravate it. It must be a time when he is ready to reprove and when she is ready to be

---

53. Whately, *A Bride-Bush*, 124.
54. Baxter, 154.
55. Cf. Westminster Shorter Catechism, Q. 83.

reproved. Whately therefore offered two rules to help determine when this time is.

Rule 1: The husband should be calm and free from anger, grief, or any other such emotion which might cloud either his thinking or his speaking. As long as a husband's anger fills his heart he is to forbear reproving his wife, for "a man that is hot and burning with the violence of wrath…will reprove for that, which after the fit is over, his own heart will say deserved no reproof; and he will do all things with such… indecent, unsavory speeches and gestures as will utterly mar…all his actions."[56] Whately continued, "In wrath a man shall speak, not what is fit for the occasion, but what is agreeable to his passion; not what the matter requires, but what his ill affected heart carries him to…. It cannot be wisdom for a man to set about a business, wherein the use of wisdom is needful, at such times as he has lost his wisdom…. A man is out of his wits in these fits; for anger is a short madness [and] how can a mad man rule well?"[57] Therefore, whenever a husband feels the fire of his anger burning in his own heart, he is in no shape to reprove others, but must take himself aside and quench his own fire with repentance and mortification before God before endeavoring to reprove his wife for her fault (Prov. 14:29). He must wrestle with his anger, his bitterness, his unforgiveness, and whatever else will clog the wheels of his judgment and cause him to disgrace his own authority by reproving where there may be no fault, or by reproving his wife for the speck in her eye while the beam of his own sin sticks out of his eye (Matt. 7:1–5).

Rule 2: The husband must chose a time when his wife is capable of receiving reproof, when she herself is also calm and free from anger, grief, and the like. If anger will prevent his ability to give reproof, then surely it will preclude her ability to receive it. If he needs a clear and calm heart to address the wrong, then she also needs a clear and calm heart to admit the wrong. "Due time and place must be observed when you reprove and admonish your wife; you must not do it when either yourself or your wife is in a pelting chafe, or passion, for then you are

---

56. Whately, *A Bride-Bush*, 135.
57. Whately, *A Bride-Bush*, 136.

not fit to give, nor she fit to receive reproof…; while men and women are in passion they are not themselves."[58]

But what should a husband do if his wife fails to receive his correction and instead counters it with angry railing? Whately gave this counsel: "Better that she speak last, than both speak foolishly; and better that she talk alone, than that you, by talking, should be cast into the same frenzy. For it is extremely difficult to take with an angry body and not grow hot for company. Walk not with an angry man (said Solomon), lest you learn his ways [Prov. 22:24–25]."[59] As wisdom must guide the husband in choosing a fit time for reproof, so wisdom must teach him when to say nothing. Even if he finds himself on the receiving end of his wife's ranting, unless he would be counted as a fool for not holding his own words in, he must be quiet, patient, and bear with his wife's infirmity until he can help her with it at a calmer hour. "Wherefore, as you look that every other thing should be fit to receive the things that you would put into them, the vessel the liquor, the ground the seed, the chest the clothes, the house the guest…; so take care that your wife's heart be fit to entertain your directions or admonitions, and that there be room for them in her mind, before you send them there for lodging. Look that she be quiet, well-pleased, pacified; not leavened with wrath, or embittered with grief, or soured with discontent. Every man is a fool in his fits of passion, and Solomon has spoken it once for all, *Speak not in the ears of a fool: for he will despise the wisdom of thy words* [Prov. 23:9]."[60]

The husband must also choose the best place. And as a rule, the best place is a secret place. Christ's own rule in Matthew 18:15 is, "if thy brother shall trespass against thee, go and tell him his fault between thee and him alone." When the husband waits until he can take his wife aside and speak to her heartily, freely, and tenderly, it will do far more towards her repentance than rebuking her openly in the presence of others (Prov. 16:21). If he corrects her in public, she will hardly believe that he did not mean to shame her; but if he takes her aside, it will greatly encourage her repentance because it proves that he cares

58. Scudder, 96–97.
59. Whately, *A Bride-Bush*, 142.
60. Whately, *A Bride-Bush*, 143–44.

about her reputation and truly desires her reformation. "If he shall have occasion to reprove her," wrote Ambrose, "he must keep his words until a convenient time, and not do it in [the] presence of others, and then utter them in the spirit of meekness and love."[61] Baxter also provided a rule for the husband on this note. He said the husband is to see that "none of their own matters, which should be kept secret, be made known to others. His teaching and reproving her should be for the most part secret."[62]

Fifth, another guideline concerns the virtue of *mildness*. We mentioned earlier that mildness ought to govern a husband in directing his wife; but it is important to see that it must also govern a husband in reproving his wife. Both the matter and the manner of his reproofs should be marked by mildness. With regard to the *matter*, his mildness should manifest itself by not finding fault with every trifling mishap that he sees. Just as in a narrow passageway two people can hardly pass by without bumping shoulders or forcing each other up against the wall, so in such a close and tight-knit relationship as marriage small offenses will abound, not only in each other's own walk but against each other. Most of these, like small sores or pinpricks, will amend themselves and can be easily overlooked. Therefore unless it is a great offense or one done in a proud and presumptuous manner, the husband ought lovingly to overlook it (1 Cor. 13:7). Where he must proceed to reprove her, it should be with genuine reluctance, feeling himself compelled more by the offense than by his willingness to reprove it (cf. Lam. 3:33). "As a mother's tenderness of love causes that she takes no notice of divers little deformities in her own child, so stand…affected to your own wife. Pray to God against all her faults, see and commend all her virtues, but petty wants and natural ordinary weaknesses, never take notice of, never reprove…. [For] your unwillingness to see and reprove shall make her more willing to see and reform."[63]

With regard to the *manner* of the husband's reproving, he must see that his reproofs are very gentle. Whately's counsel captured it best:

---

61. Ambrose, 235.
62. Baxter, 154.
63. Whately, *A Bride-Bush*, 166–67.

"The words and gestures used to press a fault upon the wife's conscience must be mild and amiable, such as breathe out love and [compassion] both at once. A reproof must be applied as a [bandage], not with [scolding], but with moaning.... The husband must ever remember to use no more roughness than is fit to his own flesh. Reproofs of themselves...go enough against the stomach; we need not by our bitterness make them more loathsome."[64] Could a sick patient be persuaded to drink down a medicine which is scalding hot? No more can a wife bear that reproof which scalds the ear, as it were, with hurtful and bitter words, and which comes with a fiery look, angry eyes, and threatening gestures. Such a reproof will never reach her heart and will have the opposite effect which her husband intends it to have (Prov. 15:4). "Rough language, and overmuch heat in reproving (though the cause be never so just) will be like a good potion administered scalding hot. This will not be forced down; she can hardly take it so hot, but will belch it up in the face of him that gives it, and the virtue of it is utterly lost."[65] Therefore if he must reprove her of sin, let him do it with the love and tenderness due to her as his wife (Prov. 15:1–2; 16:23–24).

In order to press this point home, we offer concluding and summary counsel from two Puritans. Their length, we believe, is fully warranted by their profitability.

First, consider Steele's summary advice:

The husband demonstrates his love *by gentle reproof of his wife when she does amiss.* —He must indeed overlook many infirmities; for "love covereth a multitude of sins." And as he that is always using his sword, will make it dull at length; so he that is continually reproving shall have the less regard given to his reproofs. But yet he cannot love her, if he do not, when need is, reprove her; but then, let it be with all the wisdom and tenderness imaginable; not before strangers, and rarely before the family; not for natural defects, seldom for inadvertencies; and when he does it, let him make way for his reproof by commending in her what is good; and when he is done, back [the reproof] with a reason. He must be sure to mingle the oil of kindness with the myrrh of reproof;

---

64. Whately, *A Bride-Bush*, 167.
65. Scudder, 96.

for if he give her this potion too hot, the operation is hindered, and his labor worse than lost. Admirable was the carriage of Job, when his wife had highly offended him with her words; yet hear how mildly he rebukes her…"Thou speakest as one of the foolish women" (Job 2:10). Sooner or later, if she be not brutish, she will be thankful, and amend.[66]

Steele continued,

The effects of a husband's love are to be seen in…*the mild use of his authority.* —This God has, in His wisdom invested him withal at his creation (Gen. 2:23) and not divested him at his fall (Gen. 3:16). The light of nature gives it to him (Esther 1:22) and the gospel has nowhere repealed, but confirmed the same (1 Cor. 11:3). And none but proud and ignorant women will ever dispute it. But herein lies an act of the husband's love: 1) wisely to keep; 2) mildly to use, this authority. 1) He must *keep it* by a religious, grave, and manly carriage; this will be his chiefest fort and buttress to support it. It will be hard for her, though doubtless her duty, to reverence him, who himself has forgotten to reverence his God. If his behavior be light, she will be apt to set lightly by him. If he be weak and effeminate, it loses him. But he ought to answer his name; to be a head for judgment and excellency of spirit and to be truly religious. This will maintain his authority. But then 2) herein shines his love, *to use the same* [authority] with all sweetness, remembering that though he be superior to his wife, yet that their souls are equal; that she is to be treated as his companion; that he is not to rule her as a king does his subjects, but as the head does the body; that though she was not taken out of Adam's head, so neither out of his foot, but out of his side near his heart. And therefore his countenance must be friendly, his ordinary language to her mild and sweet, his behavior obliging, his commands sparing and respectful, and his reproofs gentle. He must neither be abject nor magisterial. If his rule be too imperious, his love is destroyed; if his love be not discreetly expressed, his sceptre is lost, and then he is disabled from doing God service, or his family good. He should never imagine that a rude insolence, or perpetual bitterness, is either the way to keep or use his authority aright. Indeed, the Spirit of God expressly said, "Husbands, love your

---

66. Steele, *Puritan Sermons*, 2:287.

wives, and be not bitter against them" (Col. 3:19). If meekness of wisdom will not prevail with your wife, you are undone in this world and she [is undone] in the world to come.[67]

Consider now Whately's concluding counsel:

The husband must use his right eye, as well as his left, and hearten duty, as well as dishearten sin. Good things must be commended as well as evil amended; virtue cherished as well as vice checked.... Have we not gracious promises, alluring to all uprightness and fidelity, as well as terrible threats to affright from sin? Does not Christ hearten His Church by the consolations of the Word and Spirit, as well as chasten it with divers chastisements if need require? Men must imitate Christ in governing, if they will govern happily. And he that does not do this shall never live comfortably with a wife, but shall make his own life tedious together with his wife's. For to be always chiding is no less vexation than to be always chided. If a man be [purposely] left-eyed and left-handed [and] can neither see nor feel good qualities, because he is sometimes nettled with [his wife's] evil; [or] if he [purposely] let the good go unregarded and unrewarded, [because sometimes] discredited by [his wife's] evil; [or] if he have no leisure to see anything well, because he sees divers things amiss [in her conduct]; this will fill them both full of endless discontentment, this will make his love to decay and in ceasing to love, he shall cease to be loved. This will make him sour and crabby and withal to allow himself in his sourness. This also will make the wife at first heartless in being good, because good deeds are ill considered of, [and] at last desperate in evil doing, because well or ill, all is one, [she is] still [scolded] at, still frowned upon. So both feed upon the sour of marriage and let the sweet pass by; and this is the bane of love on both sides, causing perpetual [discord], privy heart-burnings, secret dislikes, and at last also open contention, and an irreparable breach betwixt them. Wherefore if you will live happily in matrimony, feed virtue, nourish obedience, confirm all good qualities, water and refresh the tender buds of thrift, dutifulness, and other graces which begin to bud forth, and to appear a little above ground. Consider what good you enjoy by your wife, as well as what trouble; what comfort she affords you, as what cumber; what

---

67. Steele, *Puritan Sermons*, 2:289–90.

virtues she shows, as what vices; what goodness as well as what badness, that you may strengthen the one as well as weaken the other. [Indeed] let your wife see that you do much more willingly look upon the best things and much more often remember them, and that you had much rather be telling of her good than of her evil, and making much of her, than reprehending. For doubtless when all is done, experience shall prove it, that the sweet herbs grow fairest and safest in the sunshine; and many a wife had been very good, if the husband could have seen and fostered a little goodness at the first.[68]

Study Questions

1. What are the two main ways husbands fail to exercise righteous authority?

2. What does it mean that a husband's authority is a *stewardship*?

3. What positive advice did William Whately give for how a husband should maintain his headship properly and use it honorably?

4. What negative faults should the husband avoid in order to keep his wife's respect?

5. What is the purpose of a husband's authority? How should that affect how he uses it?

6. Gouge compared the husband's authority to a sword given to him for the protection of his wife. How might he instead drop the sword? How might he, as it were, "stab" his wife with it?

---

68. Whately, *A Bride-Bush*, 126–28.

7. What practical guidelines should a husband follow to wisely use his authority in such a way as avoids provoking, overwhelming, or demeaning his wife?

8. What warnings did Whately give against micromanaging your wife, giving too many commands, or being severe and unreasonable?

9. Read Proverbs 31:28–31. What does this reveal about a husband's duty? Why is this important for your wife, your family, and society as a whole?

10. Summarize the instructions that the Puritans gave about how a husband should or should not correct his wife for her faults. What changes should you make in giving and receiving correction in your marriage?

Concluding Counsel 10

We began this book by pointing out that the divine institution of marriage is under attack in our society and that something must be done to restore it to its rightful and blessed place in our minds, hearts, and experiences. We then expressed our conviction that the only remedy is a hearty and entire return to the teachings of God in the Bible with regard to marriage. Having created marriage for His own glory and for the good of humanity, He alone can crown a marriage with honor and blessing and guide the married into the full enjoyment of the honor and blessing which come from His hand.

In defense of that conviction, we proceeded to show from the Bible and Puritan writers that God instituted marriage as a part of creation and that He has placed a very special honor upon it. We then described the many purposes and benefits of marriage and showed that marriage is not only an honorable institution, but a desirable and beneficial one. We explained that matrimonial honor can only be procured by making a good entrance into marriage. One must marry in the Lord, that is, one must be united to Christ in salvation and then marry another who is likewise joined to the Savior.

But a treasure gained is nothing to rejoice over if it is soon lost, whereas acquired riches, upon which one lives fruitfully and enduringly, is a treasure indeed. Therefore we proceeded to explain that the honor God places upon marriage, once procured by marrying in the Lord, must be preserved by walking faithfully in the several duties of marriage. Since marriage is a covenant before the Lord with obligations, its refreshing stream of blessings flows freely only into the lives of those who strive, by His grace, to walk faithfully in those obligations. Much time was spent on what these duties are for the wife, for the husband, and for both of them together. It is now our desire to offer some concluding counsel, first to the unmarried and then to the married.

To the Unmarried

The unmarried are either so anxious about marriage or so thoughtless of it that they do very little to prepare themselves for it. When they could be laying the best of foundations for life in the married state, they neglect to lay any and threaten themselves with troubles that, with a little preparation, could have been easily cut off at the root. Therefore if you are unmarried and believe the Lord would have you marry, there are six directives we advise you to heed. If you follow these directives, you will be able to enter into marriage honorably and be well prepared for the duties which belong to it.

First, heed the counsel of Paul in 1 Thessalonians 4:4 by carrying yourself faithfully in purity and chastity in your singleness.[1] Marriage includes the privilege of delighting sexually in your spouse before the Lord (Heb. 13:4; Prov. 5:18–19), and this privilege serves, in the Lord's kindness, as a preventative to lust (1 Cor. 7:2); but unless you learn to mortify the sin of lust in your singleness, the marriage bed may serve to enflame it until, in the end, it defiles the marriage bed. The reason for this is because a man given to lust often remains unsatisfied—even with his wife. To such a man, a wife may come to mean little more than a means to the end. Such a man will grow tired of his wife and before long desire someone else. Understand, then, that marriage is not given by God to make a lustful heart chaste; rather, marriage is given by God to preserve and satisfy a chaste heart. If you give the reins to your lusts before marriage, they will prove unruly and destructive in marriage. Beware of the precursors and forerunners of lust (like immoral company, provocative media, and idleness) and cultivate pure thoughts and chaste desires by setting your mind and affections on things above (Col. 3:1–3; Phil. 4:8).

---

1. Steele, *Puritan Sermons*, 2:299.

As a true believer, behave as the chaste bride of Christ that you are (Isa. 54:5) and bring that chastity into your marriage, where it may be both preserved and satisfied by the spouse of your youth.

Second, wait upon the Lord for a good and fit spouse. Anxiety has led many to rush hastily into marriage, only to cause them to meet with troubles and be filled with regrets. The demands of marriage prove to be more than they realized and the person they married proves to be less than they realized. How much better would it have been had they only taken the time, through wise counsel and due examination, to make sure that the partners they chose were both married to the Lord in faith and compatible with themselves by providence. Pray for patience to wait until the Lord sees fit to bring you into marriage with a good and fit spouse of His choosing. He knows when you are ready and He knows the one whom He's made ready for you. So entrust yourself into His good and wise hands and wait until He brings you and your spouse together. Until then, devote yourself to two things: praying for the person whom the Lord is preparing for you, that He might sanctify him or her in body and soul, and laboring by diligent use of the means of grace to become the person for whom another is praying and waiting.

Third, when the time comes, you must choose your spouse wisely.[2] If your own relationship to Christ is secure, this may very well be the most important counsel we could give. Many of the troubles that usually accompany marriage can be avoided by choosing more wisely at the beginning. Those who choose upon such grounds as riches, beauty, or amiableness and consider godliness only in the last place, if at all, put the cart before the horse and will not travel far before meeting with a host of trials and surprises. You must guard your affections and not let them seize upon such outward and external enticements without first considering the person's relationship with God and walk with Christ. To let godliness be your first criterion is to acknowledge God in your choice; and He will direct your choice if you submit trustingly to Him (Prov. 3:5–6). If you first choose one who is godly then you will be free to love your choice.

---

2. Whately, *A Care-Cloth*, 71f.

It is therefore absolutely necessary that you marry a Christian (1 Cor. 7:39) who embraces the Word of God and its doctrines of grace, whose godliness is evident to you, whose good works go before him or her, whose life bears the fruit of the Spirit, and whose family and friends testify to the same. A Christian who has learned the grace of self-denial will come into the marriage ready to love and serve you. A Christian lives humbly upon Christ's fullness and looks to Christ for strength, contentment, and grace. A Christian will be conscientious about the duties of marriage. A Christian will sincerely heed the counsel, admonitions, and reproofs of Scripture, will repent of failures in marriage, and will cultivate the grace of God given for a godly marriage. Whatever a Christian may lack in comparison with an unbeliever, he has that which none other has: the grace of Christ to daily die to himself and to live unto God, with an active love for you. If a Christian does not prove to be the best possible husband or wife, it is not because of godliness but because of the lack of it, which can itself be made up by repentance and grace. A Christian is therefore what Whately called a "curable" suitor,[3] because there is nothing amiss with him or her which cannot be cured or made up by faith and repentance.

Fourth, you must be realistic in your view of the marriage state. Many falsely imagine marriage to be a condition free of hardship and full of bliss and therefore find the troubles and challenges of marriage to be unbearable. We have argued from the beginning that marriage is an honorable condition and that those who enter upon it in the Lord and walk faithfully in its duties do indeed know the blessings, happiness, and great joy of this condition. However, marriage has its crosses as well as its comforts, and its sorrows as well as its joys (1 Cor. 7:28). It is not all honey, said Reyner, but has some bitterness intermingled with it.[4] The reason for this is simple. For all the godliness a man and a woman may bring into their marriage, their marriage remains a thing "under the sun" and is therefore subject to the same vanity and vexation of spirit that beset all other earthly things (Eccl. 1:13–14; 9:9). In other words, marriage is an earthly institution intended for the present time and its

---

3. Whately, *A Care-Cloth*, 72.
4. Reyner, 49.

comforts and joys will always be mingled with the crosses and sorrows which accompany *all things* this side of heaven. Every earthly fountain will run dry; every earthly rose has its thorns; every earthly day is followed by night; and it must be so—otherwise, who would ever long for heaven? If the blessings of this life were trouble-free, none would look with longing for the life to come or to the Lord whose sudden coming will bring it. Therefore think realistically about the condition of marriage, not expecting from it more troubles than grace can manage, but neither looking to it for more bliss than earth can render.

Fifth, with a realistic view of marriage, prepare yourself for the troubles that sin inevitably brings into it.[5] Reason with yourself this way: "I find that God would have me marry, and I am content to be in His will; but I also see that God forewarns me that marriage will have its troubles, and I am content to believe His Word. By God's help I will bear the troubles of marriage with quietness, respond to them with grace, and look for them to be made subservient to my growth in Christ and my progress heavenward. I will look to Him for strength, rest on Him for help, and comfort myself in His providence, for only then can I be sure of His blessings." Who that thus reasons with himself in light of Scripture could be surprised by marriage's crosses or fail to improve them for God's glory and his own good when they come?

Finally, be sure if God calls you to marry that you do not enter into marriage lightly. You will very soon have your hands full of duty, and it will be too much for you if you do not first get your heart full of the grace of God and your mind full of the wisdom of God.[6] Do you have the grace to lead and govern a wife and children in the ways of God? Do you have the grace to submit to a husband's authority and bring up children for the Lord? You must get these graces from Christ beforehand and cultivate them unto fruitfulness, or else marriage will require more of you than you are able to give and will render to you less contentment and happiness than you hoped for. "He that leaps over a broad ditch with a short staff, shall fall into the midst; and he that enters upon matrimony without care to attain great grace, shall be mired and doused

---

5. Cf. Whately, *A Care-Cloth*, 74–78; Reyner, 49–72.
6. Whately, *A Bride-Bush*, 216–17.

in…vexation,"[7] said Whately. See that you prepare for the demands of this condition by becoming fully acquainted with your own emptiness and learning to live upon Christ's fullness, whose grace alone can enable you to fulfill the duties and enjoy the happiness of marriage. Only then will you be able to consent to the marriage covenant understandingly, deliberately, heartily, in the fear of God, with a clear sense of your duty, and with a fixed resolution to perform it out of obedience to and for the glory of God.[8]

To the Married

By God's rich and abundant grace to them in Christ, the married find themselves in the most blessed condition this side of heaven, for they find themselves in the estate instituted by God to show forth the relationship between Christ and His church. In this condition they therefore meet not only with grace sufficient for their calling, but with a calling so high that they must learn to depend entirely upon that grace to enable them to fulfill it. If you are married and are resolved to honor God in your marriage, there are six directives you should heed. If you do so, you will be able to preserve the honor of your marriage and come to the end of it without regret or shame but with the greatest of joy and peace.

First, give thanks to God for your marriage. If you enjoy a blessed and lovely spouse, to whom do you owe the thanks? Is it not to God? If you enjoy more comforts in marriage than most and suffer fewer troubles in marriage than many, should not God be thanked? If you have a spouse ready to serve you, ready to reform by repentance, and ready to improve upon every trial for good, should you not give thanks to Him from whom alone a good spouse comes (Prov. 18:22; 19:14)? If you have a spouse who loves you, cheers you, encourages you, and helps you heavenward, should you not render unceasing praise and thanks to God? The Lord's blessings are more often lost by ingratitude than by exhaustion. Indeed, the Lord's blessings flow from the purchase of the cross and can never run dry; but when we neglect to return thanks for them, it is just for the Lord to withdraw them in order to teach us to be grateful. Give

---

7. Whately, *A Bride-Bush*, 217.
8. Baxter, 47.

thanks to God for your happy marriage. Let His praise be upon your lips and let your thankfulness be seen in your ready acknowledgment of Him as the Giver of every good and perfect gift (James 1:17).

Second, settle your affections fully upon your spouse. The temptations will be many that beckon your affections in every direction away from your spouse. Being unable to separate Christ and His bride, the devil tries to separate husbands and wives, hoping thereby to mar the reputation of Christ's marriage among men. So you must be on guard against those temptations by fully loving your spouse. If you fully love your spouse then you will be more able to bear provocations, more ready to forgive wrongs, more quick to see good and not evil, and more attentive to your own duties than to your spouse's. Unsettled affections leave a person "on the fence," as it were, suspicious of his spouse's motives and actions, expecting to be wronged and disappointed, ready to retaliate, and, if need be, to leave for another. By settling your affections fully upon your spouse you will guard against all wrongs that might be done to you and will set in motion all good that might be done towards and for your spouse, thereby securing for yourself a solid foundation for a happy marriage.

Third, thoroughly acquaint yourself with the duties of marriage and give yourself sincerely to them for Christ's sake.[9] Your spouse is not worthy of them, but God is; and it is He who has laid them upon your shoulders to perform. Therefore, though your nature may storm against them, see them as God's good commands for you and resolve to give yourself to the performance of them. Too many husbands busy themselves with the wife's duties lest they miss something owed to them. Likewise, too many wives busy themselves getting versed in the husband's duties, lest they miss something owed to them. This leads to nothing but bickering, murmuring, self-centeredness, and both of them falling short in their respective duties. Care more for your own marital duties than for your spouse's.

To the knowledge of your duties you must add the performance of them. You cannot be pleasing to God or a blessing to your spouse

---

9.. Steele, *Puritan Sermons*, 2:301.

until you sincerely give yourself to your duties. To kick against them is to rebel against God and to bring unutterable grief upon both you and your spouse. Likewise, you cannot know the blessings and honor of the married estate without sincerely taking up the yoke of your duties towards your spouse. It may be true that any man and woman may live civilly and quietly together in marriage; but what is that to enjoying the blessing and honor of God? Can two sinners living quietly under one roof and sleeping quietly in one bed even begin to be compared to a Christian marriage in which the Spirit of God dwells to bless and sanctify, upon which the blessings of Christ rest to protect and guide, and by which God is glorified and honored? Therefore know your duties well and give yourself fully to them, being comforted by the fact that the very God who places them upon you will, for the asking, fill your heart with grace to perform them to His glory.

Fourth, mark and amend your failings more than your spouse's. Just as too many husbands and wives are more ready to know their spouse's duties than their own, so too many are more ready to mark their spouse's failings than their own. They complain to others about how far short of duty their spouses come but see nothing of their own failings. Whately said this makes husbands and wives "ill paymasters one to another, because they look often [at] what is owed to them, not what they owe."[10] "What folly is this! Understand idle man and woman, that it is not the requiring or receiving of duty from others, but the knowing and performing of what pertains to yourself, that will prove you a Christian, comfort you in temptations, rejoice you in death, and stand for you in judgment," concluded Whately.[11]

Fifth, prevent as many troubles in marriage as you can.[12] Here are five directives to assist you:

1. Fear God and walk in His ways because the blessing of God will always accompany those who fear Him and walk conscionably in His commandments (Prov. 14:27; 22:4). If godliness is profitable for all things, as Paul says (1 Tim. 4:8), then it is profitable for marriage

---

10. Whately, *A Bride-Bush*, 218.
11. Whately, *A Bride-Bush*, 219.
12. Whately, *A Care-Cloth*, 77–85.

and cannot help but bring God's blessings upon you. Moreover, if we consider that God's usual purpose in sending troubles is to bring us to repentance for our sins and draw us nearer to Him in holiness, then should not the fear of God—which leads a man to depart from iniquity and walk in faithfulness—keep many unnecessary troubles out of our marriage? Godliness prevents many troubles in marriage because it precedes them by removing the occasion for them.

2. Instruct your family in the fear of God. If you labor by godly instruction and example to teach your children to walk in the fear of the Lord, then they most likely will, by the Spirit's grace, bring much happiness into the home. As they learn to fear and obey God so they will learn to obey and honor you for His sake. Otherwise, if your children reject your instruction, spurn your example, and choose to walk contrary to the Lord, at least your conscience will be clear with regard to your duty. Your faithfulness in your duty will serve as the ground of hope upon which you can send frequent and fervent prayers to the Lord, that He might yet be pleased to bring forth a harvest.

3. Pray often together and for each other. Praying together and for each other will maintain the communion and fellowship with God that will fortify you both against the troubles and trials of marriage. Many couples think their greatest security against future hardships is a bank account well stocked with money; but what if the hardship has shattered something that money cannot buy? What if the loss is something that money cannot replace? Without minimizing the need for due preparation and saving against future unknowns, your greatest security against all hardships is in the Lord. He possesses the strength you need to face trials, the wisdom you need to navigate hardships, and the grace you need to respond to suffering in a way that honors Him. A vibrant communion and fellowship with God will not prevent the trials of marriage, but it will do much towards preventing you from responding to them dishonorably or shamefully.

4. Let your heart be moderate towards the world and your hands be diligent in the world. The things of this world are to be held loosely because one of two things will surely and quickly come to pass: either they will be taken away from you by loss or you will be taken away from

them by death. You must not set your heart idolatrously upon anything in this world. You may love it for the blessing that it is and for the happiness that it affords you, but you must ever remember that, besides His Son as your Savior, God gives you nothing to own; everything you have is on loan. He is free at any time, in love, to take back what He bestowed; and if He sees it is better for you to be without it, then He most certainly will. Keeping your heart moderated to the things of earth will make it easier and less troubling to you when you must let go of them. You will be able to say with Paul, "I have learned, in whatsoever state I am, therewith to be content. I know both how to be abased, and I know how to abound: every where and in all things I am instructed both to be full and to be hungry, both to abound and to suffer need" (Phil. 4:11–12).

Moreover, if a moderate heart brings contentment in every situation, then diligent hands bring sufficiency in every situation. Scripture and experience teach us that many troubles come upon the slothful and negligent (Prov. 13:4). If this slothfulness is brought into a marriage in which a man becomes responsible for a wife and children, then it cannot be but that his troubles will multiply. Diligence therefore prevents many unnecessary troubles that slothfulness invites; for by giving yourself diligently to your calling you will enjoy both the fruit of your labors and the blessing of the Lord upon it (Prov. 10:4; 2 Peter 3:14).

5. Patiently bear the troubles of marriage when they come. If you walk before the Lord and your family in the fear of God, if you instruct your children to do the same, if you pray together with your spouse, if you live in communion with God as your strength, and if you live with moderate hearts towards the world and with diligent hands in the world, then what reason do you have to faint under the troubles that you meet with in your marriage? Can you think of a single reason why you should give up hope and give way to despair? Why you should forfeit your joy in the Lord and be overcome with sadness? Has not your God ordered the trouble, and does He not know what is best for you? Is not His grace sufficient to help you bear it and improve it to your sanctification? Then you should bear your trouble patiently and wait upon Him for the grace to see it through, the grace to profit by it, and the grace to praise Him for it.

Finally, keep your separation from your spouse in view.[13] The time you have together as husband and wife cannot be but short when life itself is no more than a vapor and a few days at best (James 4:14; Job 14:1). This perspective, said Scudder, will cause you to redeem the time "enjoying each other and doing good to each other, as well as in receiving good one from another, while you may; lest else it prove to the surviving party, great grief of heart, that he or she did let slip that good opportunity which God had given them."[14]

Therefore you must keep in view that the end of your marriage is coming, when death will part you from each other and when you must give an account to God for how you treated each other. You are both traveling the road that leads to death and you will both shortly enter into that eternal estate in which your marriage will be no more (Matt. 22:30). You will soon stand before God and answer for your marriage covenant and the vows you made when you contracted it. You will very soon be examined with regard to your marital duties, both those mutual and those particular to you. You will soon give an account of the great privilege you had of representing to the world the relationship and marriage between Christ and His church. See that you help each other along the way as husbands and wives should, serving and supporting each other as one flesh ought to do. And do what you can to make your journey easier by clinging to Christ in faith for the good of your soul, loving each other heartily for the good of your calling, and serving each other faithfully for the good of your conscience. Only then, as Whately said, will "your loves be sure, your hearts comfortable, your example commendable, your houses peaceable, your selves joyful, your lives cheerful, your deaths blessed, and your memories happy forever."[15]

Conclusion

It may be that by now, after all that has been said about marriage and with the help of the seventeenth-century English Puritans, many of our readers feel the standard has been placed too high—so high, in fact,

---

13. Baxter, 47–48.
14. Scudder, 108.
15. Whately, *A Bride-Bush*, 220.

that they feel either defeated in their marriages or discouraged from even pursuing marriage. But consider the following.

First, let it be understood that while it *is* our conviction that no one has provided a more comprehensive and practical view of the Bible's doctrine of marriage than the Puritans, we set forth the above ideal for Christian marriage not because it was "the Puritan view" but rather because the Puritans convincingly showed the biblical view. The Puritans lived in a time when the reformation of the church was well underway and when many practical questions had to be answered. The church was hungry for and in great need of specific answers to specific questions. The Puritan pastors sought, before God in prayer and with the Bible in hand, to provide those specific answers. When it came to marriage, in typical Puritan fashion, they sought to address every area of concern and outline and explain every duty, all the while gathering their light, truth, and warrant from Scripture. What they gathered is so foundational to biblical marriage that it transcends their time and place and therefore warrants a fresh hearing today.

Thus, rather than presenting only "a Puritan view of marriage" to you, we have attempted to cull and collate from their writings a perspective on marriage that is grounded in Scripture and that we believe can ably answer the demands of our own troubling day, when marriage is in desperate need of biblical reorientation. Much ground has already been lost and more slips away every day. Men and women marry without a clear view of marriage or the duties incumbent upon them in it. They marry ignorant of the honor and blessings of God they might procure, enjoy, and preserve unto their parting day if they would only marry in the Lord and live in marriage unto the Lord. We are convinced that, generally speaking, those who strive before God to apply the counsel we have outlined will enjoy, for Christ's sake, the many blessings that belong to Christian marriage.

Second, you need not be discouraged that where you are in your marriage falls short of what you have learned in this book, nor throw up your hands in despair, feeling that since you never will clear the high bar set for you that you ought not to marry. What has been set before you is the biblical ideal for marriage. To lower it would be to say both less than and other than what God's Word says, which would do us all great injury. To set it before you as the ideal for marriage is to speak the truth in love, for our own peace of conscience and for your own good. Moreover, to tell you the truth, knowing that you will inevitably see where you fall short of it is to lovingly drive you to Christ, in whom there is forgiveness for your failures, grace for your calling, and reward for your sincere and diligent effort to please Him. And it is with *that* in mind that we have set the bar for marriage where you see it set in the above pages and chapters. Never forget, dear believer, that you are hidden savingly in Christ. While you look to the merit of His obedience for your justification, you may also look to the work of His Spirit for your sanctification (Phil. 2:12–13; 1 Thess. 5:23–24).

We conclude with the counsel with which Daniel Rogers ended his book *Matrimonial Honor*. Rogers's excellent treatment of marriage provided the theme which runs through and reverberates in our own: the procuring and preserving of matrimonial honor. May his counsel greatly encourage you to look to God to enable you to live faithfully in marriage:

> My large discourse may dismay some for coming so short of practice as they do. Beseech the Lord therefore to behold your defects with a merciful eye, to read the short lines of your obedience often over in the glass and perspective of the Lord Jesus; and so, by His large interpreting and much looking upon your honest endeavor, [your obedience] shall be esteemed as full and large.
>
> God help! Our discourses of these matters are far larger than the practice of the most is. [We] who write and [others like us] are poor, and unsuitable to our rules! Howbeit, [we are] not contrary, nor willfully opposite; and where there is but endeavor, God will accept [it]. Give, Lord, power to do as Thou dost direct, and command what Thou wilt!
>
> Speak, and spare not upon these terms; for your servants and handmaids (mourning for their deaf ears and dead hearts) desire to hearken and to obey. Look not at what is ours, it is vile, but at that which is Thine in us, which is precious![16]

---

16. Rogers, 299.

Study Questions

1. How can single people who desire to get married cultivate:

   - Sexual purity?

   - Patience and contentment with God's will?

   - Discernment to choose a good spouse?

   - Readiness to endure hardship in marriage?

2. How can married people cultivate:

   - Gratitude and affection for their spouses?

   - Humility to be more critical of themselves than critical of their spouses?

   - Prayer, biblical instruction, and worship with their spouses and children at home?

   - Moderation in their earthly desires and patience in earthly sorrows?

3. Why is it crucial that "to the knowledge of your duties you must add the performance of them"? What will happen if you read this book but do nothing differently?

4. What are three specific duties of marriage that particularly impressed you from reading this book? Which one of them will you strive by grace to implement first?

5. How should we respond when we are convicted and discouraged by the lofty biblical ideals of marriage?

Appendix:
George Swinnock's Prayers for Husbands and Wives

In his well-known treatise, The Christian Man's Calling, *Swinnock ends each of his sections on (1) the spouses' mutual duties, (2) the wife's duties, and (3) the husband's duties with a lengthy sample prayer. Though they are long and a bit quaint at places, these prayers are reprinted here as an appendix as they can be of immense help in providing husbands and wives with rich substance so as to enflame and improve their own prayers to God for their respective duties.*

A Prayer for Mutual Duties in Marriage

Lord, who art the guide of all relations, and the God of all grace, be pleased to grant us affections suitable to our condition, that our whole carriage therein may be as becomes Christians, and such as are married to the Lord Christ; that as Abraham and Sarah, we may be famous for faith, as Isaac and Rebecca, we may live together in the dearest love; and that, as that pious pair, Zacharias and Elizabeth, we may walk in all the commandments and statutes of the Lord blameless, and we, walking in company, may walk the more cheerfully in the way which leads to everlasting life.

We wish, considering how marriage, though a human conjunction, is of divine institution; how the Father appointed it, and that in paradise, and the Son hath approved it by his own glorious presence, that the Spirit with its gracious beams may so overshadow our souls, that many Barnabases, many sons of consolation, may be the issue and effect of our conjugal relation. Oh that we might both reverence this golden relation for His sake whose image and superscription it bears, and never by our unworthy and unholy conversations deface and defile it! Those that are honored by a prince will seek to honor him in their places, if they be ingenuous persons. How different is men's carriage, answerable to the difference in their conditions! Lord, since Thou hast exalted us, let us never debase Thee; though others whom Thou hast lifted up make it their business to cast Thee down, and the more helps Thou dost afford them to sweeten their pilgrimage, the more they abound in profaneness, yet let Thy goodness to us be improved by us for Thy glory, and let us be holy as Thee, who have called us to this relation, art holy, in all manner of conversation.

We wish that the meditation of each other's frailty may quicken us to greater fidelity, especially in the immediate concern of eternity. The next arrow which death shoots may light upon one of us, and our relation will die with us; though now it shines pleasantly and refreshes us with its warm rays, yet it will shortly set and never arise more; and then, oh then, we shall never have the least season to advantage each other's souls, or to further one another's salvation. Oh that this weighty thought might sink so deep into our hearts, that we may pray the more frequently and the more fervently for and with one another, because within a few days we shall never pray more; that we may persuade and admonish one another the more seriously and the more affectionately, because within a few days we shall never do it more; that we may in our several places work the work of him that sent us into the world while it is day, because the night comes wherein neither of us can work. Lord, make us so mindful of our deaths, that we may be the more faithful in our duties; and whatsoever our hands find to do, in reference to Thy praise, and our eternal peace, let us do it with all our might, because there is no knowledge, nor wisdom, nor device, in the grave, where we are both going.

We wish that the covenant which we have solemnly entered into with each other, before God, angels, and men, may be like that which the Jews entered into with the Lord (Jer. 50:5), "an everlasting covenant never to be forgotten." If we forget our God, and deal falsely in His covenant, He will search it out, for He knows the secrets of the heart. Why should we, as young gallants, enter into bonds, never minding them more till the day of payment be past, and the sergeant of death be ready to arrest us, and haul us to the prison of hell! Should we, as the harlot, forget the covenant of our God, He would remember it to our loss and ruin; if it be dangerous to break the covenant of a man, that vengeance from heaven hath often fallen on their heads, how dreadful is it to break the covenant of a God! His curse has broken in upon many a couple for breaking His covenant. Oh that all our action in this relation might be so answerable to the gospel, that our God may never have cause to complain of us, as once of Israel, "What hast thou to do to take my covenant in thy mouth, seeing thou hatest instruction, and castest my words behind thee?" Lord, help us, as persons in debt that are honest, to be so mindful of our bonds, that we may be careful to discharge them in the performance of the conditions, and let the consideration thereof be an impregnable bulwark, to defend us against all the assaults which the flesh or world shall make to draw us from our duties.

We wish, since by a married condition we are more remote from our parents' care, which formerly was our haven, and are launched into the ocean of this world, in which we must expect to be tossed up and down with storms and tempests, that we may be diligent to make God our guide, and Scripture our compass, to prevent our perishing. They who have trouble in the flesh, had need to live after the Spirit. If it be foul underfoot, it will be but ill traveling if it be not fair overhead. How sad will it be to have storms on our heads, and no cover! to have qualms come over our hearts, and no cordial! to have afflictions, sickness, nay death, in our house, and to have the God of all consolations, and the Lord of life, far from our house! Oh that, whatever stony or dirty ways providence may call us to walk in on earth, yet we may so walk by rule, as to enjoy a comfortable sunshine from heaven! Lord, let us so own Thee in prosperity, that Thou mayest own us in adversity; let us be so careful to keep good consciences, that in all estates Thou mayest be our comfort, going before us as our cloud by day, and pillar of fire by night, to direct and cheer us in our passage through this wilderness, till we come to Canaan.

We wish that our affections may be as close as our relation; and since our God has tied this knot with His own blessed hands betwixt us, we may never so much as in angry thoughts, much less in wrangling deeds, do anything which may tend to loosen it. We are one flesh, why should we not have one spirit? What a dreadful, doleful spectacle is a house in a flame! What a blessed, blissful sight is a family of love! When bells clash and jangle, how harsh and displeasing is their noise! when they keep tune and time, how harmonious and grateful is their sound! Oh that our house may be a church, and its name Philadelphia, or brotherly love, and that we especially, who are the chief in it, may be like Jerusalem—compact together, and at unity within ourselves; that all our thoughts of each other may be sweetened with love, and all our words to each other seasoned with love; and that in our actions towards each other, love, as a sample of a predominant quality, may give a relish and savor to them all! Our Redeemer, who has given us this precept, and set Himself for our pattern, is love; His name is love, His nature is love, His sacraments are seals of love, His Spirit is the earnest of love, His Scripture is His letter of love, His providences are all written in the characters of love; His ordinances are love's banqueting house, wherein His banner over us is love. He has commanded us, as we are Christians (Eph. 5:1–2), to be "followers of him as dear children, and to walk in love, as he hath loved us." Oh then, what love should we have each to other! how close should we cleave in our affections, who are bound together by God Himself, both with the bond of religion and relation, and are provoked to it by such loving precepts, and such a lively pattern! Surely such cords should not be easily broken. Love is the bond of perfection, and the perfection of all bonds; it is the perfect bond which will tie all our duties and graces together, without which they will fall asunder. "Behold, how good and how pleasant is it for husband and wife to dwell together in unity! It is like the precious ointment upon the head, that ran down upon the beard, even Aaron's beard, that went down to the skirts of his garment; as the dew of Hermon, and as the dew that descended upon the mountains of Zion, for there the Lord commanded the blessing, even life for evermore," (Ps. 133). Oh that love may be our strength, wherewith we may bear one another's burdens; that love may be our mantle, wherewith we may cover one another's infirmities; and that love, like the fire in Elijah's trench, may lick up all the water of opposition which may ever arise between us! Lord, who art the God of love, let Thy Spirit so kindle and increase this heavenly flame in our hearts, that we may be always ascending up unto Thee in love of desire, and for Thy sake be carried out towards each other, with unfeigned and constant love of delight. Though others, who live always quarreling, curse their wedding day more than Job did his birthday, and desire a divorce as earnestly as he did death, let our lives be so sweetened with love, that, from the comfort of it, we long the more for our meeting together in heaven with Thyself, and amongst all Thy saints.

We wish that faithfulness may be the girdle about both our loins, which may keep us close each to other, and to our duties, notwithstanding all attempts by the flesh and devil to part us asunder. Our interests are the same—we are equal sharers both in gains and losses; neither can rise by the other's ruin, but we stand and fall together. Oh that what wealth our God has given us through His providence may never be wasted through our prodigality; but as those that trade in a joint stock, we may be equally solicitous, and, in the use of lawful means, industrious for its preservation and increase. Why should we be so foolish as to steal from ourselves either goods or good name, when the treasure and honour of both are embarked in the same bottom? Surely it behooves us to join in our diligence; ordinary thieves are unrighteous in wronging others; but we, if unfaithful, are unnatural in robbing ourselves. Lord, make us so faithful about the unrighteous mammon, that Thou mayest trust us with the true riches; but let us be more tender of each other's reputation than of the apple of our own eyes, and to imitate Thy Majesty in covering and forgiving one another's infirmities. Let neither of our bodies be sinks of uncleanness, but temples of holiness; teach us so to possess our vessels in sanctification and honor, that the very thoughts of dishonesty may be more dreadful to us than death itself. Why should we make Thy house Satan's harlot? Can we imagine that our Savior, because His bodily presence was once in an unclean stable, will vouchsafe His spiritual presence in an impure body? Do not we expect that our bodies should outshine the sun in glory and purity at the last day? And shall they resemble ditches for dirt and defilement at this day! Oh that we might never, like an adulterer and an adulteress, either in soul

or body go a-whoring from Thee, but that all the members of our bodies may be instruments of righteousness, and all the faculties of our
souls set apart for Thy service, that hereafter both soul and body may
be satisfied fully with Thy salvation.

We wish that, as head and body, we may conspire for each other's
welfare; and as we are one flesh, so we might have one spirit in seeking its real comfort, and endeavoring its lawful contentment. Domestic
burdens will be more tolerable if we put under both our shoulders; personal hardships will be more acceptable while we conjoin in our help;
the potion which is most bitter will go down the better if each drink a
part. Oh that, as fellow-commoners, we might always eat of the same
dish, whether sour or sweet; and since we are fellow-travelers, cheer up
one another, to make our journey the more pleasant, till we come to
rest in the true paradise! The head and body do not stand out against
each other in terms of defiance. Christ and His church do not rise up in
arms against each other in a warlike fashion. Lord, help us in our family affairs to live as those that draw in the same yoke, and in all our civil
and natural concernments to bear one another's burdens, and so fulfill
the law of Christ.

We wish, above all things, that we may, with the greatest faithfulness, be serviceable to each other's souls; and while others conspire
together to indulge their flesh, and like Ananias and Sapphira, to tempt
God, we may conspire together to live after the Spirit, and with the
greatest advantage to exercise ourselves to godliness, that we may
both, like the two cherubim, look one to another, and both towards
thy mercy-seat. And oh do Thou, who sittest between the cherubim,
meet us, and commune with us now, that at last we may meet at Thy
seat of mercy. Yet a little while and the light is with us; yet a little while
and we may pray together, and we may fast together, and we may read
together; within a few days the shadows of the evening will stretch
themselves upon us, and it will be no longer day with us. Oh that we
might be so far from living like those beasts, who mind little save bed-
ding and boarding together, that we may, like angels, always stand in
God's presence, and join in admiring His boundless perfections! Lord,
let us not, like Herod and Herodias, join together against Thy saints;

nor, as Herod and Pilate, agree together against our Savior, lest at last we burn together in the unquenchable fire. But let us take sweet counsel together, and go often to the house of God, and to the throne of grace in company; and do so assist us, that our house now may be a Bethel, none other than the house of God; and when this fast knot betwixt us shall be untied by the king of terrors, we may be more closely united to the King of saints, in that place where there is neither marriage nor giving in marriage, but all are as angels, bathing their souls in the rivers of Thy pleasures, and warming their hearts in Thy bosom and embraces. Oh, if there be such a help in a fit spouse, what a heaven is there in marriage to Thy dear Son! If converse with flesh and blood yield such comfort, what infinite delight, and unconceivable consolation will flow from immediate, uninterrupted, and eternal communion with Thy blessed self! Oh, blessed are they that are called to the marriage supper of the Lamb!

Lord, enable us (husband and wife) to shine as the sun and moon, and our children and servants as stars, so gloriously and powerfully with the light of holiness, that our house may be Thy lesser heaven, and that when we have finished our courses, by declaring Thy glory in our several relations, and showing forth Thy spiritual handiworks in our whole conversations, we may be elevated to those higher orbs, and heavenly mansions, where we shall never set, be eclipsed, or clouded; where the light of the moon shall be as the light of the sun, and the light of the sun as the light of seven days; where the crosses and encumbrances of all relations shall be removed, and the true comfort only of them all remain, yea, where the light of all relations shall be swallowed up, as the lesser celestial lights in the sun, in our great relation to God through Christ. For there "the sun shall no more be our light by day, nor the moon our light by night, but the Lord our God, our everlasting light, and our God our glory." Amen.[1]

A Prayer for the Wife's Duties in Marriage

The eternal and living God, who in the making of the world was pleased, out of His curious and manifold wisdom, to delight in order

---

1. Swinnock, 1:481–87.

(appointing all His creatures their several places, some to be inferior, others superior, and therein to continue and obey His pleasure), having created me of the weakest sex, a woman, and called me to the relation of a wife, in both which respects I am bound to subjection by His word, I wish that I may never, by endeavoring to start from that station in which He hath set me, question His prudence, or quarrel at His providence, and pervert His end and honor in the creation; but may adorn His gospel by adorning myself, not with broidered hair, or jewels, or gold, or costly apparel, but as becometh a woman professing godliness, with shame-facedness and sobriety, in the hidden man of the heart, with that which is incorruptible, even the ornament of a meek and a quiet spirit, which in the sight of God is of great price (1 Tim. 2:9–10; 1 Peter 3:4–5). Lord, let my heart, like the heart of Lydia, be so opened to Thy word, my hands, like the hands of Dorcas, be so full of good works, and my whole behavior in this relation be so conformable to Scripture, that at last I may be presented a chaste virgin to my Lord Jesus Christ.

I wish that the crosses incident to this condition may make me the more careful to please Him in my carriage, who is the God of all consolation. Godliness only is the salt that can heal these bitter waters, which all in this estate must drink. I can never walk cheerfully in this thorny, stony way, unless my feet be shod with the preparation of the gospel of peace. How many are the miseries which I must undergo! I conceive sorrow, when I conceive a son, carry my woe up and down in my womb. How am I terrified to think of my approaching travail! The very thoughts of those sharp throes, threaten beforehand to overthrow me. If I continue to my appointed hour, in what danger am I of unloading my babe and my life together! When I have passed these pikes, and through many pangs and much pain have brought my child forth, what frights and fears shall I suffer in bringing him up! Possibly children prove undutiful, servants unfaithful; nay, and my very husband, which should be my greatest comfort, becomes my greatest cross. What personal, domestic, civil, natural maladies must I meet with! And how can I encounter them unless godliness be my strength and cordial? In these and the like cases, whither shall I go, if not to my God? And will He know me if I be a stranger, a worker of iniquity? I had need to know, and to be known, to that house well, in which alone I can expect harbor in stormy weather. Lord, enable me to walk so purely, that though in the world I meet with trouble, yet in Thee I may have peace, and even rejoice in tribulation, whilst I may ease my heart by emptying it into Thine ears, and support it in all hardships with the lively hope of heaven; for I know assuredly that I can never sink so low in these waters, as to be past the help of Thy gracious and almighty hand.

I wish that I may not, like a whorish woman, forsake the guide of my youth, and forget the covenant of my God (Ps. 78:57); should my heart, like a deceitful bow, turn aside as the Israelites, and cause the arrows of my sacred promises to fly at random and miss the mark I seem to engage at, how certainly would they fall down on my head to my ruin! O, it is ill jesting with such edged tools. I have read that the Jews, when they took a solemn covenant (Jer. 34:18), did cut a beast in twain, and passed between the parts thereof, signifying by that ceremony that they wished, and were worthy to be so served and severed if they brake their covenant. They entered into an oath (Neh. 10:29) and a curse at the same time; and can I think to loose the bands of my oath, and not find and feel the blow of the curse! Hath not my God told me that if I break my covenant, He will not spare me (Deut. 29:20–21) but have His full stroke at me with His almighty arm; and the anger of the Lord, and His jealousy, infinitely worse than the hottest fire, shall smoke against me, and all the curses, heavier than mountains of lead, written in His book, shall lie upon me, and the Lord shall blot out my name from under heaven, cause my very remembrance to rot as an unsavory carcass; and the Lord will separate me unto evil (as a beast is separated for the slaughter, and a malefactor set apart for a gibbet), according to all the curses of the covenant (not a blessing shall fall on me, not a judgment shall fall beside me) that are written in the book of the law. O my soul! what fearful fire and fury, what dreadful death and damnation, is here threatened by the God of truth against you, if you break His oath! Lord, unite my heart to fear Thy name, and let the dread of Thy majesty be as a bridle to prevent my wanderings from Thy covenant, and to preserve me in the way of Thy commandments.

I wish that this fear of my God may be evidenced to myself and others by my fear of my husband; and that as the moon, though in the sun's absence she ruleth in the heavens, outshines all those glistering stars, yet puts on her veil when once the sun appeareth, and is contented to let her glory stoop to his, that whatsoever power I have in my family over children and servants, yet I may ever acknowledge and veil to my husband's authority and place. What destruction and confusion would it breed in the body politic, if all subordinate officers should strive to be supreme? What an unseemly and uncomely sight would it be in the body natural, if the shoulders should stand as high as the head? My God hath order in His upper heavens, and shall He, when He pleaseth to come and give me a visit, find none in His lower house? Oh let me so count this relation-grace of subjection my chiefest relation-glory, that while others are pleasing and priding themselves that they can master their masters, trample their heads under their feet, and have climbed so high above their places, that they endanger the breaking their necks, the loss of their souls. May I reverence my husband, be clothed with humility, and be contented with that condition to which my God hath called me. Lord, enable me so to behold thy power in my husband's person, that I may submit to it in such a gracious manner, that he may be either confirmed in Thy truth, or converted to Thy faith, while he beholds my chaste conversation, coupled with fear (1 Pet. 3:2).

I wish that I may not only awe him as my head, but also love him as my heart, that my fear of his authority may not in the least abate my affection to his person; but that my heart, though closed to others, may be enlarged to embrace him, and I may never give him cause to complain of me to me, as Delilah to Samson, "How canst thou say thou lovest me, when thy heart is not with me?" If I love not mine enemy, I cannot be saved; what then will be my portion if I love not my husband? When publicans and sinners love their friends, though not related, shall not I, by profession a Christian, love my greatest earthly friend and nearest relation? Oh let me never be remiss in my love, much less, like a distracted person, hate my own flesh! My God commands me to love him by His precept. Shall not His word be a sufficient warrant? Dare I disobey that order, which hath the King of kings' hand and seal to it? If

I resist His law, I proclaim myself a rebel. My God calls me to it by his providence. I am one with him by divine ordination, and shall I not be one with him in affection? I have chosen my love, and shall I not love my choice? I am joined with him in all estates, whether of prosperity or adversity, and shall I, that am partner with him in every condition, be parted from him in affection? If I deny my love, I quarrel with the Lord. My God commendeth it to me by a lively pattern. How dearly doth the church love Jesus Christ! He is her well-beloved, the fairest of ten thousands, yea, altogether lovely in her eye. She hateth all relations, and trampleth on all possessions, in comparison of Him. What a glorious dunghill, and gilded, glistering nothing is this whole world to her in competition with Him! And shall I be sick of my husband, when she was so sick of love to hers? Lord, let me never be so unlike the church, my mother; let me not so far degenerate from a Christian, yea, from a heathen, as to deny my hottest love to my husband, but give me to forget my own people, my father's house, and my own self, out of love to my second self.

I wish that I may manifest my love by my cheerful obedience, that as the church is subject to Christ, so I may be subject to my own husband in all things. I disobey the Lord, if I obey not my husband in all things that are lawful. The law of nature teaches me this lesson; the body is ruled by the head. The law of nations also; those that receive protection from others, yield subjection to them. Oh that no pretense whatsoever which Satan or my stubborn heart may suggest, may ever be my cloak for disobedience. How clearly will my nakedness appear under all the fig leaves which I can sew together to cover it! If he hath not wisdom enough to govern well, why did I voluntarily take him for my guide? If he hath, why do I refuse his government? However it be, now I am bound, with a knot tied by my own hands, I must obey in the Lord; whilst I murmur, I do but quarrel at my Maker. If he fail in his love and duty to me, it is my suffering; if I fail in my obedience and duty to him, it is my sin. The former is a bitter potion, but the latter mingled with it, turns it into rank poison.

Oh, let me never, as some wives, who, by rendering evil for evil, and reviling for reviling, turn their houses into a bedlam, or…a place of weeping. I could wish that he would enjoin me nothing but what is becoming so near a relation, that according to God's precept he would always be more ready to shew the goodness of his nature than the greatness of his power, and encourage my obedience to him by his tenderness to me; but whatsoever his person or his conversation be to me, Lord, next to the pleasing of Thyself, let me make it my business to please him, and employ that time which others do in grumbling at thee for their painful servitude, in groaning for the cause thereof, my great-grandmother's sin.

I wish that I may approve myself, what my God did appoint me for, a meet help to him in everything, and a hindrance to him in nothing; that I may, in reference to my family, not be as the wife of Lamech, Zillah, the shadow of a wife, as if he married me only for his pleasure, and with no regard to his profit; but that I may write every day, in my diligence and watchfulness about my domestic concernments, after that excellent copy which a queen thought becoming one that did wear a crown (Prov. 31). I desire to this end that I may observe the command of my God, to be a keeper at home, that while others, like Dinah, are gadders abroad, till they defile themselves, and are frequenters of plays or taverns. I may, like Sarah, keep close to my tent, and therein look so well to the ways of my household, that nothing be wanted through my penuriousness, or wasted through my prodigality. Lord, since Thy care is to preserve me, let my care be to please Thee; and suffer me not to be distrustful of Thy providence, or neglectful of those persons whom Thou hast committed to my charge.

I wish that of all in my house, I may ever have an affectionate and tender respect for my head; that whilst others are Zipporahs, mourning, and Marah, bitter to their husbands, I may be Naomi, pleasant and delightful to him. My God intended me for a cordial, and if I ever, by my fierce language or frowning carriage, prove a corrosive, how directly do I thwart the end of my Maker and making! If it be my duty as a Christian, in relation to all the members of Christ, to put away all bitterness, and wrath, and anger, and clamour, and evil-speaking (Eph. 4:31–32), and to be kind and tender-hearted, surely it is much more my duty as a wife, in relation to my head.

Lord, help me, like Lydia, to be courteous to thy disciples, and, as Phoebe, to be a servant to all thy servants; but in a special manner to be serviceable to him in sickness and health, in all conditions and occasions, whom thou hast appointed to be my master.

I wish that I may be a Mary for piety, as well as a Martha for industry; that I may not be so carking and caring about many things as to neglect the one thing necessary; but in all my dealings about this world, I may demean myself, not as a servant to it, but as a mistress and commander of it, and as one that hath her hope and happiness in a better world. Let me never be as Michal, to mock at my husband for holiness, nor as Jezebel or Job's wife, to stir up my husband to wickedness; but seek with the cords of love to draw him to the Lord of glory. Oh that holiness might ever have such precedency in my heart and life, that my carriage towards my children and servants may savor of Christianity, and my love especially towards my husband may be abundantly operative night and day in persuading and encouraging him to mind heaven! Oh God, with what heaviness do I think at this day of my carnal, unbelieving husband! and oh, with what horror do I forethink of that day when I am like to be half in heaven and half in hell! Oh, be Thou pleased, who hast promised to pour out Thy Spirit upon all flesh, even upon Thine handmaids and servants, that Thy sons and Thy daughters shall prophesy, to pardon all my failings in this relation; pour the oil of grace into Thy weaker vessel, that I may, like Elizabeth, be full of the Holy Ghost; like Mary Magdalene, love Thee fervently; like Eunice, instruct my children in Thy fear; and as Priscilla, be able to commend to my husband the sweetness of Thy favor, that while men prophesy, converting and confirming others by public ordination, I may preach effectually to the consciences of others, and of my husband especially, by my pious conversation. Lord, as a woman was, through Satan's subtlety, first in the transgression, so was a woman, through Thy rich mercy, first in the resurrection of the Lord Jesus Christ. Suffer me, I beseech thee, in no case, like the first woman, to be a messenger of damnation to my husband, but make me, like that famous penitent, a messenger of salvation....

Lord, I have heard that the true Moses, the blessed Messiah, is pleased to marry with sinful mortals. I confess I cannot but stand amazed at the low stoop of Thy sacred Majesty, in matching with so mean, and so base, and stained a family. Hadst Thou married with those spotless virgins, angels, the most ancient and honorable house of Thy creatures, Thou hadst matched much more like, yet infinitely below Thyself. But what admiration and astonishment can answer Thy boundless condescension, that Thou shouldst take polluted dust and ashes into Thy bed and bosom? that Thou shouldst strike a conjugal covenant with one whose person is ugliness and deformity, whose parentage is base and beggarly, and whose portion is nothing but diseases and misery? But since it is so, holy Father, because it seems good in thy sight, suffer Thy handmaid, though it be not proper to her sex, rather to woo thy dear Son, than to miss so rich, and noble, and gainful a match. Yet, alas! why do I talk thus? He hath prevented me with His kindness many years ago. How importunately hath He courted me! What large costly tokens hath He often presented me with, to persuade my unbelieving heart that His offer of marriage is in earnest! Oh, help me rather to accept Him heartily for my Lord and Husband, and, bidding adieu to all other lovers, to cleave to Him only; that all my wants and weaknesses, sins and sorrows, may be His, and all His robes, and riches, and mercies, and merits, and life, and death may be mine. Oh, do Thou so adorn me with grace, as a bride is tiered with her jewels, that I may be fitly arrayed for so beautiful a bridegroom. Let me love, honour, please, and obey Him above all, before all, and more than all; and my husband here below, next to him, for His sake. Cause me, as a pure virgin, to keep my garments clean, whilst I walk in a dirty defiling world, and as a wise virgin, to insure oil in my vessel against the coming of my Lord, that when death shall give me a bill of divorce from my dearest husband below, I may approach nearer, and enjoy fuller, my dearer Husband above, when I shall be above all frights and fears; lest those, my Savior and my soul, whom my God hath joined together, a deceitful heart, or ensnaring world, or tempting devil, should part asunder; where my rags of misery shall be changed into robes of glory, my nakedness covered with perfect righteousness, that my beloved may bespeak me, in the fullest sense, "Thou hast ravished my heart, my sister, my spouse; behold, thou art fair my love: behold, thou art all fair; there is no spot in thee." And where as a bridegroom rejoiceth over a bride, so shall my God rejoice over me, and I in Him, for ever and ever. Amen.[2]

A Prayer for the Husband's Duties in Marriage

The relation of a husband, speaking both my dignity, that I am the head of my wife, and my duty, to study and design, as the head doth for the body, her comfort and welfare, I wish in general that I may never be so mindful of my dominion as to forget those duties which my God hath annexed to this relation; but that, as I am higher in honor, so I may also be above her in holiness, able and faithful to guide and instruct her in the path to happiness. Lord, let me never be of their number who will be figures to stand before their wives in the concernments of this world, but are cyphers alone, standing for nothing in the affairs of the other world; but enable me to carry myself as one espoused to Christ in this relation of a husband, helping her in my place and to my power in the things that relate to this life, but especially affording her my utmost assistance, that she may attain the inheritance of the saints in light. I wish that, as my God is ever faithful in His covenant to me, so I may be always mindful of my covenants to Him. All His ways to me are mercy and truth; His faithfulness never faileth. Though heaven and earth pass away, yet not a tittle of His word shall be unfulfilled. All His words are oaths for their certainty, and all His promises are the sure mercies of David. Shall I be false to Him who is so fast to me? If it be unlawful to deceive a man who deludes me, how sinful is it to be unfaithful to my God, who is thus faithful to me? If he who telleth lies shall in nowise enter into heaven, how certainly shall I, if I foreswear myself, be cast into hell? Lord, cause me so to consider that my wedding bond to my wife hath Thee for a witness, and to this day is in Thine hand, that I may never give Thee cause to put it in suit in Thy court of justice, and to take its forfeiture by my dealing treacherously with my companion, and the wife of my covenant.

---

2. Swinnock, 1:522–28.

I wish that the thought of my dissolution may make me the more holy in this relation, that because I must shortly die and leave her, I may therefore do the more good to her, and receive the more good from her, while I live and enjoy her. My life, alas! is but a small spot of time; now a flood, by and by an ebb, and then I launch into the ocean of eternity. Now I live, anon I die, and then I must answer for my carriage in this condition. Oh that the consideration of my particular reckoning may cause me to be the more religious, that I may be the more heavenly in all my conversations with my wife, because I must shortly lie down in the earth! Lord, since I must within a few days put off the garment of this relation, which is now my comfort and ornament, let thy Spirit so embroider it with grace, and enable me so to perfume it with myrrh, aloes, and cassia, that when I shall be unclothed I may not be found naked, but clothed with my house that is from heaven.

I wish that love may act its part lively in every passage of this relation, and that my heart may be seen in my hand—I mean, my affection be visible in all my actions towards her, that though I might be much bold in Christ (as Paul wrote to Philemon, v. 8) to enjoin her that which is convenient, yet for love's sake I may rather entreat her. How sad is her condition, by reason of sin! Surely she may say, in the words of Hannah, "I am a woman of a sorrowful spirit." She conceiveth with sorrow, bringeth forth with much pain, and in bringing up her children often misses her desired pleasure. Her fears disquiet her in the night, and her cares disturb her in the day. Her sons are possibly Benonis, sons of her sorrows, and her servants Barabbases, sons of confusion. Through her whole life the yoke of subjection is on her neck, and shall I rule over her with rigor (Mal. 2:13), adding affliction to the afflicted, and wounding one whom God hath wounded? Should I cause her to sigh, by reason of her bondage, and to compass the Lord's altar about with tears and weeping, her cry would go up to heaven, for God hath a tender respect for oppressed wives, as well as afflicted widows, and He would bring some judgment on me to avenge the quarrel of His covenant. Oh let me never, like a Nabal, tyrannize and trample on my wife, as if she were my footstool, when God hath made her my fellow, and making her life, like the Israelites sojourning in Marah, full of mourning and murmuring, crying and complaining; but let her be to me, as Ezekiel's wife to him, the delight of mine eyes, and as the church to Christ (Song 4:9), the ravisher of my heart, that I may always cheer her affectionately, and cherish her tenderly, as the Lord the church.

The comfort of my life doth not a little depend upon my love to my wife. If I, like Lamech, carry myself fiercely and furiously as a lion, if she be as meek as a lamb, my house may degenerate from a society of civil men into a den of savage and ravenous beasts. Oh what a sad resemblance of hell is a brawling, cursing house! Though my wife be as cold as a flint, for me to be always, as steel, grating on her, will at last bring forth fire, and, behold, how great a matter a little fire kindleth! If the chief strings in the viol jar, the music is all marred. Why should I, by my passion, turn my house, which should be a Bethel, into a Babel of confusion (1 Kings 19:11)? My God delights not to manifest himself in blustering winds, or in frightful earthquakes, but in a still, low voice. If my house be in a flame, I undo myself by forcing away my best friend; but if I live in love and peace, the God of love and peace will live with me. Lord, who hast appointed this holy ordinance, the first that ever was under heaven, to be some poor resemblance of that sweet communion which Thine shall have in heaven one with another, and all, with Thy dear self and Son; give me some knowledge of that love Thou bearest to me, and of that delight I shall one day have in Thee, by that love I bear to, and that delight I have in, her whom Thou hast given into my bosom. Thou hast commanded me to love my wife as Christ loves His spouse. My Savior's love is chaste; there is not the least shadow of impurity in any of His commands. His love is constant. Having loved His own, He loves them to the end. Death itself could not burst asunder the cords of His love. His love is fervent; He was nothing else but a lump of love. His desire is to her, and His whole delight is in her. He passes by all others as nettles and thorns, but she is in His eye the rose of Sharon and the lily of the valleys. Oh that my soul might in these things follow my dearest Savior! My God has told me that I must love my wife as myself. My love to myself is hot, above that to any other in the world. How tender am I of myself under any malady! how pitiful towards myself in any misery! how patient towards myself when I discover many infirmities!

My love to myself is hearty. None ever was false in his love to himself, though many be feigned in their love to others. Lord, help me, that my love to her whom I call my love may be perfect; that my heart may be knit to her, and I may love her as my own soul; and since she hath left father, mother, brother, and sister for me, may she find the affection of all those relations, and far more, in me. And let my love be perpetual; let not its complexion be like aguish bodies, sometimes burning hot, and at other times shivering cold, but, as the sun, let it always be going forth in its full strength; and oh that to this end it might be pure love, not for lust or lucre, but whereas others love the wealth, I may love the wife; whereas others love portions and comeliness only, I may love her person and her godliness chiefly, and that because thou, fairest of thousands, whose lovely image is beautiful in her, hast commanded and commended it.

I wish that my love to my wife may be like Christ's to His church, as well in its goodness as in its greatness; I mean, that my chiefest endeavor may be that she may be sanctified and cleansed, and at last be presented to the blessed and beautiful bridegroom, a gracious and glorious spouse, without spot or wrinkle, or any such thing. Oh how industriously did my Redeemer endeavor His church's renovation and sanctity! how affectionately doth He beseech her to be holy! how fervently doth He beg of His Father to make her holy! how willingly did He broach His heart, and pour out His blood to wash her from her unholiness! how plentifully doth He pour down His Spirit to work her to holiness! His birth was that she might be born again, and born holy; His life was to set her a copy of holiness; His death was to purchase for her a new stock of holiness. He "gave himself for her, that he might redeem her from all iniquity, and purify unto himself a peculiar people, zealous of good works." His precepts, His prayers, His tears, His blood, His birth, His life, His death, His resurrection, His intercession, are all for her holiness and purity.

His name is called Jesus, because He saves His people, not in, but from, their sins and unholiness. He doth not think Himself perfect till His body be in heaven. My soul, when wilt thou imitate this lovely, lively pattern, and work hard in thy petitions to God, and woo hard in thy persuasions to thy wife, that she may be pure! Doth not thine heart ache to think that the object of thy dearest love and favor should be the object of God's greatest hatred and fury! that the companion of thy youth, who hath lain in thy bosom, whom thou hast so often embraced, should be a companion of frightful devils, and lie in the lake of fire and brimstone for ever and ever! Canst thou see thy wife posting in the way of perdition, hastening to hell, and never warn her of her danger, or ask her why she doth so! Is this thy kindness to thy friend? Ah, where are thy bowels? Lord, since Thou hast called me to be the head, help me to guide and direct, to see and speak, both to Thy Majesty in humble supplications, and to her in hearty and serious expostulations, that I may be ministerially, what thy Son is meritoriously, the saviour of my body. I have found a costly feast in my Father's family; the house is not so full but still there is room; there is nothing wanting but comers and company, and shall I suffer one so near me to starve for want of knowledge where it is to be had? Oh, let Thy goodness to me cause me to persuade, and let Thy goodness to her enable me to prevail, that she may taste and see that Thou art gracious!

I wish that I may naturally give the honey of sweetness and love, yet when provoked by sin against God, the sting of reproof, that I may bear with my wife in all things save wickedness. If I nourish her natural diseases, I kill her body; if I cherish her spiritual distempers, I damn her soul. And shall I, through cursed fondness, flatter her into the unquenchable fire? Lord, cause me not only to wink at her weaknesses, and to hide them from the world's eye, but also to observe any wickedness she shall be guilty of, and to set it so in order before her eyes that thou mayest cast it behind Thy back; yea, Lord, help me to hearken to all her holy counsels, and to hear Thee speaking by her, as well as to desire her to hearken to me; but let me never submit to any wicked advice, lest thou judge me at last, as thou didst Adam at first, for hearkening to the voice of my wife.

I wish that I may not, as some husbands, who dwell with their wives as brutes, understanding nothing in marriage but the meaning of carnal desires and the language of lust, yet deal worse with the wives of their bosoms than with their beasts, and deny them what is convenient for their outward well-being; but that both my person and portion may be for her comfort in health, and for her cordial in sickness, and employed upon all occasions, though not for the pampering of her pride, or nourishment of any sin, yet in a moderate way for her service. When my God gave Himself to my soul, He gave me all He had also, and thought nothing too much for me, and shall I, who have not spared myself from her, think everything too good for her? If she brought a portion, what is become of it? Was it laid out to purchase her misery and poverty? If she did not, yet she is my wife, and both nature and Scripture command me to allow her answerable to my wealth and her wants. Oh that I might be as Elkanah to Hannah, better to her than ten sons, than all relations. Lord, while I live make me so loving and industrious, that rather myself than my wife may lack. Let her body never want food and raiment, nor her soul the gospel feast, or the robes of Thy Son's righteousness; and when I die, whomsoever I neglect, if by Thy providence I am able, let me make for her a comfortable provision, that when I am happy in heaven, my other half may not, through my unworthiness, be miserable on earth. If it be Thy pleasure that I shall die poor—for my portion, through infinite grace, is not in this life—then let it please Thy Majesty to grant me this mercy, that I may leave my fatherless children with Thee, and bid my widow trust in Thee. Let not my Lord be angry, and I will speak further on her behalf. In what want soever I shall leave this world, let me leave my wife the poor, or rather the rich, Levite's portion, that though she hath no part or inheritance here below (Num. 18:20), yet Thou Thyself mayest be the portion of her cup, and the lot of her inheritance. Oh, then the lines will fall to her in pleasant places, and she will have a goodly heritage.

Behold, I have taken upon me to speak unto the Lord, who am but dust and ashes. Let not my Lord be angry, and I will speak yet but this once: Do thou so adorn me with grace, suitable to this relation, as a bridegroom is decked with ornaments, that when I cease to be a husband, I may know what it is to be the bride, the Lamb's wife (Hos. 2:19), not as I do in this imperfect condition, where Thou hast only betrothed me unto Thyself in righteousness and judgment, and in loving-kindness and in mercy, and so while I am present in the body I am absent from the Lord; but in the highest degree, in that place where Thou wilt marry me to Thyself for ever. Kiss me with the sweetest kisses of Thy lips, lodge me all night between Thy breasts, where is the voice of joy and the voice of gladness, the voice of the true bridegroom and the voice of the true bride; where is the voice of them that say and sing, Praise the Lord of hosts, for the Lord is good, for His mercy endureth for ever. Amen.[3]

---

3. Swinnock, 1:497–502.

Puritans on Marriage and Family: Bibliography

Primary Sources

Adams, Richard. "What Are the Duties of Parents and Children; and How Are They to Be Managed According to Scripture?" In *Puritan Sermons, 1659–1689*, 2:303–358. Wheaton, Ill.: Richard Owen Roberts, 1981.

Allestree, Richard. *The Whole Duty of Man*, 244–52, 258–64. London: W. Pickering, 1842.

Ambrose, Isaac. "Family Duties." In *The Practice of Sanctification*. In *Works of Isaac Ambrose*, 130–36. London: Thomas Tegg, 1829.

Ames, William. *Conscience with the Power and Cases thereof*, 156–59, 196–211. Book 5, Chapters 21–22, 35–38. 1639. Facsimile reprint, Norwood, N.J.: Walter J. Johnson, 1975.

B., D. *An Antidote Against Discord Betwixt Man and Wife*. 1685. Reprint, Warrenton, Virginia: Edification Press, 2013.

B., Ste. *Counsel to the Husband; to the Wife Instruction: A Short and Pithy Treatise of Several and Joynt Duties, Belonging unto Man and Wife, as Counsels to the One, and Instructions to the Other; for Their More Perfect Happiness in This Present Life, and Their Eternal Glorie in the Life to Come*. London: by Felix Kyngston, for Richard Boyle, 1608.

Baxter, Richard. *A Christian Directory*, Part II: Christian Economics, Chapters 1–22, in *The Practical Works of Richard Baxter*, 1:394–493. Morgan, Pa.: Soli Deo Gloria, 1996.

———. *The Godly Home*, edited by Randall J. Pederson. Wheaton, Ill.: Crossway Books, 2010. (Modernized excerpt from *A Christian Directory*.)

————. *The Poor Man's Family Book*, in *The Practical Works of Richard Baxter*, 4:165–289. Morgan, Pa.: Soli Deo Gloria, 1996.

Bayly, Lewis. *The Practice of Piety: Directing a Christian How to Walk, that He May Please God*, 143–49. Morgan, Pa.: Soli Deo Gloria, 1994.

Bayne, Paul. *An Entire Commentary upon the Whole Epistle of St. Paul to the Ephesians*, 337–64. 1866. Reprint, Stoke-on-Trent, U.K.: Tentmaker, 2001.

Bolton, Robert. *General Directions for a Comfortable Walking with God*, 262–81. Morgan, Pa.: Soli Deo Gloria, 1995.

Boston, Thomas. "Duties of Husband and Wife." In *The Works of Thomas Boston*, edited by Samuel M'Millan, 4:209–218. Wheaton, Ill: Richard Owen Roberts, 1980.

Bourne, Immanuel. *A Golden Chain of Directions, with Twenty Gold-links of Love, To Preserve Love Firm between Husband and Wife, During Their Lives*. London: by J. Streater for George Sanbridge, 1669.

Bunyan, John. *Christian Behaviour*. In *The Works of John Bunyan*, edited by George Offor, 2:557–62. 1854. Reprint, Edinburgh: Banner of Truth, 1991.

Byfield, Nicholas. *An Exposition Upon the Epistle to the Colossians*, 346–61. 1866. Reprint, Stoke-on-Trent, U.K.: Tentmaker, 2007.

Cawdrey, Daniel. *Family Reformation Promoted*. In *Anthology of Presbyterian and Reformed Literature, Volume 4*, 54–73, edited by Christopher Coldwell. 1655. Reprint, Dallas: Naphtali Press, 1991.

[Cooke, Edward.] *The Batchelor's Directory: Being a Treatise of the Excellence of Marriage*. London: Richard Cumberland and Benjamin Bragg, 1694.

Davenant, John. *Colossians*, translated by Josiah Allport, 2:151–95. A Geneva Series Commentary. 1831. Reprint, Edinburgh: Banner of Truth, 2005.

Dod, John. *A Plain and Familiar Exposition of the Ten Commandments*, 166–86, 199–209. London: Thomas Man, Paul Man, and Jonah Man, 1632.

Dod, John and Robert Cleaver. *A Godly Form of Household Government*. London: Thomas Man, 1612. (First published by Robert Cleaver in 1598, then revised by John Dod)

Doolittle, Thomas. "How May the Duty of Daily Family Prayer Be Best Managed for the Spiritual Benefit of Every One in the Family?" In *Puritan*

Sermons, 1659–1689, 2:194–272. Wheaton, Ill: Richard Owen Roberts, 1981.

Durham, James. "Family Worship." In *A Practical Exposition of the Ten Commandments*, edited by Christopher Coldwell, 221–36. Dallas: Naphtali Press, 2002.

Durham, William. *A Serious Exhortation to the Necessary Duties of Family and Personal Instruction*. London: by Tho. Newcomb, 1659.

Gataker, Thomas. "A Marriage Prayer," "A Good Wife God's Gift," "A Wife in Deed," and "Marriage Duties," in *Certain Sermons*, 2:116–208. London: John Haviland, 1637.

Goodwin, Phillip. *Religio Domestica Rediviva: Or, Family Religion Revived*. London: by R. and W. Leybourn, for Andrew Kemb and Edward Brewster, 1655.

Gouge, Thomas. *Christian Directions, Shewing How to Walk with God All the Day Long*, 131–48. London: R. Ibbitson and M. Wright, 1661.

Gouge, William. *Building a Godly Home*, edited by Joel R. Beeke and Scott Brown. 3 vols. Grand Rapids: Reformation Heritage Books, 2013–2014. (Modernized version of *Domestical Duties*.)

———. *Of Domestical Duties*, edited by Greg Fox. 1622. Reprint, Pensacola: Puritan Reprints, 2006.

Greenham, Richard. *A Godlie Exhortation, and Fruitfull Admonition to Virtuous Parents and Modest Matrons. Describing the Holie Life, and Blessed Institution of that Most Honorable State of Matrimonie, and the Increase of Godlie and Happy Children, in Training Them Up in Godly Education, and Household Discipline*. London: N. Ling, 1584.

———. "Of the Good Education of Children." In *The Works of the Reverend and Faithfull Servant of Jesus Christ M. Richard Greenham*, edited by H. H., 159–68. 1599. Facsimile reprint, Amsterdam: Theatrum Orbis Terrarum, 1973.

———. "A Treatise of a Contract before Marriage." In *The Works of the Reverend and Faithfull Servant of Jesus Christ M. Richard Greenham*, edited by H. H., 288–99. 1599. Facsimile reprint, Amsterdam: Theatrum Orbis Terrarum, 1973.

Greenhill, William. *An Exposition of Ezekiel*, 441–43. Edinburgh: Banner of Truth, 1994.

Halyburton, Thomas. "The Christian's Duty, with Respect to Both Personal and Family Religion." In *The Great Concern of Salvation*. In *The Works of Thomas Halyburton*, 2:368–403. Aberdeen: James Begg Society, 2001.

Hamond, George. *The Case for Family Worship*. Orlando: Soli Deo Gloria, 2005.

Henry, Matthew. *Family Religion: Principles for Raising a Godly Family*. Ross-shire, Scotland: Christian Focus, 2008.

Heywood, Oliver. *The Family Altar*. In *The Whole Works of the Rev. Oliver Heywood*. Reprint, Morgan, Pa.: Soli Deo Gloria, 1997.

Hildersam, Arthur. *Dealing with Sin in Our Children*, edited by Don Kistler. Morgan, Pa.: Soli Deo Gloria, 2004.

Hopkins, Ezekiel. *An Exposition upon the Commandments*. In *The Works of Ezekiel Hopkins*, ed. Charles W. Quick, 1:413–26. 1874. Reprint, Morgan, Pa.: Soli Deo Gloria, 1995.

Koelman, Jacobus. *The Duties of Parents*, translated by John Vriend, edited by M. Eugene Osterhaven. Classics of Reformed Spirituality. Grand Rapids: Reformation Heritage Books, 2003.

Lawrence, Edward. *Parent's Concerns for Their Unsaved Children*, edited by Don Kistler. Morgan, Pa.: Soli Deo Gloria, 2003.

Lye, Thomas. "What May Gracious Parents Best Do for the Conversion of Those Children Whose Wickedness Is Occasioned by Their Sinful Severity or Indulgence?" In *Puritan Sermons, 1659–1689*, 3:153–84. Wheaton, Ill.: Robert Owen Roberts, 1981.

Manton, Thomas. "Sermons Upon Ephesians V." In *The Works of Thomas Manton*, 19:436–76. 1870. Reprint, Birmingham: Solid Ground Christian Books, 2008.

———. "A Wedding Sermon." In *The Works of Thomas Manton*, 2:162–72. 1870. Reprint, Birmingham: Solid Ground Christian Books, 2008.

Maynard, John. *The Beauty and Order of the Creation. Together with Natural and Allegorical Meditations on the Six Dayes Works of the Creation*, 175–84. London: William Gearing, 1668.

Mather, Cotton. *A Family Well-ordered: Or, An Essay to Render Parents and Children Happy in One Another*, edited by Don Kistler. Morgan, Pa.: Soli Deo Gloria, 2001. (Previously reprinted Bellville, Tex.: Sower's Seed, 1995.)

————. *Help for Distressed Parents*, edited by Don Kistler. Morgan, Pa.: Soli Deo Gloria, 2004.

Norman, John. *Family-governors Persuaded to Family-godliness*. London: by A. Maxey, for Samuel Gellibrand, 1657.

Perkins, William. *Christian Oeconomy*. In *The Work of William Perkins*, edited by Ian Breward, 416–39. Appleford, England: Sutton Courtenay Press, 1970.

————. *A Golden Chaine*, in *The Workes of that Famous and Worthie Minister of Christ, in the Universitie of Cambridge, M. W. Perkins*, 1:60–61. London: John Legate, 1608.

Petter, George. *A Learned, Pious, and Practical Commentary Upon the Gospel According to St. Mark*, 703–713. London: Printed by F. Streater, 1661.

Reyner, Edward. *Considerations Concerning Marriage: The Honor, Duties, Benefits, Troubles of it. Whereto are added, 1) Directions in two particulars: a. How they that have wives may be as if they had none. b. How to prepare for parting with a dear yoke-fellow by death or otherwise. 2) Resolution of this Case of Conscience: Whether a man may lawfully marry his wife's sister?* London: by J. T. for Thomas Newbery, 1657.

Robinson, John. "Of Marriage," and "Of Children and Their Education." In *New Essays, Or Observations Divine and Moral*. In *The Works of John Robinson*, edited by Robert Ashton, 1:236–50. 1851. Reprint, Harrisonburg, Va.: Sprinkle, 2009.

Rogers, Daniel. *Matrimonial Honor*. 1642. Reprint, Warrenton, Virginia: Edification Press, 2010.

Scudder, Henry. *The Godly Man's Choice*. London: Matthew Simmons for Henry Overton, 1644.

Secker, William. "The Wedding Ring, A Sermon," printed with *The Nonsuch Professor in His Meridian Splendour; Or, The Singular Actions of Sanctified Christians*, edited by Matthew Wilks, 245–69. Reprint, Harrisonburg, Va.: Sprinkle, 1997.

Smith, Henry. *A Preparative to Marriage*. In *The Works of Henry Smith*, 1:5–40. Reprint, Stoke-on-Trent, U.K.: Tentmaker Publications, 2002.

Steele, Richard. "What Are the Duties of Husbands and Wives towards Each Other?" In *Puritan Sermons, 1659–1689*, 2:272–303. Wheaton, Ill.: Richard Owen Roberts, 1981.

Stock, Richard. *A Commentary Upon the Prophecy of Malachi*, 168–91. In *Richard Stock and Samuel Torshell on Malachi and Richard Bernard and Thomas Fuller on Ruth*. 1865. Reprint, Stoke-on-Trent, U.K.: Tentmaker, 2006.

Stockton, Owen. *A Treatise of Family Instruction*. London: H. Brome, 1672.

Stuckley, Lewis. *A Gospel Glass: Representing the Miscarriages of Professors, Both in Their Personal and Relative Capacities*, 169–183. 1852. Reprint, Grand Rapids: Ebenezer Publications, 2002.

Swinnock, George. *The Christian Man's Calling*. In *The Works of George Swinnock*, 1:464–528. 1868. Reprint, Edinburgh: Banner of Truth, 1992.

Taffin, Jean. *The Amendment of Life*, 274–327. London: Georg. Bishop, 1595.

Whately, William. *A Bride-Bush or A Wedding Sermon*. 1617. Reprint, Norwood, N.J.: Walter J. Johnson, 1975.

———. *A Care-Cloth or the Cumbers and Troubles of Marriage*. 1624. Reprint, Norwood, N.J.: Walter J. Johnson, 1975.

Willard, Samuel. "Question LXIV: What Is Required in the Fifth Commandment?" In *A Compleat Body of Divinity in Two Hundred and Fifty Expository Lectures on the Assemby's Shorter Catechism*, 598–613. 1726. Reprint, New York: Johnson Reprint Corp., 1969.

Willet, Andrew. *Hexapla in Genesin, that is, a Sixfold Commentary upon Genesis*, 38, 41–44. London: by Tho. Creede, for John Norton, 1608.

Secondary Sources

Allen, Russell. "The Beautiful Mystery: Examining Jonathan Edwards' View of Marriage. *Bound Away: The Liberty Journal of History* 1, no. 1 (2015), http://digitalcommons.liberty.edu/ljh/vol1/iss1/3, accessed February 3, 2016.

Anderson, Jody Kent. "The Church within the Church: An Examination of Family Worship in Puritan Thought." PhD diss., Mid-America Baptist Theological Seminary, 2009.

Arthur, J. Philip. "The Puritan Family." In *The Answer of a Good Conscience*, 75–94. London: Westminster Conference, 1997.

Bartlett, Robert M. *The Faith of the Pilgrims: An American Heritage*. New York: United Church Press, 1978.

Beeke, Joel R. *Living for God's Glory: an Introduction to Calvinism*. Lake Mary, Fla.: Reformation Trust, 2008.

Beeke, Joel R. and Mark Jones. *A Puritan Theology: Doctrine for Life*. Grand Rapids: Reformation Heritage Books, 2012.

Benson, Elisa Jill. "Richard Baxter's Teaching on the Family: Spheres of Soul Care and Sacrifice." Master's Thesis, Regent College, 2010.

Beougher, Tim. "The Puritan View of Marriage." *Trinity Journal* 10, no. 2 (1989): 131–60.

Braund, E. "Daily Life Among the Puritans." In *The Puritan Papers: Volume One*, 155–66. Edited by David Martin Lloyd-Jones. Phillipsburg, N.J.: P&R Publishing, 2000.

Bremer, Francis J. *The Puritan Experiment: New England Society from Bradford to Edwards*. New York: St. Martin's Press, 1995.

Bunge, Marcia J. *The Child in Christian Thought*. Grand Rapids: Eerdmans, 2001.

Byington, Ezra Hoyt. *The Puritan in England and New England*. Boston: Roberts Brothers, 1897.

Carpenter, Roy. "Sexual Politics in Eighteenth Century Pelham, Massachusetts: The Jonathan Edwards Clan, Divorce Law, and the Eleanor Gray Case." *Jonathan Edwards Studies* 1, no. 1 (2011): 22–44.

Chamberlain, Ava. *The Notorious Elizabeth Tuttle: Marriage, Murder, and Madness in the Family of Jonathan Edwards*. New York: New York University Press, 2012.

Cliffe, J. T. *The Puritan Gentry: The Great Puritan Families of Early Stuart England*. London: Routledge & Kegan Paul, 1984.

Cooke, Kathy. "Generations and Regeneration: Sexceptionalism and Group Identity among Puritans in Colonial New England." *Journal of the History of Sexuality* 23, no. 3 (2014): 333–57.

Crampton, W. Gary. *What the Puritans Taught*. Morgan, Pa.: Soli Deo Gloria, 2003.

Daniels, Bruce C. "The Progress of Romance: Sex and Courtship." In *Puritans at Play: Leisure and Recreation in Colonial New England*, 125–40. New York: Palgrave Macmillan, 2005.

Davies, Gaius. "The Puritan Teaching on Marriage and the Family." *The Evangelical Quarterly* 27 (1955): 19–30.

Davies, Kathleen. "The Sacred Condition of Equality: How Original Were Puritan Doctrines of Marriage?" *Social History* 2, no. 5 (1977): 563–80.

Demos, John. *A Little Commonwealth: Family Life in Plymouth Colony.* New York: Oxford University Press, 1970.

Doriani, Daniel. "The Godly Household in Puritan Theology, 1560–1640." PhD diss., Westminster Theological Seminary, 1985.

Durston, Christopher. *The Family in the English Revolution.* New York: Basil Blackwell, 1989.

Earle, Alice Morse. *Customs and Fashions in Old New England.* Detroit: Omnigraphics, 1990. (Published earlier in New York: Charles Scribner's Sons, 1893)

Fleming, Rachel. "Those Loose Ladies: An Examination of Scandalous Puritan Women in Massachusetts from 1635 to 1700." Master's Thesis, Salem State University, 2015.

Frye, Roland. "The Teachings of Classical Puritanism on Conjugal Love." *Studies in the Renaissance* 2 (1955): 148–59.

Graham, Judith. *Puritan Family Life: The Diary of Samuel Sewall.* Boston: Northeastern University Press, 2000.

Greven, Philip J. "Family Structure in Andover." In *Puritanism in Early America*, 123–42. Edited by George M. Waller. Lexington, Mass.: D.C. Heath and Company, 1973.

Haller, William and Malleville. "The Puritan Art of Love." *Huntington Library Quarterly* 5 (1942): 235–72.

Hambrick-Stowe, Charles E. "Ordering Their Private World: What the Puritans Did to Grow Spiritually." *Christian History* 13, no. 1 (1944): 18.

Harrison, Graham. "Marriage, Divorce in Puritan Thinking." In *The Fire Divine*, 27–51. London: Westminster Conference, 1996.

Haykin, Michael. "A Puritan Wife." *Table Talk* 36, no. 5 (May 2012): 36–37.

Hulse, Errol. *Who Are the Puritans: And What Do They Teach?* Darlington, England: Evangelical Press, 2000.

Johnson, James Turner. "The Covenant Idea and the Puritan View of Marriage." *Journal of the History of Ideas* 32, no. 1 (1971): 107–18.

————. *A Society Ordained by God: English Puritan Marriage Doctrine in the First Half of the Seventeenth Century.* Nashville: Abingdon Press, 1970.

Knappen, M. M. *Tudor Puritanism: A Chapter in the History of Idealism.* Chicago: University of Chicago Press, 1983.

Lamson, Lisa Rose. "Strange Flesh in the City on the Hill: Early Massachusetts Sodomy Laws and Puritan Spiritual Anxiety, 1629–1699." Master's Thesis, Bowling Green State University, 2014.

Lane, Belden. "Two Schools of Desire: Nature and Marriage in Seventeenth Century Puritanism." *Church History,* 69, no. 2 (2000): 372–402.

Leites, Edmund. "The Duty to Desire: Love, Friendship, and Sexuality in Some Puritan Theories of Marriage." *Journal of Social History* 15, no. 3 (1982): 383–408.

Mathes, Richard Perry. "English Puritan Attitudes toward Child-Rearing, 1560–1634." PhD diss. Northeast Missouri State University, 1975.

Moran, Gerald and Maris Vinovskis. "The Puritan Family and Religion: A Critical Reappraisal." *William and Mary Quarterly* 39, no. 1 (1982): 29–63.

Morgan, Edmund. *The Puritan Family.* Revised ed. New York: Harper & Row, 1966.

Morris, Michelle Jarrett. *Under Household Government: Sex and Family in Puritan Massachusetts.* Cambridge: Harvard University Press, 2012.

Ozment, Steven. *When Fathers Ruled: Family Life in Reformation Europe.* Cambridge: Harvard University Press, 1983.

Packer, J. I. *A Quest for Godliness: The Puritan Vision of the Christian Life.* Wheaton, Ill.: Crossway, 1990.

Parsons, Michael. "Marriage under Threat in the Writings of George Swinnock." *Scottish Bulletin of Evangelical Theology* 20, no. 1 (2002): 29–50.

Ratner, Helen. "The Puritan Family." *Child & Family* 9, no. 1 (1970): 54–60.

Rutman, Darrett B. *Winthrop's Boston: A Portrait of a Puritan Town, 1630–1649.* New York: W. W. Norton Company, 1972.

Ryken, Leland. *Worldly Saints: The Puritans as They Really Were.* Grand Rapids: Zondervan, 1986.

Sather, Kathryn. "Sixteenth and Seventeenth Century Child-Rearing: A Matter of Discipline." *Journal of Social History* 22, no. 4 (1989): 735–43.

Schucking, Levin Ludwig. *The Puritan Family: A Social Study from the Literary Sources*. New York: Schocken Books, 1970.

Schweitzer, Ivy. "John Winthrop's Model of American Affiliation." *Early American Literature* 40, no. 3 (2005): 441–69.

Setran, David. "Igniting the 'Family Sacrifice': Cotton Mather and Familial Christian Education in Puritan New England." *Christian Education Journal* 11, no. 2 (2014): 351–66.

Sisemore, Timothy. "From Doctrine to Practice: the Influence of the Doctrine of Original Sin in Puritan Child-Rearing." *Children's Spirituality: Christian Perspectives, Research and Applications*. Edited by D. Radcliffe and M. McQuitty. Eugene, Ore.: Cascade Books, 2004.

Stewart, Carole Lynne. "A Revolutionary Marriage Deferred." In *Strange Jeremiahs: Civil Religion and the Literary Imaginations of Jonathan Edwards, Herman Melville and W.E. DuBois*. Albuquerque: University of New Mexico Press, 2010.

Stone, Lawrence. *The Family, Sex and Marriage in England, 1500–1800*. New York: Harper & Row, 1977.

Todd, Margo. "Humanists, Puritans and the Spiritualized Household." *Church History* 49, no. 1 (1980): 18–34.

Ulrich, Laurel Thatcher. "Good Wives: A Study in Role Definition in Northern New England, 1650–1750." PhD diss. University of New Hampshire, 1980.

Vaughan, David J. *A Divine Light: The Spiritual Leadership of Jonathan Edwards*. Nashville: Cumberland House, 2007.

Verduin, Kathleen. "Our Cursed Natures: Sexuality and the Puritan Conscience." *New England Quarterly* 56, no. 2 (1983): 220–37.

Weisberg, Kelly. "Under Greet Temptations Heer: Women and Divorce in Puritan Massachusetts." *Feminist Studies* 2, no. 2 (1975): 183–93.

Westerkamp, Marilyn. "Puritan Women, Spiritual Power, and the Question of Sexuality." In *The Religious History of American Women*, 51–72. Edited by C. Brekus. Chapel Hill: University of North Carolina Press, 2007.

Wiebracht, Ben. "First Cousin Marriage in Tudor and Stuart England, 1540–1688." *Journal of Family History* 40, no. 1 (2015): 24–38.